Hiking Marin

121 Great Hikes in Marin County

Don and Kay Martin
Illustrated by Bob Johnson

Copyright 1995 by Don Martin and Kay Martin

Inquiries should be addressed to:
Martin Press
P.O. Box 2109
San Anselmo, CA 94979

ISBN 0-9617044-5-4

Printed in the United States of America

Cover Photo Locations: Chimney Rock, Muir Woods, Tennessee Valley, Cataract Creek and Bon Tempe Lake

Acknowledgments

This book includes material from two other books, *MT TAM* and *Point Reyes National Seashore*. We are extremely grateful to everyone who has helped us in producing both previous books as well as this book. We are especially thankful to Ron Angier, Greg Archbald, Lincoln Fairley, Wilma Follette, Jim Furman, Tom Gaman, Dave Gould, Jim Locke, Eric Mohr, Brian Simon, Casey May, Al Molina, Eric McGuire, Jerry Olmsted, Fred Sandrock, Bob Stewart, Solange Russek, Lanny Waggoner, Chris Hansen, Tim Warner, Mary Vedovi, Fred Lew, Jeff Price, Leonard Page, Pat Robards, Larry Perkins, Rand Knox, Ron Miska, Meryl Sundove, Mia Monroe, Ted Wurm, John Del'Osso, Jack Williams, Bill Michaels, Dewey Livingston, Geoff Geupel, Joe Mueller, Sue Baty, Ron Paolini and to the folks at Desktop Publishing Inc.

We would also like to thank our hiking and running friends who have shared many enjoyable times on the trails of Marin with us: Dick and Sharon Shlegeris, Bill and Dixie James, Ruth and Steve Nash, Shel and Joy Siewert, Arlene Hansen, Mary Lou Grossberg, Sue Steele, Mel and Pam DeWeerd, Dave and Rozanne Stringer, Jim and Joanne Kambur, Bill and Els Tuinzing, Edda Stickle and Gillian Clark. We especially want to thank the members of our family, Daryl Odnert and Jennifer, Theresa, Susan and Greg Martin, for their enthusiastic and valuable support.

Although these people have helped us in many ways, we are responsible for all errors that have occurred.

Photo Credits

22 *S.S. Tennessee*: National Maritime Museum, San Francisco
44 Gravity Car: A.C. Graves-Ted Wurm Collection
48 Muir Woods Inn: Muir Woods National Monument
80 Tamalpais Tavern: photo courtesy of Joseph A. Baird, Jr.
138 Papermill: Samuel P. Taylor State Park
140 Hotel: Samuel P. Taylor State Park
194 Bear Valley Country Club: Anne T. Kent California Room, Marin County Library
202 The Oaks: Jack Mason Museum
246 Schooner *Point Reyes*: Point Reyes National Seashore
250 Lighthouse: Dewey Livingston, Point Reyes National Seashore
260 Tule Elk: photo by John Aho, Point Reyes National Seashore

All other photos by the authors.

Table of Contents

How to Use this Book
Topographic Map and Shaded Relief Map of Marin County

Region F: Point Reyes South - 18 Hikes

Region G: Point Reyes North - 19 Hikes

Appendices

This book is dedicated

To the citizens of Marin County, past and present, who have had the foresight, energy and perseverance to protect the natural beauty of Marin and thus create the finest urban park system in the world.

To the park rangers and volunteer associations who love and maintain this park system for our education and enjoyment.

Public lands visited in this book include

Golden Gate National Recreation Area
Muir Woods National Monument
Point Reyes National Seashore

Angel Island State Park
China Camp State Park
Olompali State Park
Samuel P. Taylor State Park
Tomales Bay State Park
Mt. Tamalpais State Park

Audubon Canyon Ranch
Las Gallinas Sanitary Wildlife Ponds
Marin Municipal Water District
Marinwood Community Services District
McInnes County Park
Ring Mountain Preserve
Stafford Lake County Park

Baltimore Canyon Open Space
Blithedale Ridge Open Space
Cascade Canyon Open Space
Deer Island Open Space
Ignacio Valley Open Space
Indian Tree Open Space
Indian Valley Open Space
King Mountain Open Space
Loma Alta Open Space
Loma Verde Open Space
Lucas Valley Open Space
Mt. Burdell Open Space
Pacheco Valle Open Space
Roy's Redwoods Open Space
San Pedro Mountain Open Space
Terra Linda-Sleepy Hollow Divide Open Space

How to Use this Book

Choosing a Hike

Not sure where to go? We usually plan our hikes around the season and weather. In the winter, we look for creeks, waterfalls and views. In spring, wildflowers are the main attraction. In the fall, we head out to the coast. Check out Appendices H1 and H2 for many more ideas.

Hike Descriptions

Here is a sample entry of a hike description with a brief explanation.

> *Distance:* 6.9 miles   Shaded: 60%
> *Elevation Change:* 1300'   Occasionally steep.
> *Rating:* Hiking - 10   Difficulty - 7   Some poison oak.
> *When to Go:* Excellent anytime, best from March to June.

Distance and Shade

Distance measurements refer to the total hike distance. Shaded refers to the percent of tree cover. Shaded 60% means that the total distance is shaded about 60% by trees or tall shrubs.

Elevation Change

Elevation change helps determine how strenuous the hike is. A 1300' change means the hike climbs 1300' and descends 1300'.

Hiking and Difficulty

The Hiking Rating depends on aesthetics. How interesting is the hike? For example, the Bear Valley-Old Pine-Sky trails, Hike F3, has a variety of flora, rolling terrain and good views. We consider it interesting 90-100% of the time and so, rated it a 10.

Hiking Rating
8   Interesting 70-80% of the time
9   Interesting 80-90% of the time
10   Interesting 90-100% of the time

Obviously, this rating system is subjective and depends on what we like. Also, our rating of hikes is based on the best possible conditions, the best season, views, weather and wildflowers.

The Difficulty Rating ranges from 1 to 10 depending primarily on footing and steepness. For example, Hike D3, in Cascade Canyon, has a short 30' section of trail that is very steep and slippery. It has been given a difficulty rating of 9.

1

Difficulty Rating
1-2   Easy
3-5   Moderate
6-8   Difficult
9-10   Very difficult

Note that Easy and Moderate hikes can develop poor trail conditions. For example, during the storms of 1995, dozens of trails were closed due to fallen trees, slides and washouts.

When To Go

The When to Go rating is based on flora and fauna, weather, season, views, trail and road conditions. Since winter provides rainfall and water runoff, and late winter and spring produce wildflowers, these two seasons are the best times to go on most hikes.

Using The Maps

The lower 3-dimensional map contains "3-D slices" as shown in the figure below. The bottom map is displayed so that no part of the map is any closer to the observer than any other part. Scales shown on the map are approximate since elevations have been exaggerated.

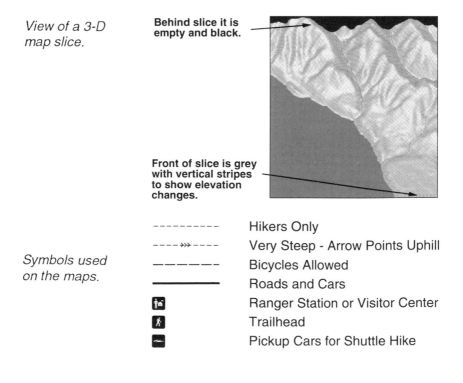

View of a 3-D map slice.

Behind slice it is empty and black.

Front of slice is grey with vertical stripes to show elevation changes.

Symbols used on the maps.

----------	Hikers Only
----»»----	Very Steep - Arrow Points Uphill
——————	Bicycles Allowed
▬▬▬▬▬	Roads and Cars
🚻	Ranger Station or Visitor Center
🚶	Trailhead
🚐	Pickup Cars for Shuttle Hike

2

Suggestions and Precautions

As hiking becomes more popular, it attracts a wider variety of people with different levels of hiking experience. We offer the following suggestions and precautions, especially for beginning hikers.

What to Take on a Hike

Some of the hikes in this book, like those in open space lands are short and often in full view of civilization. The only essential item to take is water. However, when hiking in more remote areas, such as Mt. Tamalpais or Point Reyes, it is best to be prepared. Here is a sample check list of things to take.

Adequate Fluids	First Aid Kit
Light Jacket	Extra Food
Poncho in Winter	Hat
Suncreen in Summer	Knife
Book or Map	Flashlight
Binoculars	Compass

Hiking Boots

Most of the trails described in this book are uneven, rocky or rutted. Hiking boots are preferred. They protect the feet and provide stable support. They reduce the chance of injuries, such as sprained ankles.

Hiking Alone

Hiking alone is not recommended. However, if you do go out alone, tell someone where you are going and when you will return or leave a note in your car at the trailhead with this information.

Fluids

Fluids are essential when hiking or staying outdoors. Often, people go hiking or go to the beach and wind up the day with a mild headache. Usually, this is attributed to too much exposure, too much sun or too much wind. Many times, the problem is too little fluids. Hiking requires a minimum of 1/2 quart of fluid per hour, or more, depending on the temperature and elevation change.

Plan to drink at least 1/2 quart of fluid per hour on hikes.

Alcohol does not count. It is a diuretic, which means that it removes fluid by osmosis in the stomach. It is always a good idea to carry water on a hike and to drink it regularly whether you feel thirsty or not.

Do not drink water from streams or lakes. It may contain giardia, which can cause severe stomach problems until treated.

Hikers and Bicyclists

Hikes in this book have been laid out to minimize contact between hikers and bicyclists. Where possible, hikes have been routed off bike roads and onto trails. Also, hikes that include roads for part of the trip usually head uphill, so that hikers can see bicyclists coming downhill. All bike roads are marked on the maps.

Poison Oak

Poison oak for some is a minor irritation, for most, a major irritation and for a few, a medical emergency. The best advice is to learn to identify the plant by its leaves and avoid touching it. An old saying is,

Poison Oak

"Leaves of three, leave it be."

In fall, poison oak leaves turn crimson red and drop off. In winter, the bare branches are difficult to identify, yet still retain their toxic oils. It helps to stay on designated   trails and to watch out for branches that lean out onto the trail. If you are allergic to it, carry small individually packaged Handi-wipes and wash an affected area within ten minutes.

Ticks and Lyme Disease

Ticks are common in Marin and are especially noticeable during the rainy season from November to May. Recent studies have shown that 1-2% of the western black-legged ticks in Marin County carry Lyme disease.

Western Black-Legged Tick - enlarged 8 times

The best way to avoid ticks is to stay on trails. It also helps to wear light clothing so that ticks can be seen. Be sure to brush yourself frequently, especially after passing through tall grass or shrubs. After a hike, check yourself completely. Ticks anesthetize the skin before biting so you'll seldom feel the original bite.

Early removal of a tick reduces the risk of infection. Use tweezers. Grab the tick mouth parts as close to the skin as possible and pull straight out. Wash hands and clean the bite with an antiseptic.

The first recognizable symptom of Lyme disease is usually a ring-like rash that occurs 3-30 days after the tick bite. One or more rashes may occur and not always at the bite. However, a rash only appears 60-80% of the time. Other symptoms may include flu-like fever, chills, fatigue, headaches and a stiff neck. Since early diagnosis of Lyme disease is crucial, see a doctor if you think you have it.

Rattlesnakes and Mountain Lions

Both are present and dangerous, but rarely seen in Marin. Rattlesnakes will often sun themselves in open areas in the spring. The best way to avoid rattlesnakes is to stay on the trail and avoid climbing over loose rocky areas.

If you do see a mountain lion, don't run. Stand your ground, keep eye contact, make yourself look bigger, perhaps using your jacket or daypack. Then, slowly back away. If attacked, fight back.

Parking

When parking on narrow streets, please respect local neighborhoods. Most cities require a 12' pavement clearance for emergency vehicles. Also, remember to lock your car and don't leave valuables in view. Vandalism and theft at trailheads in Marin is not common, but it does happen. You might check with park rangers about problem areas.

Wildfires

Wildfires are part of the natural history of Marin. These fires can be deadly. During periods of extreme fire danger, called "Red Flag Days", public lands may be closed. In late summer and fall, avoid hilltops and ridges during hot, dry or windy days.

Accuracy of the Maps

We have tried to show every official trail on the map for each hike. Thus, you can use the maps to lengthen, shorten or change the hikes as you wish. Most unofficial trails are not shown.

Getting Lost

It is surprisingly easy to get lost on hikes, even when using an up-to-date book with good maps. There are four major reasons for this: there are lots of deer trails, a few trails are overgrown, some junctions lack signs, and people take short-cuts. If you are in a new area, our advice is to follow the book carefully and note each junction on the map. Stay on trails and don't take shortcuts.

Disclaimer

Although we have tried to provide valuable information, there are errors. Also, nature is not static. Hillsides erode. Trees fall down. Trails get rerouted. Signs change and hikes change. In winter, some trails are impassable. This book is only a guide. *We can not accept responsibility for trail conditions or for trail information.* This is our disclaimer that we do not accept liability or legal responsibility for any injuries, damage, or losses allegedly caused by using this book. For the best information, check the local ranger stations.

Marin County
Topographic Map

This topographic map uses grey scale to indicate elevation. White is 2600' elevation and black is 0' elevation. The map was created by taking USGS digital elevation data and converting it to shades of grey.

Because the eye is very sensitive to changes in grey, the map clearly shows the main geological features of Marin. The most prominent feature is the Point Reyes peninsula, which is separated from the rest of Marin by the Olema Valley or San Andreas Fault Zone.

Mt. Tamalpais is the highest (whitest point on the map) mountain in Marin County and the mountain crest can be seen running down to Rock Spring, then turning northwest and following Bolinas Ridge, which parallels Olema Valley. Just to the north of Bolinas Ridge, Lagunitas Creek drains into Tomales Bay.

Selected Mountains of Marin

Mt. Tamalpais	2571'	G6	Mt. Wittenberg	1407'	E3
Big Rock	1887'	D5	Firtop	1324'	F3
Pine Mountain	1762'	F5	Pt. Reyes Hill	1336'	D2
Loma Alta	1592'	E6	Mt. Vision	1282'	D2
Mt. Burdell	1558'	C6	Black Mountain	1280'	D3
Hicks Mountain	1532'	C4	Oat Hill	1200'	F5
Mt. Barnabe	1466'	E4	Pilot Knob	1187'	F6
Shroyer Mtn.	1458'	D5	Bald Hill	1141'	F6
White Hill	1430'	F5	San Pedro Mtn.	1058'	E7

Note that Mt. Tamalpais includes an entire ridgeline running from East Peak at 2571' through West Peak at 2560' to Rock Spring at 1970' (marked at G5), all points higher than any other mountain in Marin.

/

A - Southern Marin - 15 Hikes

Starting from East Fort Baker at 60'
A1 ..... Bay Trail and Fire Road 1.6 and 1.0

Starting from along Conzelman Road
A2 ..... Kirby Cove and Hawk Hill Trails 1.8 and 0.5
A3 ..... Coastal - SCA - Bobcat Trails 7.1

Starting from Rodeo Beach at 20'
A4 ..... Rodeo Beach to Point Bonita 3.7
A5 ..... Coastal - Wolf Ridge - Miwok Trails 5.2

Starting from Tennessee Valley
A6 ..... Oakwood Valley - Bobcat - Miwok Trails 5.1
A7 ..... Tennessee Valley Trail 3.8
A8 ..... Miwok - Coyote Ridge - Coastal Trails 5.1

Starting from Panoramic Hwy at 660'
A9 ..... Diaz Ridge - Redwood Creek Trails 6.3

Starting from Muir Beach at 20'
A10 ... Coastal - Coyote Ridge - Green Gulch Trails 5.0

Starting from Tiburon Peninsula at 20'
A11 ... Ring Mountain Nature Preserve 2.8

Starting from Angel Island at 2'
A12 ... Northridge Trail to Mt. Livermore 6.2
A13 ... Angel Island Perimeter Trail 5.2

Starting from Mill Valley at 200'
A14 ... Glen - Warner Cyn. - Blithedale Ridge FR 4.3

Starting from Larkspur at 170'
A15 ... Baltimore Canyon to Blithedale Ridge 3.9

Pets allowed on hikes 5, 14 and 15.

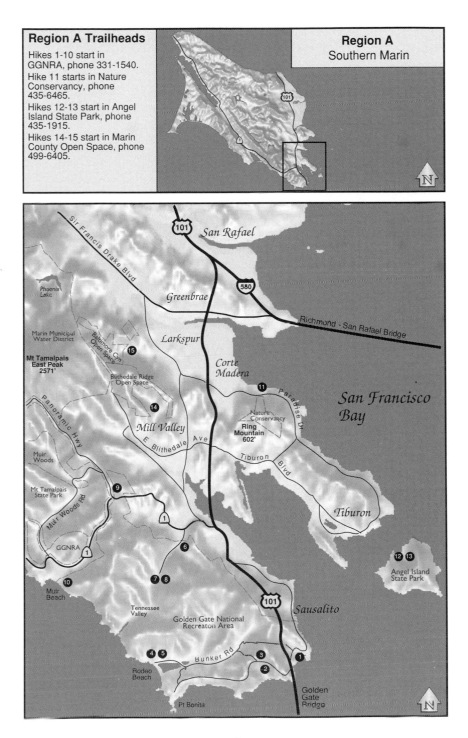

Region A Trailheads

Hikes 1-10 start in GGNRA, phone 331-1540.

Hike 11 starts in Nature Conservancy, phone 435-6465.

Hikes 12-13 start in Angel Island State Park, phone 435-1915.

Hikes 14-15 start in Marin County Open Space, phone 499-6405.

Region A
Southern Marin

A1 Bay Trail and Fire Rd. in Fort Baker

Distance: 1.6 and 1.0 miles   Shaded: Bay Trail 0%, Fire Rd. 60%
Elevation Change: 30' and 200'   Some auto traffic along route.
Rating: Hiking - 8   Difficulty - 2
When to Go: Best when calm and clear. Bring binoculars.
One hike explores the shoreline in East Fort Baker. The other hike climbs up a ridge to offer a classic view of the Golden Gate Bridge.

To the Fishing Pier and Back - 1.6 miles and 30' Change

0.0 From the Bay trail parking area, head downhill 70 yds. to pick up the Bay trail that starts down a flight of stairs. At the bottom of the stairs, head right in front of the long warehouse building.

0.1 Bay Area Discovery Museum and junction. The children's museum is open afternoons except Mondays (and Tuesdays during the school year.) Head left along the gravel road and follow it in the opposite direction of the one-way auto traffic.

0.2 Junction and bunker. Head left to explore the cliff and area around Battery Yates, which was built in 1906. Then return here to continue along the road.

0.6 Cavallo Pt. and the Presidio Yacht Club. At the old gun platform, head right around the rock towards the breakwater. **Option:** You can walk out along the breakwater to view the sailboats and small craft.

0.7 At the end of the parking area, head left across the gangplank in front of the Yacht Club building. Continue west along the beach.

0.9 Coast Guard Station. Continue around the beach area.

1.0 Fishing pier and turnaround pt. #1. The end of the pier offers great views of the bridge and also of Lime Pt., which is directly under the bridge. Lime Pt. is named after a 20 ton schooner that shipwrecked there in 1878. Return to the parking area.

Fire Rd. to the Ridge and Back - 1.0 miles and 200' Change

0.0 From the Bay trail parking area, head downhill 80 yds. to pick up the Fire Rd. that heads up to the right.

0.4 Junction. The road heads left. A spur trail climbs the ridgeline to two small, sandbagged bunkers offering a classic view of the bridge.

East Fort Baker was constructed in 1897 as a harbor defense site. It is named after Colonel Edward Baker, a civil war hero, lawyer, U.S. Senator and friend of Abraham Lincoln.

0.5 Viewpoint and turnaround pt. #2.

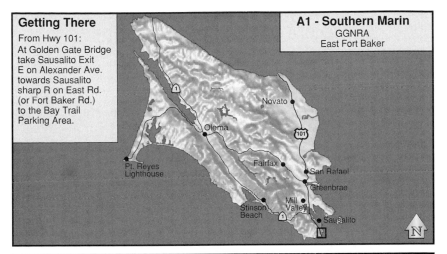

Getting There

From Hwy 101:
At Golden Gate Bridge
take Sausalito Exit
E on Alexander Ave.
towards Sausalito
sharp R on East Rd.
(or Fort Baker Rd.)
to the Bay Trail
Parking Area.

A1 - Southern Marin
GGNRA
East Fort Baker

Novato

Olema

101

Pt. Reyes
Lighthouse

Fairfax

San Rafael

Greenbrae

Stinson
Beach

Mill
Valley

1

Sausalito

N

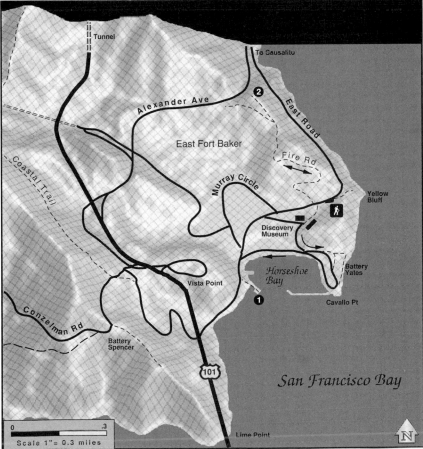

Tunnel

To Sausalito

Alexander Ave

East Road

2

East Fort Baker

Fire Rd

Coastal Trail

Murray Circle

Yellow
Bluff

Discovery
Museum

Horseshoe
Bay

Battery
Yates

Vista Point

1

Cavallo Pt

Conzelman Rd

Battery
Spencer

101

San Francisco Bay

0   .3

Scale 1"= 0.3 miles

Lime Point

N

A2 Kirby Cove and Hawk Hill Trails

Distance: 1.8 and 0.5 miles   Shaded: Kirby C. 30%, Hawk Hill 10%
Elevation Change: 400' and 50'   Can be windy.
Rating: Hiking - 9   Difficulty - 3   Moderately steep hills.
When to Go: Best when calm and clear in September and October.

These two out-and-back hikes explore the southern Marin Headlands offering unparalleled views. Observe fall raptor migration at Hawk Hill.

To Kirby Cove and Back - 1.8 miles and 400' Change

0.0 Park at Battery Spencer on Conzelman Rd. right above the Golden Gate Bridge. Be sure to lock your car and take any valuables with you. **Option**: Take a short stroll out the ridge to a lookout point above the Golden Gate Bridge. The hike to Kirby Cove starts on the right by passing through a gate and heading down a paved road.

0.7 Junction. At a Y in the road, head left through the group camping area located under the pine trees.

0.9 Bunker and beach at Kirby Cove and turnaround pt. #1. There are trails to the beach at both ends of the beach.

To Hawk Hill and Back - 0.5 miles and 50' Change

0.0 Park at the top of Conzelman Rd. just before it becomes a one-way road. Take the upper tunnel through to the other side. An information sign at the start of the tunnel describes Battery 129.

At the other end of the tunnel, there is a great view of Pt. Bonita and the lighthouse. From here, follow the trail signs right.

0.1 Gun emplacement. The lower tunnel leads out to an enormous gun mount, built to house a 16" naval gun. Although the gun was brought to the site, it was never mounted. By 1943, the war had shifted to the western Pacific. Over one million cubic yds. of concrete were poured into this battery with walls and floors eight to twelve feet thick. The hike continues to the right, up the stairs.

0.2 Junction. Head left to explore the hilltop.

0.3 Hawk Hill and turnaround pt. #2. During the   *Red-tailed Hawk*
peak season, over 2000 hawks a day have been
counted passing overhead. These hawks concentrate here to catch the rising wind currents necessary to cross the waters of the Golden Gate. When ready to continue, return to the junction and take the paved road left downhill.

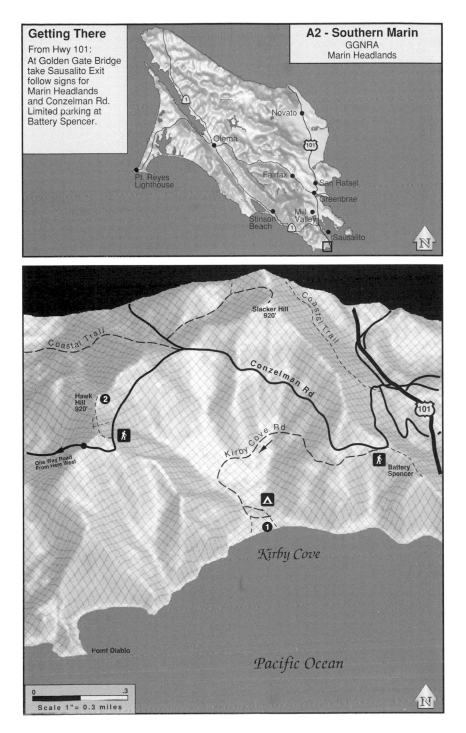

Getting There

From Hwy 101:
At Golden Gate Bridge
take Sausalito Exit
follow signs for
Marin Headlands
and Conzelman Rd.
Limited parking at
Battery Spencer.

A2 - Southern Marin
GGNRA
Marin Headlands

Novato

Olema

Pt. Reyes
Lighthouse

Fairfax

San Rafael

Greenbrae

Stinson
Beach

Mill
Valley

Sausalito

N

Coastal Trail

Slacker Hill
920'

Coastal Trail

Conzelman Rd

Hawk
Hill
920'

❷

Kirby Cove Rd

One Way Road
From Here West

Battery
Spencer

101

❶

Kirby Cove

Point Diablo

Pacific Ocean

0   .3
Scale 1" = 0.3 miles

N

A3 Coastal - SCA - Bobcat Trails

Distance: 7.1 miles   Shaded: 10%
Elevation Change: 1000'   Heavy bicycle traffic on weekends.
Rating: Hiking - 9   Difficulty - 5   Some poison oak.
When to Go: Good when calm and clear. Best in March for flowers.

This is a great hike that travels above Rodeo Valley and down Gerbode Valley. It offers sweeping views and beautiful wildflowers.

0.0 Park near the junction of Conzelman Rd. and McCullough Rd. and walk down McCullough Rd. 50 yds. to the trail gate. Take the Coastal trail uphill. The hike starts out in dense coastal scrub that includes coyote bush, cow parsley, blackberries, sage, poison oak, bracken fern and wild cucumber. Up ahead, on the right, notice the large rock precariously perched on the hillside.

0.3 Junction #1. Take the short spur trail right to Slacker Hill.

0.6 Slacker Hill at 920'. Incomparable views. Return to junction #1.

0.9 Junction #1. Go right. Ahead, after crossing the ridgetop, look for a variety of spring flowers. Also, watch out for poison oak.

1.2 Junction and wind funnel. Stay on the ridge on the SCA trail. In the fall, afternoon winds are funneled up Rodeo Valley to roar over this low spot in the ridgeline.

2.2 Junction #2 with the Rodeo Valley trail. Head straight, then right, then left towards the eucalyptus trees. Pass through the gate and enter a small rain forest created by the tall trees and heavy fog drip. Notice the growth of ivy 50' up the trunks of the eucalyptus.

2.4 Junction. Continue past the Morning Sun trail, then take a short spur trail right to a viewpoint. Return down the road to the left.

2.9 Junction #3. Go left, then left again to take the Bobcat trail down.

3.0 Junction. In April, a carpet of yellow lotus marks this junction. Stay right on the Bobcat trail to make a long downhill descent.

5.0 Junction. Take the Rodeo Valley trail left.

5.4 Double junction #4. Go right, then left to cross a small bridge that leads to a paved road. Head right out to Bunker Rd.

5.5 Bunker Rd. Cross the road and take the Coastal trail into the meadow. Ahead at the gate, continue straight. Wildflowers include poppies, blue lupine, Indian paintbrush and yellow mimulus. As you head uphill, stay right. Watch for bicycles and more great flowers.

7.1 Gate and parking area.

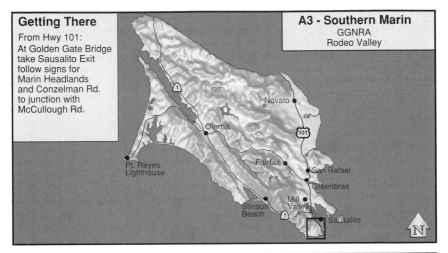

Getting There

From Hwy 101:
At Golden Gate Bridge
take Sausalito Exit
follow signs for
Marin Headlands
and Conzelman Rd.
to junction with
McCullough Rd.

A3 - Southern Marin
GGNRA
Rodeo Valley

Novato

Olema

Pt. Reyes
Lighthouse

Fairfax

San Rafael

Greenbrae

Mill
Valley

Stinson
Beach

Sausalito

Bobcat Tr

FAA
Tower
1041'

Hawk
Campground

Morning
Sun

Wolfback Ridge Rd

Gerbode
Valley

Miwok Trail

Bobcat Trail

Rodeo
Valley

SCA Trail

Tunnel

Rodeo Valley Trail

Road

McCullough Rd

Coastal

Slacker
Hill
920'

Trail

Bunker

Coastal Trail

Conzelman Rd

Hawk
Hill
920'

Kirby Cove Rd

Lower
Fishermans
Trail

Upper
Fishermans
Trail

One Way Road
West from Here

Kirby Cove

0   .7
Scale 1"= 0.7 miles

Point Diablo

15

A4 Rodeo Beach to Point Bonita

Distance: 3.7 miles   Shaded: 10%
Elevation Change: 350'   Hike parallels road for 0.5 miles.
Rating: Hiking - 9   Difficulty - 4   Can be very windy.
When to Go: Good anytime. Often great weather in fall and winter.

This hike explores the beach, coastal area and old military fortifications from Rodeo Beach to Pt. Bonita. Great views.

0.0 From the Rodeo Beach parking area, head south along the beach. Up ahead, notice Bird Rock extending from the shoreline. To the west of Bird Rock lies the "Potato Patch", a dangerously shallow sandbar that can increase the height of northerly swells.

0.3 Junction #1. Follow the trail up the ridge through the iceplant.

0.5 Junction. Take the old road right towards the YMCA building.

0.8 Junction. Enter the YMCA area and follow the sidewalk along the front of the long dormitory. At the end of the dormitory, go right.

1.0 Junction. Take the paved road right past Battery Mendell. Be sure to follow the road counterclockwise to get the best views.

1.2 Bird Rock overlook. Great views of the coast north and south. To continue the hike, take the trail along the cliff past the two "pillboxes".

1.4 Far end of Battery Mendell. Continue along the clifftop another 70 yds. to a sign and a view down to the remains of a wrecked ship. Then backtrack and take the trail towards the lighthouse.

1.6 Junction #2. Take the road right towards the lighthouse. Ahead, at the low point on the trail, you can see remains of the Life Saving Station established in 1899 because of the more than 20 shipwrecks on the nearby Marin coast. (The lighthouse trail may be closed due to cliff erosion.) The hike returns to the entrance road.

1.9 Junction #2 with the entrance road. Take the main road right.

2.0 Junction. Head right uphill towards Battery Wallace.

2.3 Junction #3. **Option:** A trail right drops 250' to a small sandy beach that offers shelter from the wind and great views. Otherwise follow the road sign that says "Beach" past the old missile site.

The Nike missile site is open the first Sunday of each month.

2.8 Junction #4 and Visitor Center. It's worth a stop at the Visitor Center to see the displays. Then, take the Lagoon trail left.

3.7 Back at the parking area with water, tables and restrooms.

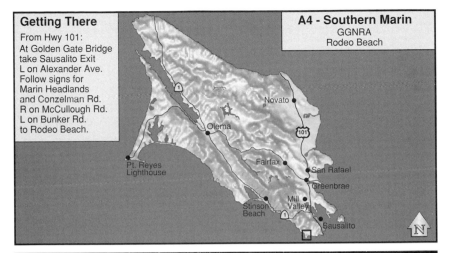

Getting There

From Hwy 101:
At Golden Gate Bridge
take Sausalito Exit
L on Alexander Ave.
Follow signs for
Marin Headlands
and Conzelman Rd.
R on McCullough Rd.
L on Bunker Rd.
to Rodeo Beach.

A4 - Southern Marin
GGNRA
Rodeo Beach

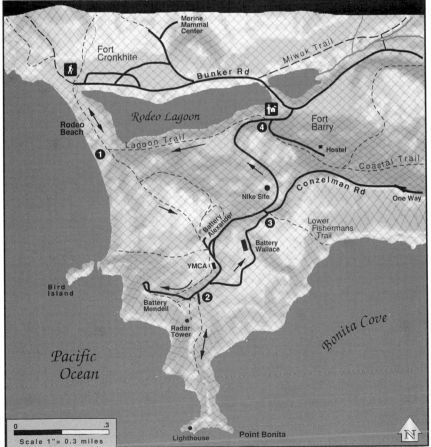

A5 Coastal - Wolf Ridge - Miwok Trails

Distance: 5.2 miles   Shaded: 0%
Elevation Change: 1000'   Trail rutted in places. Can be muddy.
Rating: Hiking - 7   Difficulty - 7   One steep section.
When to Go: Good when clear, calm. Best March-May for flowers.

This is one of the best ridge hikes in the Marin Headlands offering great coastal views, many old bunkers and hills of wildflowers.

0.0 From the parking area, go past the gate and up the paved road.

0.1 Junction. Take the trail left towards the ocean and a fortified lookout point. At the bunker, continue uphill and parallel the road.

0.2 Steep cliffs. The trail skirts a steep cliff that drops off dramatically to a small ocean cove. Stay back from the cliff edge!

0.3 Junction. Continue left on the dirt road. Good ocean views.

0.4 Junction #1. Take the trail right. The road left ends at a fence.

0.5 Junction. The trail joins the paved road and heads inland. Up ahead, the road passes Battery Townsley, an underground bunker system that held two 16-inch naval guns. After the bombing of Pearl Harbor, this battery housed 150 men on 15 minute alert.

0.7 Junction. The road right heads downhill. Continue left. Ahead, part of the road is closed due to a major slide. Take the path on the right, which heads through dense coastal scrub up to stairs.

1.1 Junction. The trail joins the paved road again. Continue uphill.

1.2 Junction #2. Take the red gravel road left towards a bunker and some great views north to Tennessee Valley. Continue up the road, which, if open, is steep and rocky, but much more interesting than the paved road. At the top, walk carefully around the collapsing bunkers.

1.5 Junction. The trail joins the road. Continue east.

1.6 Junction #3 with Wolf Ridge trail. Continue up the road to Hill 88.

1.8 Hill 88. This was once a Nike missile radar station. Now, it is a group camp site. Great 360 degree views. Return to junction #3.

2.0 Junction #3. Take the Wolf Ridge trail right. Good flowers ahead.

2.7 Junction #4. Take the Miwok trail right downhill. Look for fields of flowers in April, fragrant blue lupine and yellow poppies.

4.1 Junction #5. Continue right on the Miwok trail.

4.5 Warehouse. Cross Bunker Road and take the trail west.

5.2 Back at the parking area with water and restrooms.

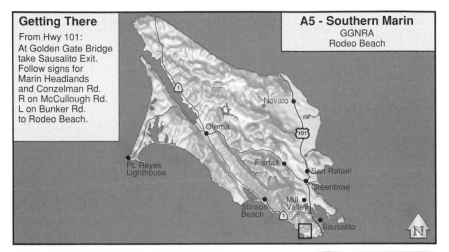

Getting There

From Hwy 101:
At Golden Gate Bridge
take Sausalito Exit.
Follow signs for
Marin Headlands
and Conzelman Rd.
R on McCullough Rd.
L on Bunker Rd.
to Rodeo Beach.

A5 - Southern Marin
GGNRA
Rodeo Beach

Novato

Olema

Pt. Reyes
Lighthouse

Fairfax

San Rafael

Greenbrae

Mill
Valley

Stinson
Beach

Sausalito

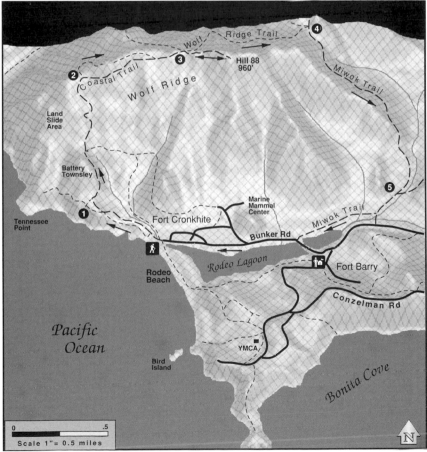

Ridge Trail

Wolf

❹

❸

Hill 88
960'

Miwok Trail

❷

Coastal Trail

Wolf Ridge

Land
Slide
Area

Battery
Townsley

❺

Tennessee
Point

❶

Fort Cronkhite

Marine
Mammal
Center

Miwok Trail

Bunker Rd

Rodeo Lagoon

Fort Barry

Rodeo
Beach

Conzelman Rd

Pacific
Ocean

YMCA

Bird
Island

Bonita Cove

0   .5
Scale 1"= 0.5 miles

19

A6 Oakwood Valley - Bobcat - Miwok

Distance: 5.1 miles   Shaded: 30%
Elevation Change: 1000'   Some poison oak. May be windy.
Rating: Hiking - 7   Difficulty - 6   Can be muddy.
When to Go: Good when clear and calm. Best in April for flowers.
This hike climbs out of Oakwood Valley to the second highest point in the Marin Headlands, then returns via Tennessee Valley.

0.0 Park along the road just past the small one-lane bridge. There are two parallel routes up Oakwood Valley. It's best to take the road just before the bridge if the ground is wet. This hike describes the alternate route, a trail that starts just past the bridge and heads to the right of the open meadow. At the top of the meadow, watch out for poison oak, which crowds the trail if it has not been cleared recently.

0.7 Bridge and junction. The trail crosses a bridge to join the road.

0.9 Small ranch pond. Continue left on the road.

1.0 Junction #1. One hundred yds. before the road deadends in a thicket of broom, take the trail to the right.

1.4 Hilltop and junction. Continue 50' past an old road to the main road and bear right. Good views east.

1.8 Junction and viewpoint. Stay on the road to the right.

1.9 Two junctions #2. Go right, then right again to take the signed Bobcat trail, which heads north towards power lines.

This "trail" was once a 60' wide road that was part of Marincello, a proposed city of 30,000 planned for the headlands in the 1960s. The development was blocked in court and the land sold to the Nature Conservancy for $6.5 million. Later, it was given to the GGNRA.

2.7 Junction #3. Continue on the Bobcat trail towards the antenna.

3.0 FAA antenna. For a good view south, walk 100 yds. along the south side of the fenced FAA transmitter, then backtrack to junction #3 and take the north Miwok trail downhill.

4.3 Stables, road and junction #4. Go down the gravel road 100 yds. to the parking area, then down the paved road 100' to take the Miwok trail which starts out on the left side of the road.

4.4 Junction. Continue downhill to the right. The Miwok trail goes uphill. Watch for poison oak, especially near the eucalyptus groves.

5.1 The trail crosses the creek to return to the parking area.

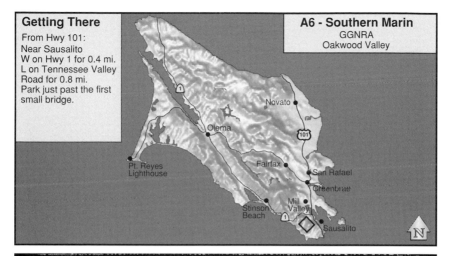

Getting There

From Hwy 101:
Near Sausalito
W on Hwy 1 for 0.4 mi.
L on Tennessee Valley
Road for 0.8 mi.
Park just past the first
small bridge.

A6 - Southern Marin
GGNRA
Oakwood Valley

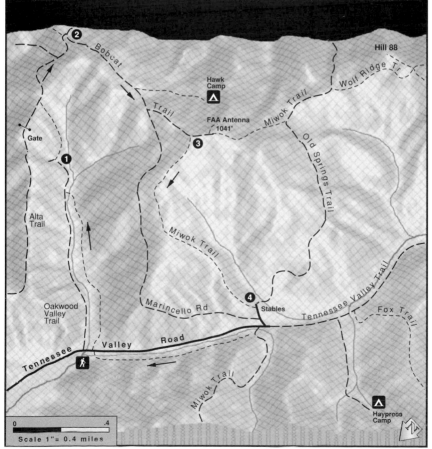

Scale 1"= 0.4 miles

21

A7 Tennessee Valley Trail

Distance: 3.8 miles   Shaded: 0%
Elevation Change: 200'   Crowded on weekends. Bicycles likely.
Rating: Hiking - 8   Difficulty - 1   Can be very windy.
When to Go: Best when clear, calm and low tide.

This is one of the most popular hikes in Marin as it offers easy, level access to the beach and ocean. Good flowers on cliffs by the beach.

0.0 From the parking area, head west past the gate on the road.

0.7 Junction and ranch house. Continue straight on the dirt road.

1.0 Junction #1. Take the trail left which does not allow bicycles. You may notice scat on the trail, most likely from bobcat, fox or skunks. In the 1840s, this valley, also known as "Elk Valley", was abundant with mammals. Historian Jack Mason writes that, "the ground was white with the bones of deer, elk and wild cattle killed for their hides."

1.7 Lagoon and dam. The old stock pond invites a variety of shorebirds, mallard ducks, coots, sea gulls and occasionally pelicans.

1.8 Beach and junction #2. Head down to the south end of the beach.

1.9 Wreck of the *S.S. Tennessee*. During certain times of the year, when the sand is lowered by wave action, it is possible to see remains of the *Tennessee* (usually the engine), which beached here on a foggy March 6, 1853. The *Tennessee* was a side-paddle steamer that carried 551 passengers bound for San Francisco and the gold rush. Eventually, they all made it, as did much of the cargo. Two smaller vessels also wrecked here, the *Tagus* in 1851 and the *Fourth of July* in 1878. The only casualty was the captain of the fifty-ton *Fourth of July* who was killed when enormous waves tossed his ship end over end onto the sand.

S.S. Tennessee
Shipwrecked here in 1853

Option: At low tide, it may be possible to get around the southern rocks to another small, sandy beach with interesting rock formations.

2.0 Junction #2. **Option**: A small trail makes a moderately steep climb to a bunker and great view point. Otherwise, retrace your steps.

3.8 Back at the parking area with restroom and picnic tables.

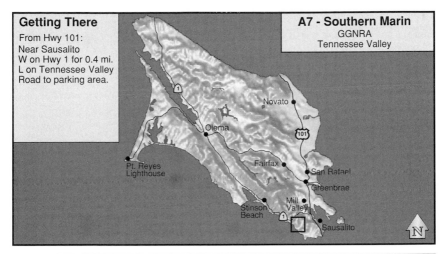

Getting There

From Hwy 101:
Near Sausalito
W on Hwy 1 for 0.4 mi.
L on Tennessee Valley
Road to parking area.

A7 - Southern Marin
GGNRA
Tennessee Valley

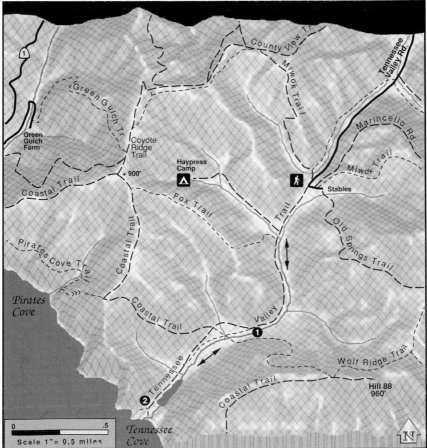

23

A8 Miwok - Coyote Ridge - Coastal Trails

Distance: 5.1 miles   Shaded: 0%
Elevation Change: 1000'   Can be windy. May be overgrown.
Rating: Hiking - 7   Difficulty - 5   Moderately steep in places.
When to Go: Good when clear. Best weather often in fall and winter.

This hike climbs out of Tennessee Valley to Coyote Ridge, then returns down the Coastal trail. Great views of the ocean and valleys.

0.0 From the east end of the Tennessee Valley parking lot, take the signed Miwok trail, which starts out paralleling the road downhill.

0.1 Bridge and junction. Continue left, uphill on the Miwok trail.

0.9 Junction #1. Take the far left trail to head across the top of the ravine. Good views down to the valley. Tennessee Valley, also known as "Elk Valley", was once part of the 19,000 acre Rancho Saucelito granted to William Richardson in 1838. Captain Richardson was the first port captain for San Francisco Bay. His all-Indian crew used a tule raft to meet incoming ships and guide them into the bay.

1.2 Ridgetop and Y-junction. A trail right leads to a road and good views to Mt. Tamalpais. Continue left. Note: There are three to four parallel routes on the ridgetop (only 100 yds. apart). Generally, this hike follows the trail farthest south, which is also the narrowest trail.

1.5 Rocky outcrop. This rocky ledge is easy to climb, offering good views south down the valley. Caution: Rattlesnakes often like to sun on rocks, especially in spring. Always watch where you walk. The hike continues on a narrow, overgrown trail to a rock outcrop.

1.7 Junction with an abandoned road. Head right uphill. At the top, check your clothes for ticks if grasses crowded the trail.

1.8 Junction #2 with Coyote Ridge trail. Head left uphill on the road.

1.9 High point at 1031'. Wonderful views in all directions.

2.1 Junction with the Green Gulch trail. Continue left.

2.3 Junction. Go left on the Coastal trail.

2.4 Junction with the Fox trail. Continue straight on the Coastal trail.

3.1 Junction #3. Before heading left down the Coastal trail, take the small trail west for 50 yds. to a bluff overlooking the ocean.

3.8 Junction. Take the Tennessee Valley trail left. **Option**: Go right if you want to visit the beach at Tennessee Cove.

5.1 Back at the parking area with restroom and tables.

Getting There

From Hwy 101:
Near Sausalito
W on Hwy 1 for 0.4 mi.
L on Tennessee Valley
Rd. to parking area.

A8 - Southern Marin
GGNRA
Tennessee Valley

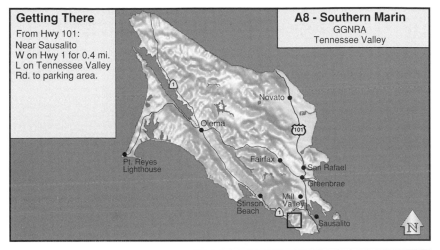

Novato

Olema

101

Pt. Reyes
Lighthouse

Fairfax

San Rafael

Greenbrae

Stinson
Beach

Mill
Valley

Sausalito

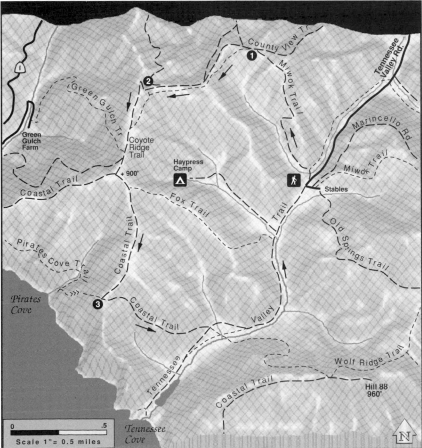

25

A9 Diaz Ridge - Redwood Creek Trails

Distance: 6.3 miles   Shaded: 20%
Elevation Change: 1000'   Can be windy. May be dusty in fall.
Rating: Hiking - 7   Difficulty - 7   Some steep downhill sections.
When to Go: Good in spring. Best weather often in fall and winter.

This hike follows Diaz Ridge down to Muir Beach, then circles back through Frank's Valley before making a gradual climb to the ridge.

0.0 Park about 0.1 mile past the switchback on Panoramic Hwy. Take the Diaz Ridge trail southwest through grasslands. This ridge is named after George Diaz who operated a ranch here and the Sausalito Creamery in the early 1900s.

0.4 Junction with the Miwok trail. Continue straight on Diaz Ridge.

1.2 Junction #1 and gate. Go through the chained gate and take the trail downhill. Be sure to refasten the chain. This pastureland is often used to graze horses. Ahead, great views to Muir Beach.

1.9 Junction and rock. The trail levels out on a knoll with a large rock outcrop. Head right downhill on one of an assortment of trails carved out by the horses. Aim for the back of the stables.

2.1 Junction #2 with Hwy 1. Cross the highway and take the paved road past the Pelican Inn to Muir Beach. This grove of Monterey pines along the road is winter home to thousands of Monarch butterflies that migrate here in the fall.

Monarch Butterfly

2.2 Junction. Take the fire lane to bypass the road.

2.5 Junction, bridge and beach. Follow the creek out to Muir Beach. Retrace steps back to junction #2 when ready to continue.

3.1 Junction #2. Carefully walk along the left shoulder of the highway.

3.3 Highway intersection and junction. Go up the Muir Woods Road for 50' to pick up the Redwood Creek trail.

4.5 Junction and option. You can take a 1.2 mile detour to a small, but lovely, waterfall in Kent Canyon. The trail goes through the creek, crosses the road and heads up Kerri Lane past the aluminum barn.

4.8 Junction #3. Take the signed Miwok trail right to begin a long, gradual climb into a bay-filled canyon. Look for shooting star, trillium and hounds tongue in early March. Poison oak may crowd the trail.

5.9 Junction. Take the Diaz Ridge trail left.

6.3 Back at the parking area. No facilities.

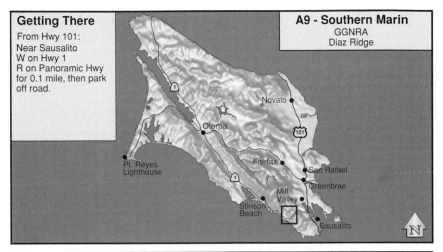

Getting There

From Hwy 101:
Near Sausalito
W on Hwy 1
R on Panoramic Hwy
for 0.1 mile, then park
off road.

A9 - Southern Marin
GGNRA
Diaz Ridge

Novato

Olema

101

Pt. Reyes
Lighthouse

Fairfax

San Rafael

Greenbrae

Mill
Valley

Stinson
Beach

Sausalito

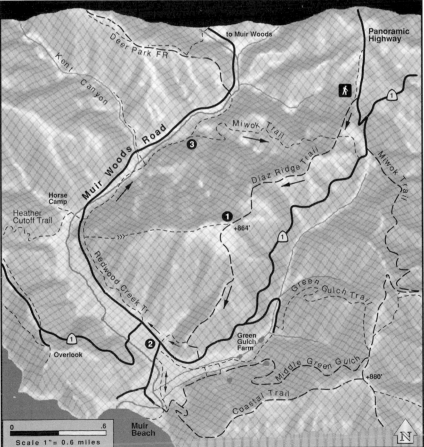

Deer Park FR

to Muir Woods

Panoramic
Highway

Kent Canyon

1

Miwok Trail

Muir Woods Road

3

Diaz Ridge Trail

Miwok Trail

Horse
Camp

Heather
Cutoff Trail

1

+864'

1

Redwood Creek Tr

Green Gulch Trail

1

Overlook

Green
Gulch
Farm

2

Middle Green Gulch

+880'

Coastal Trail

0   .6
Scale 1"= 0.6 miles

Muir
Beach

N

A10 Coastal - Coyote Rdg. - Green Gulch

Distance: 5.0 miles   Shaded: 10%
Elevation Change: 1300'   Poison oak possible.
Rating: Hiking - 9   Difficulty - 9   One very steep uphill section.
When to Go: Great whenever clear and not windy.
This hike out of Muir Beach passes through wild and remote coastal hills offering striking views of the ocean. Good wildflowers in spring.

0.0 From the end of the parking lot, head west towards the ocean, then cross the footbridge over Redwood Creek. After the first heavy rains, salmon pass here on the way to spawn in Muir Woods. On the other side of the bridge, go left to pick up the Coastal trail.

0.1 Junction with Green Gulch trail. Head right on the Coastal trail, which climbs gradually uphill with good views back to Muir Beach. Near the top of the hill, take the spur trail right to a fence that overlooks a peregrine falcon nest site.

0.7 Junction #1. Take the Pirates Cove trail (may be signed Coastal Trail) right, with spectacular views down plunging cliffs to the ocean.

1.5 Junction. At the bottom of a ravine, a short spur trail drops steeply 100' to a small plateau and a superb view of the coast and rugged cliffs. From here, the next section of trail is very steep.

1.7 Junction #2. After reaching a plateau, head left on the Coastal trail, which climbs more gradually.

2.4 Junction. The Fox trail joins from the right. Continue left.

2.5 Junction. Head right on the Coyote Ridge trail.

2.6 Junction #3. Take the Green Gulch trail left downhill. Look for spring flowers here including tidy tips, lupine and poppies.

2.9 Junction with a crossing trail. Continue straight downhill.

3.0 Hope Cottage. A small rock-wall cottage, originally built in 1888, is being restored by volunteers from Green Gulch Farm.

4.0 Junction #4 with road. Go right 50', then take the stairs down to the paved road. Continue left to pass through Green Gulch Farm, a non-profit farm and Zen center. Follow the main road past the plant nursery, down the center of the valley through the crop fields.

4.8 Junction and gate. Head left along the tall deer-fence, then right towards the ocean and wooden bridge.

5.0 Back at the parking area and restrooms.

Getting There

From Hwy 101:
Near Sausalito
W on Hwy 1
to Muir Beach, then
L to parking area.

A10 - Southern Marin
GGNRA
Muir Beach

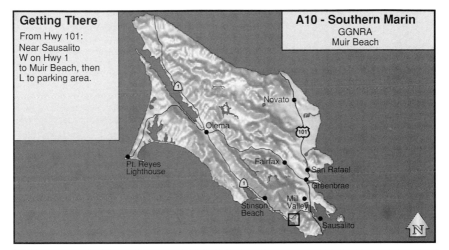

Novato

Olema

101

Pt. Reyes
Lighthouse

Fairfax

San Rafael

Greenbrae

Stinson
Beach

Mill
Valley

Sausalito

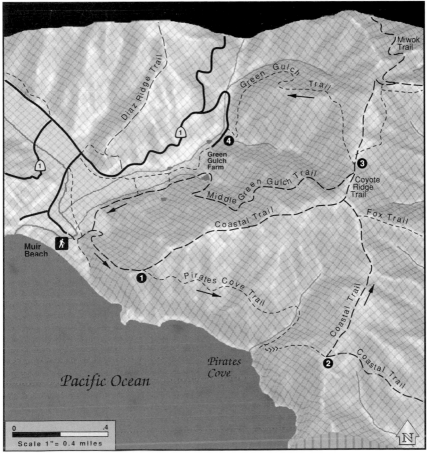

Miwok
Trail

Diaz Ridge Trail

Green Gulch Trail

Green
Gulch
Farm

4

3

Coyote
Ridge
Trail

Middle Green Gulch Trail

Coastal Trail

Fox Trail

Muir
Beach

1

Pirates Cove Trail

Coastal Trail

Coastal Trail

2

Pacific Ocean

Pirates
Cove

0   .4
Scale 1"= 0.4 miles

A11 Ring Mountain Nature Preserve

Distance: 2.8 miles   Shaded: 10%
Elevation Change: 700'   Can be muddy. Strong winds possible.
Rating: Hiking - 10   Difficulty - 6   Rocky and rutted areas.
When to Go: Best on clear, calm days in March to May for flowers.

This climb up the grassy slopes of Ring Mountain provides some of the best views and wildflower displays in the bay area.

0.0 Park on Paradise Drive just past Westward Drive. Look for the Nature Preserve sign and gate. The trail crosses a small bridge to an information display. Pick up a nature guide if it's available.

0.2 Junction #1. Head left at the signed "Loop Trail". Up ahead, the trail crosses a small creek. Look for the white Oakland star tulip.

0.3 Post 4 and junction. There are several unofficial crossing trails. Continue right on the main trail. Numbered posts mark the way.

0.9 Knoll, road and junction #2. After climbing a knoll offering grand views south, the trail drops down to a road. Continue across the road to Turtle Rock. From the south side of the rock, take the footpath uphill to the east, aiming to the right of the water tank.

1.0 Junction. Continue across the road and head uphill on the unofficial trail, which soon passes over a white serpentine outcrop.

1.2 Junction #3. The trail meets the road, but again, leave the road and head right, up towards the highest point.

1.3 Ring Mountain at 602'. The summit of Ring Mountain was flattened to house anti-aircraft guns after World War II. The broad hilltop is worth exploring for its magnificent views and wildflowers. The hike continues by taking the paved road back towards the west.

1.5 Junction. The hike leaves the paved road and heads west.

1.6 Junction #2. Go back to Turtle Rock again and now take the path to the right, west down a rocky outcrop towards another large rock with the sign, "Protect Rare Lichens." Continue past the rock uphill.

1.8 Hilltop and junction #4. You can add another two miles to this hike by taking the dirt road left, out and back, along the ridge. Otherwise, head right downhill and right again at another junction.

2.0 Junction #5. Take the Phyllis Ellman trail. At post 13, take the upper trail left to look for the rare Tiburon Mariposa Lily, a tan-colored calochortus that grows only on Ring Mountain and flowers in late May.

2.8 Back at the parking area with no facilities.

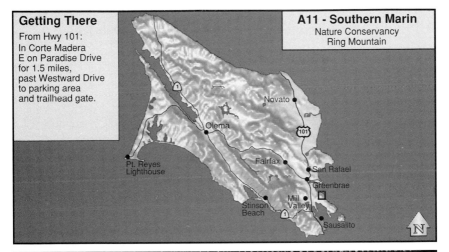

Getting There

From Hwy 101:
In Corte Madera
E on Paradise Drive
for 1.5 miles,
past Westward Drive
to parking area
and trailhead gate.

A11 - Southern Marin
Nature Conservancy
Ring Mountain

Novato

Olema

Pt. Reyes
Lighthouse

Fairfax

San Rafael

Greenbrae

Mill
Valley

Stinson
Beach

Sausalito

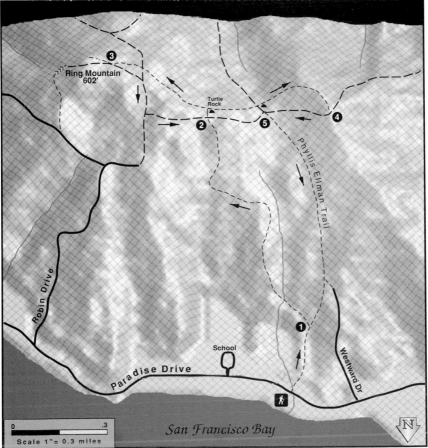

Ring Mountain
602'

Turtle
Rock

Phyllis Ellman Trail

Robin Drive

Westward Dr

School

Paradise Drive

San Francisco Bay

Scale 1" = 0.3 miles

0   .3

A12 Northridge Trail to Mt. Livermore

Distance: 6.2 miles   Shaded: 50%
Elevation Change: 800'   For ferry info from Marin, call 435-2131.
Rating: Hiking - 9   Difficulty - 6   Afternoons can be windy.
When to Go: Best anytime when clear. Pretty spring wildflowers.
Bring binoculars and camera to climb to the highest point on Angel
Island with one of the most spectacular views in the world.

0.0 When you get off the ferry, immediately head left and take the
signed Northridge trail uphill. The trail starts out under oaks and
pines, passes a small picnic area, then climbs a series of stairs.

0.2 Junction #1 with Perimeter Rd. Continue uphill on the Northridge
trail which is much less steep. Good views down to Ayala Cove and
north to Tiburon and Mt. Tamalpais. Wherever the trail enters the
northeast side of the island, vegetation is dense.

1.2 Junction with Fire Rd. Go left 50' and continue up the trail.

2.3 Junction #2 with the road and Sunset trail. Great views south to
Alcatraz Island and San Francisco. Take the paved road uphill.

2.6 Mt. Livermore at 781' and picnic benches. Spectacular views in
all directions. Be sure to look at the information display signs.

2.9 Junction #2. Take the Sunset trail right, which starts out in an
area where non-native eucalyptus trees were cut and then removed
by helicopter. Angel Island was once known as Wood Island and most
of the island's trees were cut to supply steamships entering the bay.

3.7 Ridgeline, bench and junction #3. Go left on the Fire Rd.

4.2 Junction. Take the trail downhill to the right which aims straight
for the Golden Gate Bridge. The trail gets rocky and steep for a short
distance as it descends over a serpentine outcrop. Down below, the
trail passes a water tank, campsite and Battery Wallace, built in 1898.

4.6 Junction #4. Take Perimeter Rd. to the right.

4.8 Junction. Head left on the road to Camp Reynolds and the West
Garrison. Fortifications were first built here in 1864 to help defend
San Francisco from Confederate raiding ships.

If possible, take the docent-led tour of the recently restored
bakehouse and officer quarters. After exploring the area, continue
north up the stairs to rejoin the Perimeter Rd.

5.9 Junction #5. Take the paved road left downhill.

6.2 Ayala Cove, Visitor Center, snackbar and ferry dock.

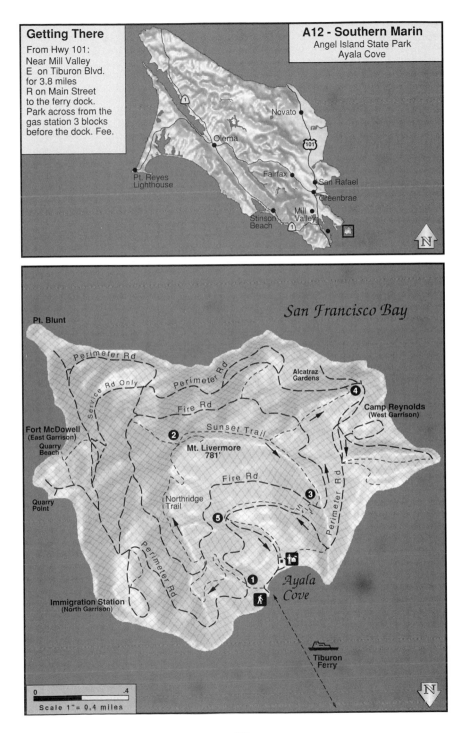

Getting There

From Hwy 101:
Near Mill Valley
E on Tiburon Blvd.
for 3.8 miles
R on Main Street
to the ferry dock.
Park across from the
gas station 3 blocks
before the dock. Fee.

A12 - Southern Marin
Angel Island State Park
Ayala Cove

Novato

Olema

Pt. Reyes
Lighthouse

Fairfax

San Rafael

Greenbrae

Stinson
Beach

Mill
Valley

N

San Francisco Bay

Pt. Blunt

Perimeter Rd

Perimeter Rd

Service Rd Only

Perimeter

Rd Only

Alcatraz
Gardens

Fire Rd

4

Camp Reynolds
(West Garrison)

Fort McDowell
(East Garrison)

Sunset Trail

2

Quarry
Beach

Mt. Livermore
781'

Perimeter Rd

Fire Rd

Quarry
Point

Northridge
Trail

3

5

Perimeter Rd

1

Ayala
Cove

Immigration Station
(North Garrison)

Tiburon
Ferry

0   .4

Scale 1"= 0,4 miles

N

A13 Angel Island Perimeter Trail

Distance: 5.2 miles   Shaded: 30%
Elevation Change: 300'
Rating: Hiking - 9 Difficulty - 3   Lots of bicycles.
When to Go: Best when clear. Afternoons can be windy.
This hike on the main road around Angel Island visits all the historical areas including the Immigration Station. Great views and picnic sites.

0.0 From the dock, walk to the picnic area and Visitor Center in Ayala Cove. Then, take the dirt road that heads west up to Perimeter Rd.

0.3 Junction #1. Take Perimeter Rd to the right to circle the island counterclockwise. Stay to the right and watch for bicycles.

0.7 Junction#2 with Camp Reynolds. The artillery batteries near here were part of the defense system of San Francisco Bay that included the Presidio, Fort Point and Fort Scott in San Francisco, Alcatraz Island, and Fort Cronkhite, Fort Barry and Fort Baker on the Marin Headlands. The various gun emplacements started with Spanish cannons at Fort Point in 1776 and ended in 1974 with the closing of a Nike missile site at Fort Barry. The local batteries started in the 1860s and were replaced in the 1900s.

1.2 Battery Ledyard. Spectacular views of the Golden Gate.

2.7 Nike missile site.

2.9 Junction #3 with Fort McDowell. Just above the group picnic area, take the stairs downhill. Then go left to pass in front of the large grey building. **Option:** Continue right to Quarry Beach.

3.2 Junction with road to the dock at Quarry Point. Continue straight. Up ahead you can explore the yellow building on the left. **Option:** You can also explore the area to the right down by the dock.

4.1 Junction #4. Take the road downhill to the Immigration Station.

4.3 Immigration Station, museum and China Cove. The museum is open weekends. This station, built in 1910, was designed as an "Ellis Island West" to handle the expected arrival of Europeans when the Panama Canal opened. That never happened as a result of World War 1 and the station wound up handling mostly Chinese immigrants. The station closed in 1940 after 175,000 Chinese had gone through.

4.5 Junction #4 with Perimeter Rd. Head right.

4.9 Junction #5. Take the trail or the road down to Ayala Cove.

5.2 Back at the ferry dock. Snackbar, bicycle rentals and restrooms.

Getting There

From Hwy 101:
Near Mill Valley
E on Tiburon Blvd.
for 3.8 miles
R on Main Street
to the ferry dock.
Park across from the
gas station 3 blocks
before the dock. Fee.

A13 - Southern Marin
Angel Island State Park
Ayala Cove

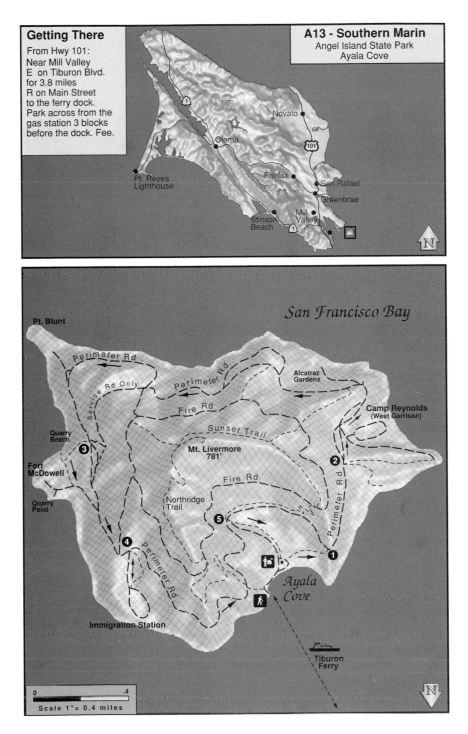

A14 Warner Cyn. FR - Blithedale Ridge

Distance: 4.3 miles   Shaded: 50%
Elevation Change: 900'   May have standing water.
Rating: Hiking - 9   Difficulty - 8   One steep uphill climb.
When to Go: Best in winter for falls and early March for trillium.

This hike circles Warner Canyon to visit the small winter falls, then climbs to Blithedale Ridge to offer great views of Mt. Tamalpais.

0.0 Start at the Open Space gate at the end of Glen Drive and take the Glen FR uphill. Ahead, you can get a good feel for Warner Canyon which has mostly redwoods on the north-facing slopes and oaks and chaparral along the south-facing Glen FR.

0.4 Junction #1. Take the Warner Canyon FR left. The road crosses the head of the canyon and a creek, then heads gradually downhill.

1.3 Junction #2. Take the signed Warner Cyn. trail left (The sign should read Warner Falls trail). The trail may be overgrown.

1.8 Warner Falls. Since the canyon is fairly small, water runoff and the series of cascades are best seen after heavy rains. Look for trillium in late winter. The trail ends here at the falls. Various paths up along the falls are very steep and unsafe. Retrace your steps.

2.3 Junction #2. Take the Warner Canyon FR right uphill.

2.4 Junction. At a sharp bend in the road, a small trail heads left through broom and into redwoods. The trail climbs steeply up the right side of a V-shaped ravine. Up ahead, a small path branches left, keep to the right.

2.5 Junction with the Maytag trail. Near the top of the ridge, at a T-junction, head left to the top of the ridge.

2.5+ Junction #3. Take the Blithedale Ridge FR right. (On hot days, you can backtrack and follow the Maytag trail as it parallels the ridge.) Up ahead, look for great views across Blithedale Canyon to Mt. Tam.

3.3 Junction #4. Take the Corte Madera Ridge FR right. About 100' ahead, the road offers a classic view down Warner Canyon and out across Richardson Bay to San Francisco. Warner Canyon was named after Alexander Warner, a San Francisco physician who bought a summer home here in 1885.

3.4 Junction. Take the Glen FR downhill to the right.

3.9 Junction #1. Continue left down the Glen FR.

4.3 Back at the parking area. No facilities.

Getting There

From Hwy 101:
Near Mill Valley
W on East Blithedale
for 1.5 miles, then
R on Carmelita
R on Buena Vista Ave.
continue on Glen Dr.
to end of street.
Limited parking.

A14 - Southern Marin
Marin County Open Space
Warner Canyon

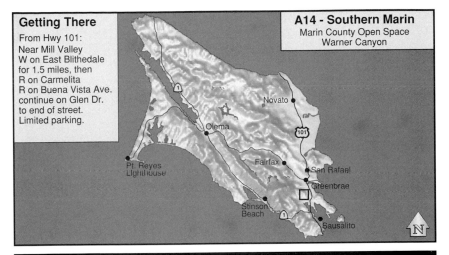

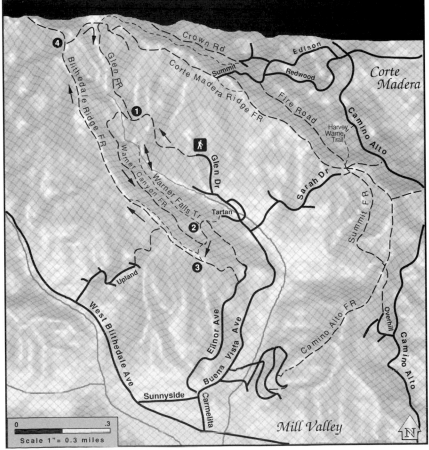

37

A15 Baltimore Cyn. to Blithedale Ridge

Distance: 3.9 miles   Shaded: 60%
Elevation Change: 700'   Can have standing water.
Rating: Hiking - 9   Difficulty - 9   One short, very steep climb.
When to Go: Best in winter for falls and early March for trillium.
This hike climbs to Blithedale Ridge for great views, then descends on the Dawn Falls trail to offer waterfalls and a redwood forest.

0.0 Follow the trail at the end of the road across the small bridge, then head right. Fifty yds. upstream, take the signed Barbara Springs trail to the left. This trail makes a short, very steep climb up a ravine. Lots of tall redwoods, moss-covered bay trees and low-growing tanoaks provide a woodsy setting.

0.3 Junction #1. Go right on Crown Rd., which is also called Southern Marin Line FR. The road was built by the water district to pipe water from the Bon Tempe treatment plant to southern Marin. The 24" pipe is buried beneath the road. Up ahead, glance down the hillside to your right. The slope is extremely steep.

0.7 Junction #2. At the exposed pipes, take the H-Line Rd. left uphill.

1.0 Junction. Take the Blithedale Ridge FR to the right. Up ahead, rewards for the steep climb are apparent with great views west to Mt. Tamalpais and east to the bay and Mt. Diablo.

1.5 Junction #3. Take the signed Hoo-Koo-E-Koo trail to the right. The hike now passes through dense chaparral: manzanita and chamise with occasional oak, bay and madrone trees. More great views down Baltimore Canyon.

1.9 Junction with Dawn Falls trail. Continue straight.

2.4 Junction #4. Take Crown Rd. to the right.

2.7 Junction. Take the Dawn Falls trail downhill to the left. This well-built trail makes several switchbacks to provide a gradual descent. Downhill, the trail skirts lovely Dawn Falls, then enters Baltimore Canyon. During heavy water runoff, sections of the trail can be flooded, which may require a detour. In early March, look for trillium that line the trail.

3.8 Old dam. The remains of a dam that provided water for the city of Larkspur span the creek. The dam, which was no longer in use, was dynamited in the 1920s, after an accidental drowning.

3.9 Back at the parking area with no facilities.

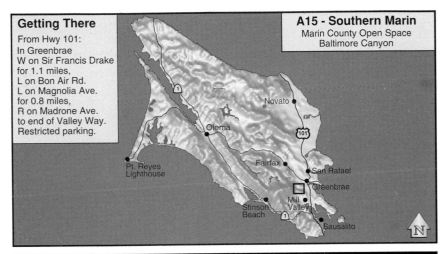

Getting There

From Hwy 101:
In Greenbrae
W on Sir Francis Drake
for 1.1 miles,
L on Bon Air Rd.
L on Magnolia Ave.
for 0.8 miles,
R on Madrone Ave.
to end of Valley Way.
Restricted parking.

A15 - Southern Marin
Marin County Open Space
Baltimore Canyon

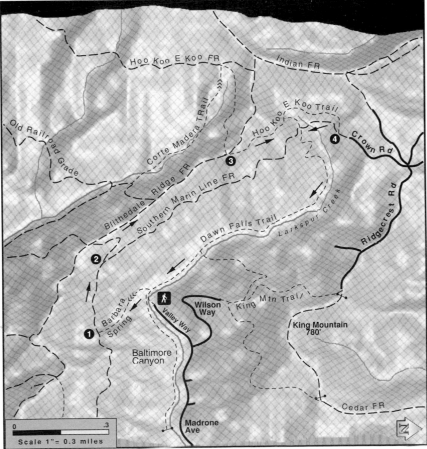

39

B - Mt. Tamalpais South - 21 Hikes

Starting from West Blithedale Ave at 240'
B1 ..... Blithedale Ridge - Corte Madera Trails 4.2
B2 ..... Old Railroad Grade - Hoo-Koo-E-Koo Road 7.4

Starting from Muir Woods at 150'
B3 ..... Muir Woods - Hillside Trails 1.9
B4 ..... Muir Woods - Fern Canyon Trails 3.6
B5 ..... Panoramic - Redwood - Sun Trails 4.2
B6 ..... Muir Woods - TCC - Dipsea Trails 6.3

Starting from Mtn. Home Inn at 920'
B7 ..... Panoramic - Lost - Sierra Trails 3.2
B8 ..... Mountain Home Inn to East Peak 4.7
B9 ..... Matt Davis - Troop 80 Trails 5.0
B10 ... Old RR Grade to West Point Inn 3.9

Starting from Bootjack at 1350'
B11 ... TCC - Alpine Trails 3.5
B12 ... Bootjack - Rock Spring Trails 4.1

Starting from Pantoll Ranger Station at 1500'
B13 ... Easy Grade to Mountain Theater 2.2
B14 ... Dipsea - Steep Ravine Trails 3.6
B15 ... Matt Davis - Coastal - Cataract Trails 6.6
B16 ... Matt Davis Trail to Stinson Beach 7.2

Starting from Rock Spring at 1970'
B17 ... Simmons - Music Camp - Cataract Trails 3.8
B18 ... Benstein - International Trails 5.4
B19 ... Cataract - High Marsh - Kent Trails 6.0

Starting from East Peak at 2300'
B20 ... East Peak Loop and Plankwalk Trails 0.7 and 0.6
B21 ... Northside - Colier - Lakeview Trails 4.3

Pets allowed on hikes 1, 2, 10, 17 and 19.

Region B Trailheads

Hikes 1-2 start in Marin Co. Open Space, phone 499-6405.

Hikes 3-6 start in Muir Woods, phone 388-2595.

Hikes 7-10 and 17-19 start in Marin Municipal Water Dist., phone 459-5267.

Hikes 11-16 and 20-21 start Mt. Tamalpais State Park, phone 388-2070.

Region B
Mt. Tamalpais South

Alpine Lake

Lake Lagunitas

Corte Madera

Marin Muncipal Water District

Mt Tamalpais East Peak 2571' ⑳ ㉑

Baltimore Canyon Open Space

Ridgecrest Blvd

Birthedale Ridge Open Space

① ②

Rock Spring ⑰ ⑱ ⑲

Panoramic Hwy

⑪ ⑫

Mtn Home Inn ⑦ ⑧ ⑨ ⑩

Pantoll ⑬ ⑭ ⑮ ⑯

Muir Woods National Mon't.

1

Panoramic Hwy

Mt. Tamalpais State Park

③ ④ ⑤ ⑥

Mill Valley

1

Muir Woods Rd

GGNRA GGNRA

1

Muir Beach

Golden Gate National Recreation Area

Pacific Ocean

Tennessee Valley

B1 Blithedale Ridge - Corte Madera Trails

Distance: 4.2 miles   Shaded: 20%
Elevation Change: 1100'   Heavy bicycle use on parts.
Rating: Hiking - 9   Difficulty - 9   One very steep section.
When to Go: Save this hike for cool, clear winter days.

Bring binoculars and camera for this roller-coaster hike that rolls along Blithedale Ridge offering stunning views of Mt. Tam and Marin.

0.0 Start near the Old Railroad Grade trailhead located near the end of West Blithedale Ave. Go through the gate and head uphill on the dirt road. Stay to the right and watch for bicycles.

0.1 Junction. Turn right and take the H-Line FR as it starts a moderately steep climb out of the canyon and into open chaparral.

0.7 Two junctions #1. You can reduce the hill climbing by 300' and cut this hike short by a mile by heading left. Otherwise, go right on Blithedale Ridge to climb to a spectacular viewpoint of Mt. Tamalpais.

1.2 Junction #2 with the Corte Madera Ridge FR. There are two great view spots near here. First, go left 50' for a great view down Warner Canyon and out towards San Francisco. Then return to this junction and continue on the road up to the next knoll.

1.3 Knoll and view spot. This picture-taking spot offers a striking profile of the East Peak of Mt. Tamalpais. Return to junction #1.

1.9 Back at junction #1. Continue straight and up along the ridge.

2.8 Junction #3 with the Hoo-Koo-E-Koo FR. Note that there is both a trail and fire road called Hoo-Koo-E-Koo, which was presumably named after a band of Miwok Indians that lived near the base of the mountain. It's worth continuing the climb another 100 yds. up to Indian FR, which offers panoramic views north.

2.8+ Indian FR. Great views of Bill Williams Canyon and points to the north. When ready to continue, backtrack 100 yds.

2.9 Junction. Take the Hoo-Koo-E-Koo FR right towards East Peak.

3.1 Two junctions #4. The Hoo-Koo-E-Koo trail heads left. Take the Corte Madera trail as it descends steeply alongside the creek. The trail crosses the creek four times, so if you lose the trail, look for it on the other side of the creek.

3.5 Junction with Horseshoe FR. Head right downhill.

3.6 Junction with the Old Railroad Grade. Continue left downhill.

4.2 Back at the trailhead.

Getting There

From Hwy 101:
Near Mill Valley
W on East Blithedale
for 1.9 miles, then
take West Blithedale
for 1.2 miles to where
the street crosses
the creek. Very limited
parking.

B1 - Mt. Tamalpais South
Marin County Open Space
Old Railroad Grade

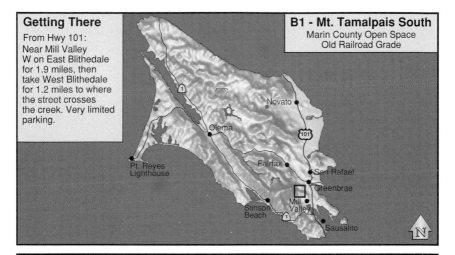

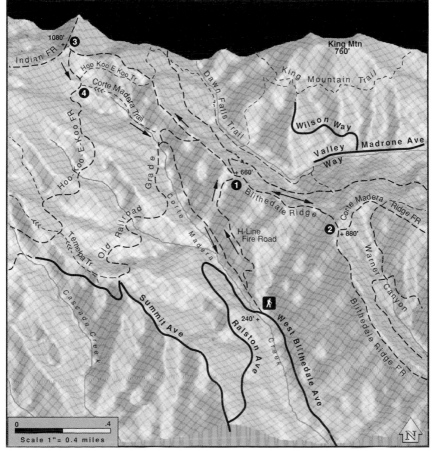

43

B2 Old Railroad Grade - Hoo-Koo-E-Koo

Distance: 7.4 miles   Shaded: 50%
Elevation Change: 1300'   Heavy bicycle traffic.
Rating: Hiking - 7   Difficulty - 9   Two steep downhill sections.
When to Go: Best on cool, clear weekdays.

This hike follows the historic Old Railroad Grade as it gradually climbs up the mountain. Open chaparral areas provide great views.

0.0 Start at the Old Railroad Grade trailhead located near the end of West Blithedale Ave. Go through the gate and head uphill.

1.8 Junction #1 with Summit Ave and Fern Canyon Rd. The hike continues uphill on the paved road for 0.6 miles. Great views.

2.9 Two junctions and the Double Bowknot. Two roads separated by 100' head left and join to form Gravity Car Grade, which leads to the Mtn. Home Inn and Muir Woods.

Continue right to pass the concrete landing, Mesa Station, where passengers could transfer to gravity cars and coast down Gravity Car Grade. This road section is part of the famous Double Bowknot where tracks make a series of switchbacks and parallel each other five times. From 1896 to 1930, the Mt. Tamalpais & Muir Woods Railway, better known as the "Crookedest Railroad in the World", attracted bay area residents and tourists to outings on the mountain.

Gravity Car

3.2 Junction #2 with the Hoo-Koo-E-Koo FR. Continue left uphill.

3.8 Junction #3. Head left, steeply down Hogback FR.

3.9 Junction. Take the signed Hoo-Koo-E-Koo trail left.

4.6 Junction. Take the Old Railroad Grade left for just 100 yds.

4.7 Back at junction #2. Leave the Old Railroad Grade and take the signed Hoo-Koo-E-Koo FR to the right. Watch for bicycles.

6.3 Two junctions #4. Take the Corte Madera trail as it descends steeply alongside the creek, which it crosses several times.

6.7 Junction with Horseshoe FR. Head right downhill.

6.8 Junction with the Old Railroad Grade. Continue left downhill.

7.4 Back at the trailhead.

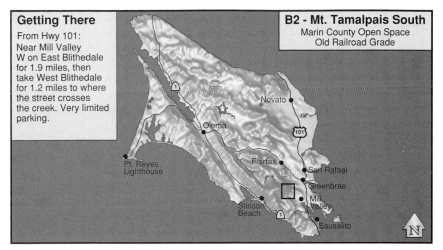

Getting There

From Hwy 101:
Near Mill Valley
W on East Blithedale
for 1.9 miles, then
take West Blithedale
for 1.2 miles to where
the street crosses
the creek. Very limited
parking.

B2 - Mt. Tamalpais South
Marin County Open Space
Old Railroad Grade

Novato
Olema
Pt. Reyes
Lighthouse
Fairfax
San Rafael
Greenbrae
Mill
Valley
Stinson
Beach
Sausalito

Eldridge Grade
East
Peak
2571'
920' +
Wheeler
Trail
④
Corte Madera Tr
Blithedale
FR
Tennelpa
1200' +
Koo
Koo E
Vic Haun Tr
Old
Railroad
Grade
Corte
Ridge FR
H-Line
FR
Old
Railroad
Grade
③
Hoo Koo E Koo Tr
Gravity
Car
Grade
Mesa
Station
1120'
Double
Bowknot
②
Hoo
Trail
①
Summit Ave
Cascade Creek
240' +
Madera Cr
Mtn Home
Inn 920'
Panoramic
Highway
Tenderfoot
Trail
Old Mill Creek
Cascade Drive
Cascade
West
Blithedale
Avenue

0 .5
Scale 1"= 0.6 miles

45

B3 Muir Woods - Hillside Trails

Distance: 1.9 miles   Shaded: 100%
Elevation Change: 200'
Rating: Hiking - 10   Difficulty - 2   Can be crowded.
When to Go: Excellent anytime, best in spring for trillium.

This Muir Woods hike is the most heavily traveled trail on Mt. Tam. It winds along the floor of a beautiful, virgin redwood forest.

0.0 Start at the Muir Woods parking lot. Follow the signed Main trail along the right side of Redwood Creek. The trail has several nature information signs describing the redwood forest. Also, you can pick up a brochure at the entrance describing points of interest.

0.5 Cathedral Grove. A beautiful redwood grove dedicated to the founding of the United Nations in San Francisco in 1945. Tanoak and western sword fern are the dominant shrub-like growth under the redwood canopy, while redwood sorrel provides most of the ground cover. Ahead, the light green leaves of western azalea, hazel and big leaf maple stand out against the dark-green, redwood background.

0.7 Junction with Fern Creek. Continue left. Notice how some redwoods have an enormous number of sprouts growing out of the base, while others have grey-green lichens growing on the bark.

0.9 Park boundary and junction #1. Bear left, cross the bridge and head up to Hillside Jct. Go left again and climb up the Hillside trail.

1.1 Ravine. The first of three small, picturesque ravines. Ferns, mosses, pink trillium, sorrel and the striking clintonia grow along the bank. Notice the large Douglas fir just past the streambed. Its bark differs from nearby redwoods in texture and in the moss covering. Redwoods often have lichens growing on them, but seldom mosses.

Trillium

1.6 Junction. The Hillside trail gently descends to the canyon floor. Stay right to enter Bohemian Grove with some of the tallest trees in the park, nearly 260'. Ahead at the bridge, look for spawning silver salmon and steelhead trout in wintertime.

1.8 Snack shop, gift shop and restroom facilities.

1.9 Parking lot. Continue walking along the creek to see several large red alders in a riparian setting. Further downstream, across from the highway entrance, notice the incredibly tangled buckeye trees with moss-covered trunks criss-crossing every which way.

From Hwy 101:
Near Sausalito
W on Hwy 1
for 3.3 miles,
R on Panoramic Hwy
for 0.9 miles to a
dangerous junction.
L on Muir Woods Rd.
Best to park in outer lot.

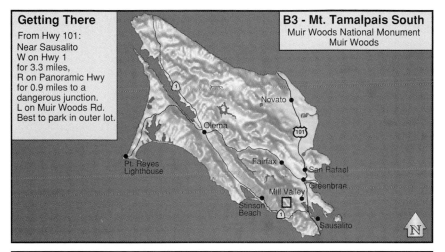

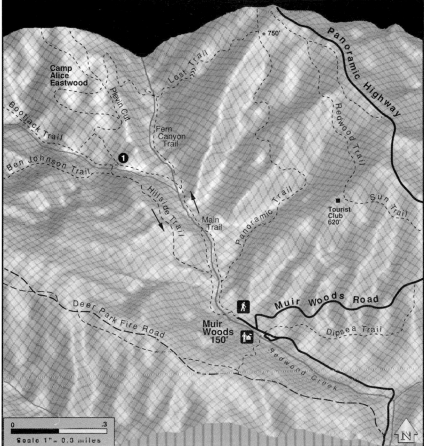

47

B4 Muir Woods - Fern Canyon Trails

Distance: 3.6 miles   Shaded: 100%
Elevation Change: 300'
Rating: Hiking - 9   Difficulty - 4   Moderately steep.
When to Go: Excellent anytime, best in February and March.

This is a great redwood forest hike that leaves the crowded Muir Woods floor to explore Fern Canyon and Camp Alice Eastwood.

0.0 Start at the Muir Woods parking lot. Follow the signed Main trail along the right side of Redwood Creek.

0.7 Junction. Take the Fern Canyon trail right along the small creek. Watch for white trillium in March and the striking pink clintonia in April.

1.1 Junction #1 and bridge. Bear left down the 50' picturesque wood-plank bridge. Continue upstream on the left bank to another junction. Then, either take the shortcut up the stairs, or go slightly further upstream. Look for iris as the trail climbs through the redwoods.

1.8 Plevin Cut and Camp Alice Eastwood junctions #2. At the first junction, continue right to the parking area. The camp, named for Alice Eastwood, avid botanist, writer and hiker, was dedicated in 1949 on her 90th birthday.

This was also the location of the Muir Woods Inn, which served visitors who coasted down on gravity cars in the early 1900s.

From the camp, cross the paved parking circle to Camp Eastwood Rd. signed to Muir Woods. The road starts downhill passing through madrone, manzanita, oak, yerba santa and non-native broom.

Muir Woods Inn 1908

2.5 Junction #3. Take the signed Bootjack Spur trail right past a large lichen-covered redwood tree down to Redwood Creek, then go left and head downstream. Look for spawning salmon in late winter.

2.7 Junction and park boundary. Continue along the creek.

3.1 Bridge and Cathedral Grove. Cross the bridge to return down the right side of Redwood Creek. Look for redwood burls. Further ahead lies Bohemian Grove with some of the tallest trees in the park at 260'.

3.6 Snack shop, gift shop, restroom facilities and parking lot.

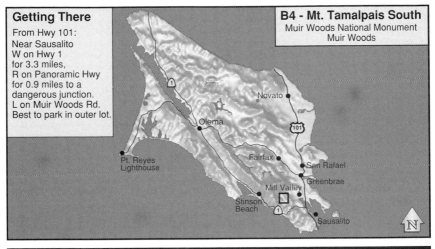

Getting There

From Hwy 101:
Near Sausalito
W on Hwy 1
for 3.3 miles,
R on Panoramic Hwy
for 0.9 miles to a
dangerous junction.
L on Muir Woods Rd.
Best to park in outer lot.

B4 - Mt. Tamalpais South
Muir Woods National Monument
Muir Woods

Novato

Olema

Pt. Reyes
Lighthouse

Fairfax

San Rafael

Greenbrae

Mill Valley

Stinson
Beach

Sausalito

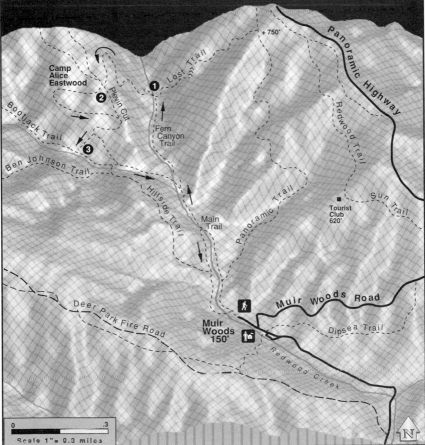

+ 750'

Panoramic Highway

Camp
Alice
Eastwood

Lost Trail

Plevin Cut

Fern
Canyon
Trail

Redwood Trail

Bootjack Trail

Ben Johnson Trail

Hillside Trail

Main
Trail

Panoramic Trail

Sun Trail

Tourist
Club
620'

Deer Park Fire Road

Muir Woods Road

Muir
Woods
150'

Dipsea Trail

Redwood Creek

0 .3
Scale 1" = 0.3 miles

49

B5 Panoramic - Redwood - Sun Trails

Distance: 4.2 miles   Shaded: 70%
Elevation Change: 700'   May be impassable, see note.
Rating: Hiking - 9   Difficulty - 7   One short steep section.
When to Go: Best February to April for flowers.

This is a great hike out of Muir Woods into mixed conifers, then on to the Sun trail where wildflowers start in February.

Note: Sections of the Sun trail may be overgrown with French broom and impassable. The hike is included here assuming that the trail will be clear. It also serves as an example of the problems with broom.

0.0 At the Muir Woods entrance, take the Main trail up the right side of Redwood Creek past magnificent redwoods.

0.2 Junction #1. Take the signed Panoramic trail right for a long steady climb. In February, watch for pink trillium and blue hound's tongue among the ferns, tanoak and redwoods.

1.5 Junction with Lost trail. Stay right and continue uphill. Look for chaparral being overgrown by taller trees: bay, fir and redwood.

1.8 Junction and highway. Take the signed Panoramic trail right. (The Panoramic trail formerly was called Ocean View trail.)

2.1 Junction #2. Bear right, downhill on the signed Redwood trail.

2.4 Bench. Here is a good spot to enjoy the views across Muir Woods to the ocean. Notice the Douglas fir about to overgrow chaparral shrubs. In spring, look for red Indian paintbrush.

Indian Paintbrush

2.8 Junction at the Tourist Club. This club was founded in 1912 by German immigrants as a branch of a European hiking club. The club is private, but often sells refreshments on weekends. The trail continues above the club to the road and then heads left for 100' to the Sun trail.

2.9 Junction #3. Head right on the Sun trail which earns its name by skirting the south-facing hillside overlooking Muir Woods. Wildflowers begin in February, building to a peak in April. (In a few years, the flowers will be crowded out by invasive French broom.)

3.5 Junction. Follow the signed Dipsea trail right as it drops steeply down the hillside and crosses the highway into a bay-filled ravine.

4.2 Parking lot, snack shop, gift shop and restroom facilities.

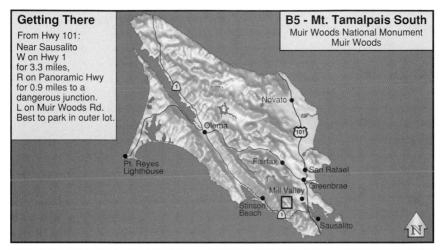

Getting There

From Hwy 101:
Near Sausalito
W on Hwy 1
for 3.3 miles,
R on Panoramic Hwy
for 0.9 miles to a
dangerous junction.
L on Muir Woods Rd.
Best to park in outer lot.

B5 - Mt. Tamalpais South
Muir Woods National Monument
Muir Woods

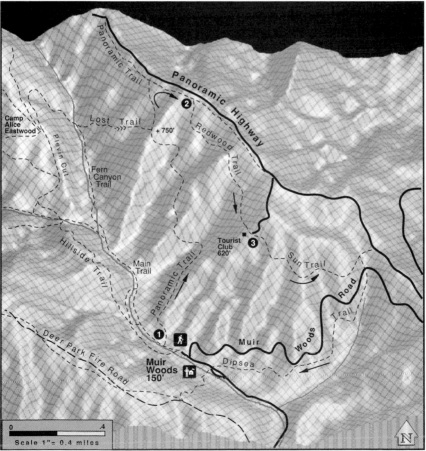

Camp Alice Eastwood

Lost Trail

+750'

Panoramic Trail

Plevin Cut

Fern Canyon Trail

Redwood Trail

Panoramic Highway

Tourist Club 620'

Sun Trail

Hillside Trail

Main Trail

Panoramic Trail

Road

Deer Park Fire Road

Woods Trail

Muir

Dipsea

Muir Woods 150'

Scale 1"= 0.4 miles
0 .4

B6 Muir Woods - TCC - Dipsea Trails

Distance: 6.3 miles   Shaded: 70%
Elevation Change: 1300'
Rating: Hiking - 10   Difficulty - 7   Steep in places.
When to Go: Good anytime, best in April after the bridge opens.
A dramatic hike into dense redwood forest with plunging creek, then down an open ridge with views and flowers, and into a lush canyon.

0.0 Start at the Muir Woods parking lot. Check at the kiosk to see if the Dipsea trail bridge is open. Follow the Main trail along the right side of Redwood Creek.

0.9 Junction #1. Take the signed Bootjack trail along the right side of Redwood Creek. Notice the light-green leaves of western azalea, hazel and big leaf maple against the dark-green, redwood needles.

1.3 Slides. Downed trees and large boulders testify to the power of fast-moving water. Look for white milkmaids, pink sorrel and trillium.

2.3 Van Wyck Meadow and junction #2. This meadow with its large picturesque rock and "population sign" has often served as a gathering and resting spot. Continue past the trail right and take the signed TCC trail left over the creek.

2.8 Manzanita. Notice the dead manzanita from an old chaparral community. Now, ferns and huckleberry lie under the conifers.

3.7 Junction #3 with the Stapelveldt trail. First go left, then right to take the signed TCC trail towards the Dipsea trail.

4.1 Junction #4. Eventually, we'll take the Dipsea trail left down to Muir Woods. However, now go right, uphill 200' to the hilltop for great views and wildflowers. This hill is known as "Cardiac Hill" to the 1500 Dipsea runners who struggle up from Muir Woods each June. Now backtrack down the trail and follow the Dipsea trail to the road. Watch for red columbine along the road in late spring.

4.5 Junction. Leave the road and go right down the Dipsea trail. The trail and the road (Deer Park FR) intersect several times.

4.7 Open hillside. This grassy ridge is called "Hogsback" by Dipsea runners. It is said to be where the Dipsea race is won or lost.

5.9 Junction #5. Take the trail left, down into a moist canyon filled with bay, hazel, berries and ferns. If the bridge is out, take the road.

6.2 Bridge. Cross the creek under red alders and head left.

6.3 Back at Muir Woods with full facilities.

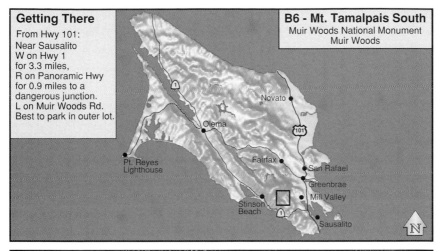

Getting There

From Hwy 101:
Near Sausalito
W on Hwy 1
for 3.3 miles,
R on Panoramic Hwy
for 0.9 miles to a
dangerous junction.
L on Muir Woods Rd.
Best to park in outer lot.

B6 - Mt. Tamalpais South
Muir Woods National Monument
Muir Woods

Novato

Olema

Pt. Reyes
Lighthouse

Fairfax

San Rafael

Greenbrae

Mill Valley

Stinson
Beach

Sausalito

N

Rock Spring Trail

Rattlesnake Tr

Spike Buck Cr

West Point Inn
1785'

Old Railroad Grade

Hoo-Koo-E-Koo Tr

Old Stage Rd

Matt Davis Trail

Gravity Car Grade

Panoramic Highway

Bootjack
1350'

Van Wyck
Meadow

Troop 80 Trail

Mtn Home
Inn 920'

②

Camp Eastwood Rd

Fern Creek

Pantoll
1500'

③

TCC
Trail

Bootjack Trail

Sierra
Trail

Lost Tr

Stapelveldt Tr

④

Ben Johnson Trail

Redwood Creek

①

Fern
Canyon
Trail

Panoramic
Trail

1400
Cardiac
Hill

Dipsea Trail

Deer Park Fire Road

Main
Trail

Coastal Fire Road

Kent Creek

Muir Woods
150'

Dipsea Tr

⑤

0   .5
Scale 1" = 0.5 miles

N

B7 Panoramic - Lost - Sierra Trails

Distance: 3.2 miles   Shaded: 60%
Elevation Change: 600'
Rating: Hiking - 9   Difficulty - 9   One very steep section.
When to Go: Good anytime, best January to March.
This is a great hike that descends steeply into Fern Canyon, then gradually climbs back through chaparral and redwoods.

0.0 From the north end of the parking lot opposite the Mtn. Home Inn, take the signed Trestle trail down the stairs. At the road, head left past chaparral consisting of manzanita and chamise.

0.1 Gate and junction. Take the signed Panoramic trail right past broom, which may crowd the trail. Good views towards the ocean.

0.2 Junction #1. Take the Panoramic trail (originally called the Ocean View trail) right towards Muir Woods. Up ahead, Douglas fir has invaded and overgrown a chaparral area.

0.5 Junction. At the redwood grove, take the Lost trail right. This trail was constructed in 1914 by members of the Tourist Club. It is very steep in places and was blocked (hence "lost") for a long time after a massive slide in the1930s.

1.1 Junction and bridge. Bear right down the 50' bridge and continue upstream along the left bank of Fern Creek. The hike came down the south-facing hill through fir and bay. Now it climbs the north-facing hill through redwoods. Notice how many redwoods are burned on the uphill side where forest debris or duff collected.

1.7 Plevin Cut and Camp Eastwood junctions #2. At the first junction, go right up to Camp Eastwood, then go right again across the parking circle and take the signed Sierra trail up the dirt road.

1.8 Water tank. At the water tank and bench, the road abruptly ends and a trail swings in and out of the transition zone between two unlikely bedfellows, redwood and chaparral. Look for huckleberry bushes, with berries ripening in late summer.

Huckleberry

2.3 Chinquapin. The trail passes a small grove of chinquapin with 2 inch leaves, green on top and gold underneath.

2.4 Junction #3. Head right on Troop 80 trail towards Mtn. Home.

2.8 Fern Creek and junction. Go left on the paved road.

3.2 Stairs. Take the stairs back up to the parking area.

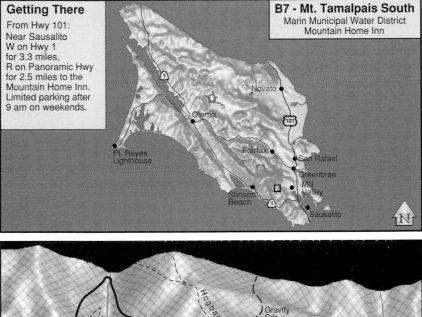

Getting There

From Hwy 101:
Near Sausalito
W on Hwy 1
for 3.3 miles,
R on Panoramic Hwy
for 2.5 miles to the
Mountain Home Inn.
Limited parking after
9 am on weekends.

B7 - Mt. Tamalpais South
Marin Municipal Water District
Mountain Home Inn

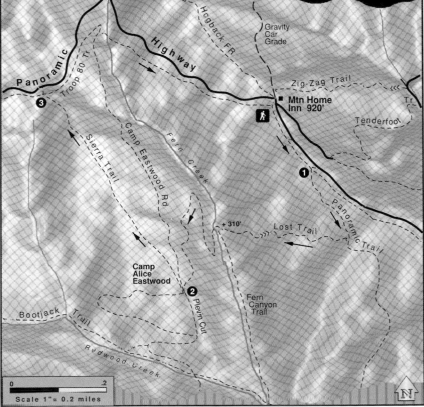

55

B8 Mountain Home Inn to East Peak

Distance: 4.7 miles   Shaded: 30%
Elevation Change: 1700'
Rating: Hiking - 9   Difficulty - 10   Very steep in places.
When to Go: Best on cool, clear, calm winter days.

This is the shortest and quickest hike to the top of Mt. Tamalpais. It offers great exercise and spectacular views in all directions.

0.0 Start at the Mtn. Home Inn and head north across the highway and up the paved road towards the fire station. Take the Hogback FR past the fire station and up past a new water tank.

0.3 Junction with the Matt Davis trail. Continue up Hogback, which gets steeper as it passes manzanita, oak, madrone, bay and fir.

0.6 Junction #1. Take the Old Railroad Grade left for a more gradual climb. The trail provides sweeping views in chaparral areas, then enters Fern Canyon with redwoods and occasional madrones.

1.0 Junction. Take the signed Fern Creek trail on the right and start a steep climb up the right side of the creek.

1.2 Creek crossing and junction #2. Tall chain ferns and a new bridge mark the creek crossing. About 100 yds. beyond the crossing, the trail enters a dense stand of bay trees, then veers right to pass a water tank and the signed Tavern Pump trail.

The hike continues on Fern Creek trail up the left side of the creek along side a metal water pipe, then heads west out of the canyon.

1.7 Junction with Ridgecrest Blvd. Cross the road, take the stairs to the parking lot and head towards the picnic area and East Peak.

1.8 Junction. Take the signed Plankwalk trail up the north side.

2.0 East Peak and fire lookout station at 2571'. Stunning views!

2.2 East Peak parking lot. The small Visitor Center is usually open weekends from 12 - 4 pm. Take the one-way paved road to the west.

2.4 Two junctions #3. Take the Old Railroad Grade left.

3.1 Junction #4. Take the signed Miller trail left. The upper 200 yds. are steep and dangerous with ruts and loose rocks. Once the trail enters an oak forest, the going is easier. Creek crossings ahead.

3.6 Junction. Take the Old Railroad Grade left to go downhill.

4.1 Junction #1. Take the Hogback FR right for a steep descent.

4.7 Mtn. Home Inn parking area with restrooms and water.

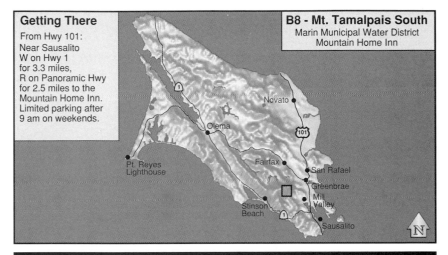

Getting There

From Hwy 101:
Near Sausalito
W on Hwy 1
for 3.3 miles,
R on Panoramic Hwy
for 2.5 miles to the
Mountain Home Inn.
Limited parking after
9 am on weekends.

Novato

Olema

Pt. Reyes
Lighthouse

Fairfax

San Rafael

Greenbrae

Mill
Valley

Stinson
Beach

Sausalito

N

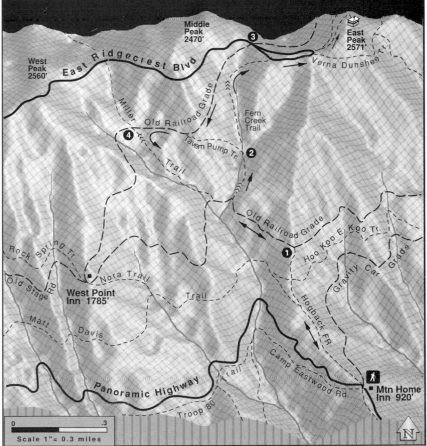

West
Peak
2560'

Middle
Peak
2470'

East
Peak
2571'

East Ridgecrest Blvd

Verna Dunshee Tr.

Miller

Old Railroad Grade

Fern
Creek
Trail

Tavern Pump Tr.

Trail

Old Railroad Grade

Hoo Koo E Koo Tr.

Gravity Car Grade

Rock Spring Tr.

Nora Trail

Old Stage Rd.

West Point
Inn 1785'

Trail

Hogback FR

Matt
Davis

Camp Eastwood Rd.

Mtn Home
Inn 920'

Panoramic Highway

Trail

Troop 80

Scale 1" = 0.3 miles

0   .3

N

57

B9 Matt Davis - Troop 80 Trails

Distance: 5.0 miles   Shaded: 60%
Elevation Change: 550'
Rating: Hiking - 9   Difficulty - 6   Rocky in places.
When to Go: Good in winter and spring for views, sun and creeks.

This is a great hike along south-facing ridges, into redwood canyons and over cascading creeks, offering views to the city and coast.

0.0 From the north end of the parking lot opposite the Mtn. Home Inn, cross the highway and take the paved road up past the fire station.

0.3 Water tank and junction #1. Just past the new water tank, take the signed Matt Davis trail left towards the west. Good views south. Matt Davis, known as the "dean of trail workers," lived in a small cabin he built above Bootjack Camp. He was paid by the Tamalpais Conservation Club to work on trails; he built this trail in the 1920s.

0.6 Fern Creek. The concrete weir above the bridge was part of a water intake system that is no longer used.

Are the densely-packed, skinny redwoods young trees or stunted growth? Old-timers report similar groves 50 years ago.

1.3 Junction with the Nora trail. Cross the bridge and continue west.

1.9 Fire! Bare branches mark the remains of a 1984 controlled burn. The Water District considers these burns necessary to reduce the fire fuel load. After the burn, monkeyflower was the first major species to return. Now, chamise covers most of the hill.

2.6 Bootjack picnic area and junction #2. Follow the paved path through the picnic area down to the parking lot. Cross Panoramic Hwy and take the signed Bootjack trail downhill.

2.7 Junction with the Alpine trail. Continue downhill under redwoods.

3.0 Van Wyck Meadow and junction #3. The meadow, originally called Lower Rattlesnake Camp, was renamed for Sidney M. Van Wyck, president of the TCC in 1920-21. At the large rock in the center of the meadow, take a spur trail left, east towards the Troop 80 trail and Mtn. Home Inn.

3.1 Junction and plaque. At the bottom of some steps, a plaque dedicates a Douglas fir tree to World War I veterans. Continue straight on the Troop 80 trail, built by the Ingleside Boy Scout Troop.

4.6 Junction with the paved Camp Eastwood road. Head left uphill.

5.0 Junction, head up the stairs to the Mtn. Home Inn parking area.

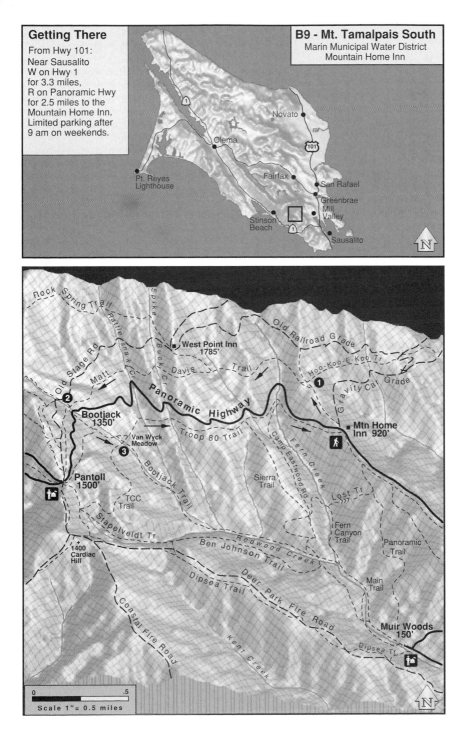

Getting There

From Hwy 101:
Near Sausalito
W on Hwy 1
for 3.3 miles,
R on Panoramic Hwy
for 2.5 miles to the
Mountain Home Inn.
Limited parking after
9 am on weekends.

B9 - Mt. Tamalpais South

Marin Municipal Water District
Mountain Home Inn

Novato

Olema

Pt. Reyes
Lighthouse

Fairfax

San Rafael

Greenbrae
Mill
Valley

Stinson
Beach

Sausalito

Rock Spring Trail

Spike

Matt Davis Trail

West Point Inn
1785'

Old Railroad Grade

Hoo-Koo-E-Koo Tr

Old Stage Rd

Rattlesnake Cr

Bucky Cr

Gravity Car Grade

Panoramic Highway

Bootjack
1350'

Van Wyck
Meadow

Troop 80 Trail

Mtn Home
Inn 920'

Camp Eastwood Rd

Fern Creek

Pantoll
1500'

Bootjack Trail

Sierra
Trail

Lost Tr

TCC
Trail

Stapelveldt Tr

Fern
Canyon
Trail

Panoramic
Trail

1400
Cardiac
Hill

Redwood Creek

Ben Johnson Trail

Dipsea Trail

Deer Park Fire Road

Main
Trail

Coastal Fire Road

Kent Creek

Muir Woods
150'

Dipsea Tr

0 .5
Scale 1" = 0.5 miles

59

B10 Old RR Grade to West Point Inn

Distance: 3.9 miles   Shaded: 50%
Elevation Change: 800'   Heavy bicycle traffic weekends.
Rating: Hiking - 7   Difficulty - 6   Steep uphill on Hogback FR.
When to Go: Best on a clear day in fall, winter or spring.

This often-used route provides the shortest round trip to West Point Inn while offering great views east and south.

0.0 Start at the parking lot opposite the Mtn. Home Inn. Cross the highway and take the paved road up towards the fire station. The road turns into Hogback FR, also called Throckmorton FR, which once led hikers all the way to East Peak, but is now closed beyond the Old Railroad Grade for erosion control.

0.3 Two water tanks and junction. Continue up Hogback, which gets steeper here, providing an opportunity to stop and enjoy the view.

0.6 Junction #1. Turn left on the Old Railroad Grade which climbs gradually; the grade is never more than 7%. The entire 8.1 miles of road and railroad track from downtown Mill Valley to East Peak took just six months to build in 1896.

1.0 Junction with Fern Creek trail. Just past the main ravine, a small spring supports graceful chain ferns.

2. 1 Junction #2 and West Point Inn. This historic railroad tavern, built in 1904, was a restaurant and stopover point for passengers taking the stage to Bolinas and Willow Camp (later Stinson Beach).

West Point Inn

The inn was called West Point Inn because this is the westernmost point of the Old Railroad Grade.

For many years, the cast of the Mountain Play stayed at the inn the week before the play and walked to rehearsals each morning.

To continue the hike, take the signed Nora trail located in front of the inn. This well-maintained trail descends under a canopy of chaparral, then enters a grove of skinny redwoods.

2.6 Junction #3. Take the signed Matt Davis trail left.

3.6 Junction and water tanks. Take the Hogback FR downhill right.

3.9 Back at the parking lot with water and restrooms.

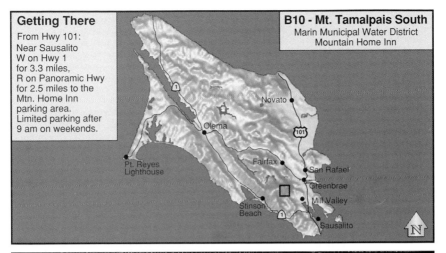

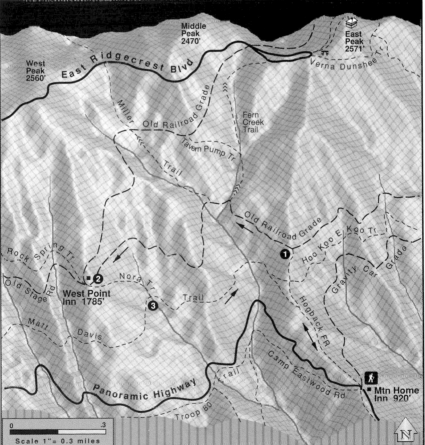

B11 TCC - Alpine Trails

Distance: 3.5 miles Shaded: 90%
Elevation Change: 500'
Rating: Hiking - 9 Difficulty - 6 Moderately steep downhill.
When to Go: Good anytime, best in early spring.

This is a good hike exploring the dense woods east of Pantoll.
Cardiac Hill on the Dipsea trail provides vistas and wildflowers.

0.0 Start at the Bootjack parking lot. Cross the highway and take the signed Bootjack trail towards Van Wyck Meadow. The trail drops steeply down past Douglas fir and bay into redwood forest. In early spring, look for white milkmaids and blue hound's tongue.

0.1 Junction with Alpine trail. Bear left to cross two small bridges ahead. Watch for white fairy bells and pink trillium.

0.4 Junction #1. Just past the bench and western azalea shrubs, continue right on the Bootjack trail. The trail goes alongside moss-covered boulders, then down past a brown sandstone slab.

0.5 Junction and Van Wyck Meadow. Take the signed TCC trail right, across the creek and into redwoods. The TCC trail was built in 1918 and named for the Tamalpais Conservation Club, often called the "Guardians of the Mountain" for their conservation activities.

1.0 Manzanita. Notice the dead manzanitas from an old chaparral community. Now, ferns and huckleberry lie under the conifers.

1.9 Junction #2 with Stapelveldt trail. First go left, then right to take the signed TCC trail towards the Dipsea trail.

2.3 Junction. Take the Dipsea trail right uphill.

2.4 Junction #3 and hill. Congratulations! You have just climbed "Cardiac", as it's called by the throng of Dipsea runners who run from Mill Valley to Stinson Beach each June. Go right on the road.

2.5 Junction with Old Mine Rd. Bear right into Douglas fir and bay.

2.7 Junction. Take the Old Mine trail right. Up ahead, an 1863 mining claim was staked out in search of gold and silver.

3.0 Pantoll and junction #4. Water, tables and restrooms. Continue past the ranger station and take the signed Alpine trail just before the highway. The trail follows the road downhill.

3.4 Junction. Take the signed Bootjack trail left.

3.5 Back at Bootjack with water, tables and restrooms.

Getting There

From Hwy 101:
Near Sausalito
W on Hwy 1
for 3.3 miles,
R on Panoramic Hwy
for 4.5 miles to the
Bootjack parking area.
Parking fee.

B11 - Mt. Tamalpais South

Mt. Tamalpais State Park
Bootjack

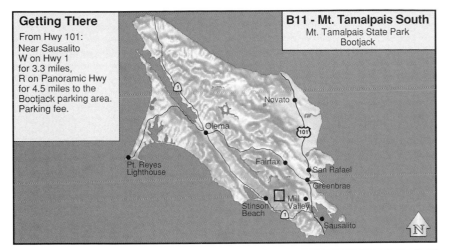

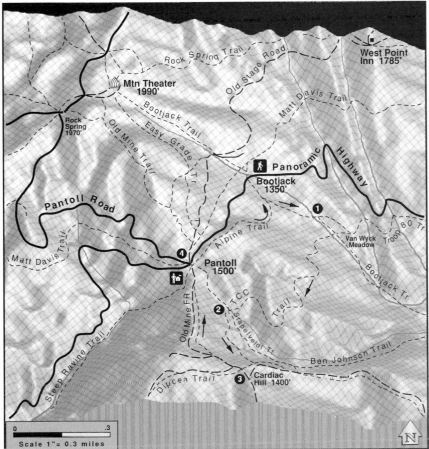

63

B12 Bootjack - Rock Spring Trails

Distance: 4.1 miles   Shaded: 60%
Elevation Change: 600'   One rocky area.
Rating: Hiking - 8   Difficulty - 5   Moderately steep uphill.
When to Go: Good any cool, clear day, best February to April.

This is a good sunshine hike mostly through chaparral, first climbing to the Mtn. Theater, then to West Point Inn and back.

0.0 Start at the Bootjack parking lot. Take the signed Bootjack trail into the picnic area. At a signed junction with the Matt Davis trail, continue on the Bootjack trail steeply up towards the Mtn. Theater.

0.2 Junction #1 with Old Stage Rd. In the early 1900s, a stage coach made a daily run from West Point Inn to Stinson Beach. Our hike just crosses the road. Go left on the road 20', then right 20', then left again to continue on the Bootjack trail. In early spring, look for blue hound's tongue, white milkmaids and purple iris.

0.7 Junction and Mtn. Theater. Turn right at the junction and head towards the theater. Go up to the top of the theater to enjoy a unique setting and view. This natural amphitheater has been the site of spring plays since 1913. To continue the hike, go across the top to the northeast corner of the theater. See map inset, Hike B13.

0.8 Junction #2. Take the Rock Spring trail towards West Point Inn. This south-facing trail gradually descends through chaparral and wooded ravines. Watch for orange monkeyflower, tree poppy, blue-eyed grass, white Oakland star tulip and red Indian warrior.

1.4 Rocky knoll. Great views to San Francisco and the East Bay.

2.3 West Point Inn. Water, restrooms and beverages are available on most weekends. A pancake breakfast is served once a month from May to September in this glorious setting. To continue the hike, take the signed Nora trail in front of the picnic area.

2.8 Junction #3. Take the Matt Davis trail right over the bridge, out of the redwoods, and into a mixture of oak, huckleberry, manzanita and chamise with occasional Douglas fir and bay trees.

3.3 Controlled burn area. The last major fire on the mountain was in 1945. Now, controlled burns are necessary to reduce the fire danger.

3.7 Bridge. The trail enters a ravine, crosses a bridge on Rattlesnake Creek, then goes up a rocky slope.

4.1 Back at Bootjack picnic area with restrooms, tables and water.

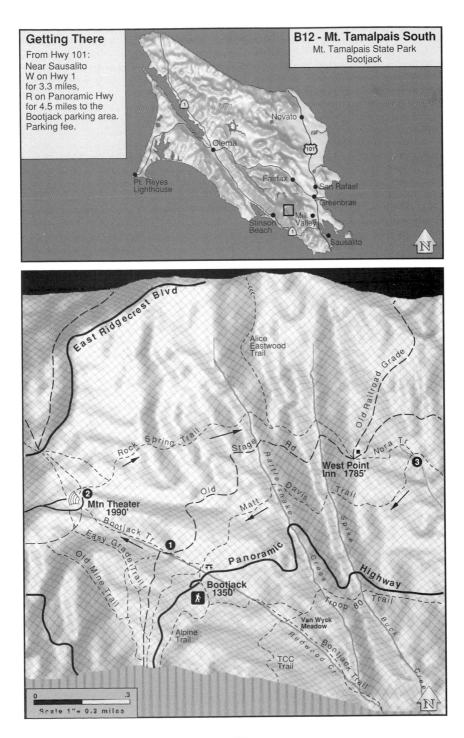

Getting There

From Hwy 101:
Near Sausalito
W on Hwy 1
for 3.3 miles,
R on Panoramic Hwy
for 4.5 miles to the
Bootjack parking area.
Parking fee.

65

B13 Easy Grade to Mountain Theater

Distance: 2.2 miles   Shaded: 60%
Elevation Change: 500'
Rating: Hiking - 10   Difficulty - 5   Moderately steep.
When to Go: Good any clear day, best in spring.

This short hike climbs from Pantoll through forest to the Mountain Theater, then over open hills with magnificent views south and east.

0.0 Start at the Pantoll parking lot. Cross the highway, bear right and go along the paved section of the Old Stage Rd. signed to East Peak. Immediately ahead, continue on the road past two junctions.

0.1 Junction. Take the signed Easy Grade trail left towards the Mtn. Theater. The trail climbs up wooded hills with occasional views east.

0.3 Junction with Easy Grade Spur trail. Keep left at the Spur trail and straight up ahead. Watch for white milkmaids and iris.

0.8 Mtn. Theater and junction. This natural amphitheater has been the site of plays since 1913. The present theater was built in 1934 using over 40,000 stones, some weighing 4000 lbs. Each stone is buried so that only a small fraction is visible. Water and restrooms nearby. To continue the hike, head up the right side of the theater, then back across the top and admire the views. Continue west on the paved road.

Map of Mtn. Theater Area

1.0 Junction #1. Head left on the signed road to Madrone Grove and explore the hilltop covered with large madrone, oak and Douglas fir trees. To continue the hike, backtrack to the road and go left (west) through the gate, cross the highway and pick up the signed trail towards Rock Spring.

1.2 Rock Spring and junction #2. From the parking area, cross the highway, bear left and take the signed Mtn. Theater fire trail uphill.

1.3 Junction with Old Mine trail. Bear right along the open hillside.

1.5 Rocky knoll and spectacular views!

1.9 Junction #3. Continue straight towards Pantoll and right ahead.

2.2 Back at Pantoll ranger station. Full facilities.

Getting There

From Hwy 101:
Near Sausalito
W on Hwy 1
for 3.3 miles,
R on Panoramic Hwy
for 4.9 miles to the
Pantoll parking area.
Parking fee.

B13 - Mt. Tamalpais South

Mt. Tamalpais State Park
Pantoll

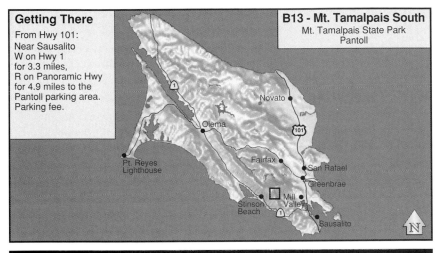

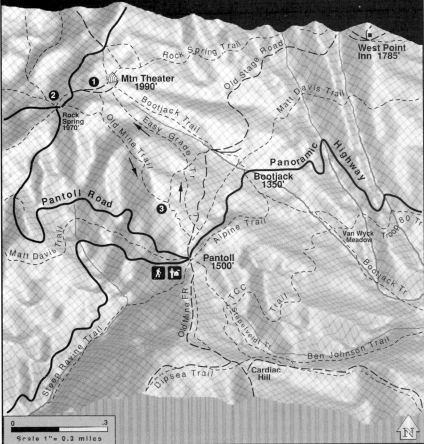

67

B14 Dipsea - Steep Ravine Trails

Distance: 3.6 miles   Shaded: 70%
Elevation Change: 1100'   Hike requires climbing a ladder.
Rating: Hiking - 10   Difficulty - 8   Steep in places.
When to Go: Good in winter and spring, best on a clear April day.

This is a breathtaking hike through forest, along coastal hills, then up spectacular Steep Ravine. Good wildflowers and good views.

0.0 Start at the Pantoll parking lot. Take the paved road next to the ranger station south 200' to the signed Old Mine trail. Go left into Douglas fir forest with some oak and bay. In March, look for white zigadene, yellow buttercup, blue hound's tongue and purple iris.

0.2 Mining claim. In 1863, prospectors dug for gold and silver.

0.3 Junction. Continue south on the Old Mine Rd.

0.5 Junction with Dipsea Fire Rd. Stay left on the road.

0.6 Junction #1. Follow the Dipsea trail right. This trail is thought to be one of the oldest on the mountain. In 1905, it became part of the famous Dipsea race that covers 7.1 miles from downtown Mill Valley to Stinson Beach.

1.3 Junction #2. Take the Dipsea trail right towards Stinson Beach.

1.4 Fence. Bear right. The trail drops down through luxuriant growth kept moist by winter rain and summer fog. Ahead, the trail drops so steeply that it's hard to believe that 1500 Dipsea runners plunge through here at full speed each June.

Dipsea Race - June 1993

2.0 Junction #3 and bridge. Cross the bridge, go right on the Steep Ravine trail and enjoy the finest scenery on Mt. Tam. Steep Ravine offers spectacular redwoods, ferns, mosses, berries, tumbled trees, wooden bridges, quiet pools and cascading waterfalls.

2.4 Notched redwood. A large redwood lying across the trail is notched to allow passage. As you duck, look for white fairy bells.

2.8 Ladder. Webb Creek is squeezed by large boulders. The only way up is to climb a 10' ladder.

3.6 Back at Pantoll with camping, restrooms, tables and water.

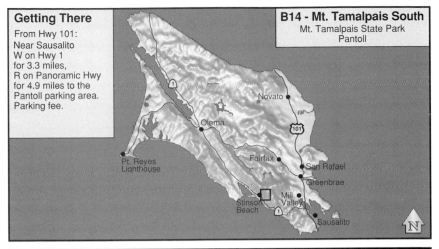

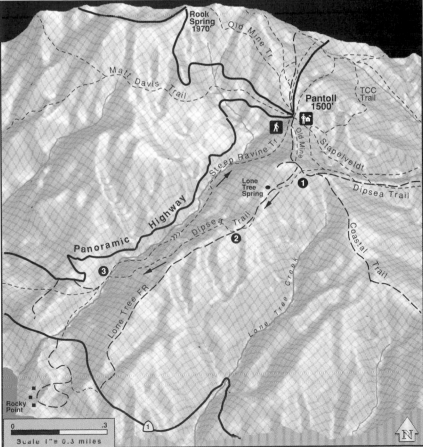

B15 Matt Davis - Coastal - Cataract

Distance: 6.6 miles   Shaded: 50%
Elevation Change: 700'   May be overgrown in summer.
Rating: Hiking - 10   Difficulty - 6   Moderately steep uphill.
When to Go: Best on a clear day in March or April.

Here is a magnificent hike through dense forest, past flowering hillsides, then along a refreshing creek. Spectacular views.

0.0 From the Pantoll parking lot, cross Panoramic Hwy and take the paved Pantoll Rd. 200' uphill to the Matt Davis trail signed to Stinson Beach. The trail starts out along open hillside, but soon enters dense woods of Douglas fir, oak and bay. Wildflowers along the trail include white zigadene, yellow poppy, yellow Mariposa lily, blue hound's tongue, blue-eyed grass, blue dicks and iris.

1.2 Open hillside. Leaving the woods, look for white popcorn flower, yellow buttercup, pink checkerbloom and lupine. Great views. Up ahead, a short spur trail leads left to a lookout point.

1.6 Junction #1. Stay right to climb gently on the Coastal trail. In summer, this trail is crowded with grasses and thistles.

2.4 Rock outcroppings. Green-grey lichens enjoy the cool and moist coastal climate on these small rocky patches.

3.3 Junction #2. Turn right and take the Willow Camp FR steeply up to the first knoll, then take the short trail left to Ridgecrest Blvd.

3.5 Highway junction. Continue on the dirt road to Laurel Dell.

3.8 Junction #3. A trail leads right, over the bridge on Cataract Creek. Go left on Cataract trail through the meadow to Laurel Dell.

4.1 Laurel Dell picnic area. Continue north on the Cataract trail.

4.2 Waterfalls and turnaround point. Beneath a big-leaf maple, moss-covered rocks and ferns, Cataract Creek starts its vigorous plunge to Alpine Lake. To continue the hike, backtrack south along the left side of Cataract Creek towards jct. #3 and Rock Spring.

4.6 Junction and airplane engine. About 100' past the bridge on the right, look for a Navy Corsair airplane engine down in the middle of the creek, the result of a mid-air plane collision October 4, 1945.

5.6 Rock Spring. Cross the highway, bear left and take the signed Mtn. Theater fire trail uphill, then right on the Old Mine trail.

5.9 Rocky knoll and spectacular views. Continue downhill.

6.6 Back at Pantoll Ranger Station. Full facilities.

Getting There

From Hwy 101:
Near Sausalito
W on Hwy 1
for 3.3 miles,
R on Panoramic Hwy
for 4.9 miles to the
Pantoll parking area.
Parking fee.

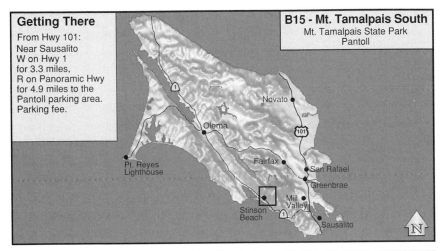

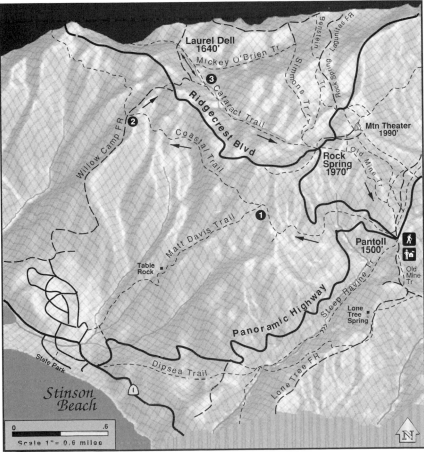

71

B16 Matt Davis Trail to Stinson Beach

Distance: 7.2 miles   Shaded: 60%
Elevation Change: 1600'   Many stairs.
Rating: Hiking - 10   Difficulty - 8   Steep in places.
When to Go: Good anytime, best in winter and spring.

This strenuous, but spectacular hike, starts out on coastal hills, then descends to Stinson Beach and returns along scenic Steep Ravine.

0.0 From the Pantoll parking lot, cross Panoramic Hwy and take the paved Pantoll Rd. 200' uphill to the signed Matt Davis trail heading west towards Stinson Beach.

0.4 Webb Creek. Mosses, chain ferns, bays and Douglas fir provide a woodsy setting next to bedrock carved by Webb Creek.

1.2 Open hillsides. Great views to Stinson Beach and Bolinas Mesa. Look for checkerbloom and lupine among the spring wildflowers.

1.6 Junction #1. Take the signed Matt Davis trail left towards Stinson Beach. The trail makes a gradual descent until it enters a Douglas fir forest where it drops more quickly. Lots of stairs.

3.5 Table Rock. At a fencepost under buckeye trees, take a spur trail 10' to the right to Table Rock. Great views of Bolinas Lagoon.

3.7 Bridge and junction #2. Go left across the creek and bridge. Up ahead, bear to the right at the Y-junction.

4.0 Paved street. The trail emerges on Belvedere Street. Continue west towards Shoreline Hwy. At the road, go left 100 yds., then take the first right to head past the Parkside Cafe to the beach entrance.

4.3 Stinson Beach State Park. The park has complete amenities: grass, trees and shade, beach, swimming, water, food and restrooms. It offers a great place for resting and picnicking, although it may be crowded on summer weekends. After enjoying the beach, retrace your steps to Shoreline Hwy.

4.6 Shoreline Hwy. Head south for 300 yds. along the highway to take the famed Dipsea trail towards Steep Ravine and Pantoll.

5.0 Open hillsides. Take the most prominent trail across the "moors" up towards the steps and fire road. Continue across the fire road.

5.6 Bridge and junction #3. Take the signed Steep Ravine trail left. This is a magnificent area offering an inspiring setting of redwoods, ferns, mosses, creeks and waterfalls.

7.2 Back at the Pantoll parking area with water and restrooms.

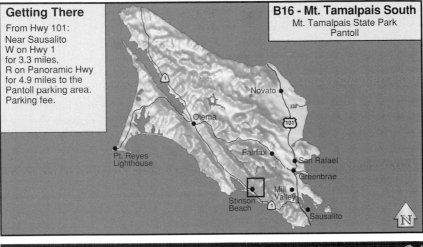

Getting There

From Hwy 101:
Near Sausalito
W on Hwy 1
for 3.3 miles,
R on Panoramic Hwy
for 4.9 miles to the
Pantoll parking area.
Parking fee.

B16 - Mt. Tamalpais South
Mt. Tamalpais State Park
Pantoll

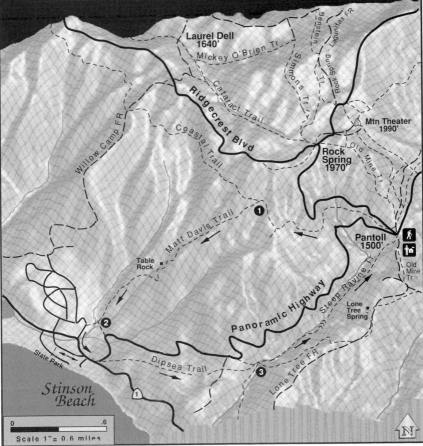

B17 Simmons - Music Camp - Cataract

Distance: 3.8 miles   Shaded: 60%
Elevation Change: 800'   Trail difficult to follow in places.
Rating: Hiking - 10   Difficulty - 8   Steep and rocky in places.
When to Go: Best in winter and spring after rain.

This is a great hike through woods and chaparral and along three cascading creeks to Barth's Retreat and magical Music Camp.

0.0 Start at the Rock Spring parking area and take the signed Cataract trail into the meadow. Up ahead, continue straight on the signed Simmons trail towards the Benstein trail.

0.2 Junction #1. Bear left on the signed Simmons trail and head downhill towards Ziesche Creek. Look for the coral root orchid in May.

0.3 Bridge and junction. Cross the bridge to make a steep climb up to a hilltop covered with tanoak and large Douglas fir trees.

0.4 Chaparral. The trail abruptly leaves the forest and enters a rocky serpentine slope, covered with chamise and Sargent cypress.

1.2 Barth's Retreat and junction #2. The trail drops down through Douglas fir, bay, oak and madrone to cross a creek at Barth's Retreat. Emil Barth, pianist and avid hiker, built his camp in the 1920s. To continue, take the dirt road north into coastal scrub.

1.3 Junction. Continue straight across the Laurel Dell FR and follow an uncertain path through chaparral and down into a rocky creek bed. Ahead, the trail descends along the left side of the creek.

1.4 Two creek crossings and junction #3. The trail crosses to the right of the creek, goes 30 yds., then returns to the left side of the creek and goes for 40 yds. to a junction next to a double-trunked fir tree. Head left, away from the creek, for 50 yds. to Music Camp.

1.5 Music Camp. This idyllic retreat, one of Mt. Tam's many hidden treasures, was built by music lover Ben Schmidt in the1950s. When ready to return, retrace your steps back up to Barth's Retreat.

1.8 Barth's Retreat. Take the Mickey O'Brien trail, which stays on the south side of Barth's Creek, downhill towards Laurel Dell.

2.6 Junction #4 with Cataract trail. Head left towards Rock Spring. About 100' past the bridge on the right, look for a Navy Corsair airplane engine down in the middle of the creek, the result of a mid-air plane collision October 4, 1945.

3.8 Parking area. Ocean view, tables and restrooms.

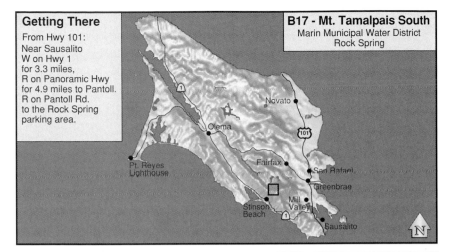

Getting There

From Hwy 101:
Near Sausalito
W on Hwy 1
for 3.3 miles,
R on Panoramic Hwy
for 4.9 miles to Pantoll.
R on Pantoll Rd.
to the Rock Spring
parking area.

B17 - Mt. Tamalpais South

Marin Municipal Water District
Rock Spring

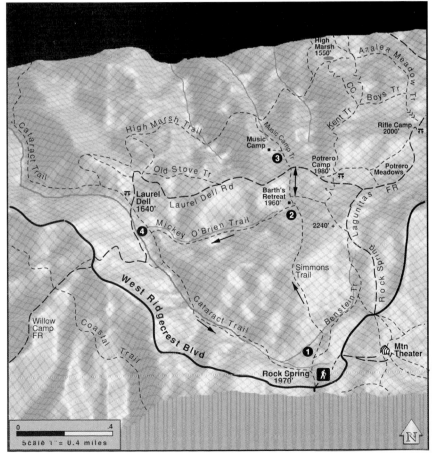

B18 Benstein - International Trails

Distance: 5.4 miles   Shaded: 40%
Elevation Change: 600'   Some bicycle traffic.
Rating: Hiking - 8   Difficulty - 8   Steep in places.
When to Go: Best when clear for views, and March-April for orchids.

This is a pleasant hike that explores woods and chaparral on both sides of the mountain offering great views and good wildflowers.

0.0 Start at the Rock Spring parking area and take the trail into the meadow. Up ahead, continue straight on the signed Simmons trail towards the Benstein trail.

0.2 Junction. Take the signed Benstein trail right into Douglas fir and tanoak trees and up past moss-covered rocks. In late March, look for the delicate and beautiful calypso orchid usually found under Douglas fir. It has a bright pink flower with a lower scoop-like petal colored to attract insects for pollination. The plant, also called "fairy slipper", is common in the Pacific northwest, but rare here.

Calypso Orchid

0.4 Junction with trail to the Mtn. Theater. Continue left towards signed Potrero Meadows.

0.7 Junction #1. Go left on the Rock Spring - Lagunitas Rd.

1.3 Junction #2 and Rifle Camp. Go down through the picnic area, cross the creek and take the signed Northside trail into woods.

1.8 Views. Great views north, east and west. Continue straight across the serpentine ridgeline; notice the stunted Sargent cypress.

1.9 Junction #3. Take the signed International trail right. Notice the manzanita being succeeded by Douglas fir, oak and some nutmeg.

2.4 Junction with Ridgecrest Blvd. Cross the road and take the Miller trail down the rocky hillside. John Miller, who worked on trails for over 30 years, was injured while working here in 1947 at the age of 80.

2.7 Junction #4. Turn right and take the Old RR Grade downhill.

3.4 Junction and West Point Inn. Water, restroom, tables and view. To continue the hike, take the Rock Spring trail west of the inn.

5.1 Mtn. Theater. Water, restrooms and picnic area. Continue right, around the top of the theater, and along the paved path to Ridgecrest Blvd. Cross the road and take the trail to Rock Spring.

5.4 Rock Spring parking area. Ocean view, tables and restrooms.

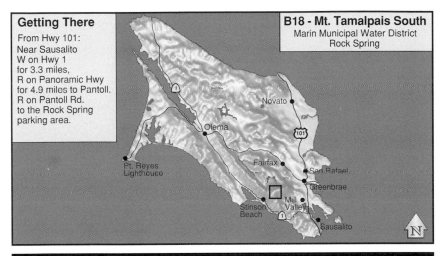

Getting There

From Hwy 101:
Near Sausalito
W on Hwy 1
for 3.3 miles,
R on Panoramic Hwy
for 4.9 miles to Pantoll.
R on Pantoll Rd.
to the Rock Spring
parking area.

B18 - Mt. Tamalpais South
Marin Municipal Water District
Rock Spring

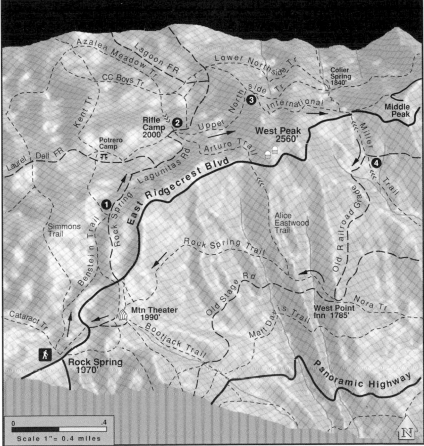

77

B19 Cataract - High Marsh - Kent Trails

Distance: 6.0 miles   Shaded: 90%
Elevation Change: 800'   Can have standing water in winter.
Rating: Hiking - 10   Difficulty - 7   Steep and rocky in places.
When to Go: Good anytime, great in winter and spring.

This is a magnificent hike that features creeks, forests, views and flowers in some of the most remote areas on the mountain.

0.0 Start at the Rock Spring parking area and take the Cataract trail down the left side of the meadow towards Cataract Creek. The Cataract trail offers some of the finest hiking on Mt. Tam with pools, waterfalls, small meadows, wildflowers and Douglas fir forest.

1.2 Junction with Mickey O'Brien trail. This area can be soggy when wet. Continue straight. Pretty flowers in the meadow in spring.

1.3 Laurel Dell picnic area with tables and restrooms. From the picnic area, take the signed Cataract trail downstream.

1.5 Junction #1, bench and waterfalls. Here, Cataract Creek starts its dramatic plunge towards Alpine Lake. At the bench, take the High Marsh trail right and right again 100' ahead. The trail climbs past a down oak tree, then skirts an open hillside with great views north.

2.3 Junction with spur trail to Laurel Dell FR. Continue on the High Marsh trail, which follows a roller-coaster pattern, downhill into forested ravines, then uphill to ridges covered with chaparral.

3.0 Creek and junction. A large 20' by 30' boulder in the streambed marks the trail right to Music Camp. Continue straight.

3.3 Unmarked junction. The Willow trail heads downhill left. Continue straight and slightly uphill past a small grove of madrone trees.

3.5 High Marsh and junction. The Cross Country Boys trail heads right and uphill. Continue straight as the trail skirts the marsh.

3.6 Junction #2. Take the signed Kent trail right which climbs slowly at first, then zig-zags up the ridge.

4.2 Junction. The CC Boys trail crosses here. Continue straight.

4.6 Potrero Camp and junction #3. Take the dirt road south to Laurel Dell FR, then go left 100' and take the signed Benstein trail uphill. The trail climbs past a serpentine outcropping with Sargent cypress trees.

5.3 Junction #4. Take the Rock Spring-Lagunitas FR right 100 yds., then head downhill on the signed Benstein trail.

6.0 Back at the Rock Spring parking area with restrooms.

Getting There

From Hwy 101:
Near Sausalito
W on Hwy 1
for 3.3 miles,
R on Panoramic Hwy
for 4.9 miles to Pantoll.
R on Pantoll Rd.
to the Rock Spring
parking area.

B19 - Mt. Tamalpais South

Marin Municipal Water District
Rock Spring

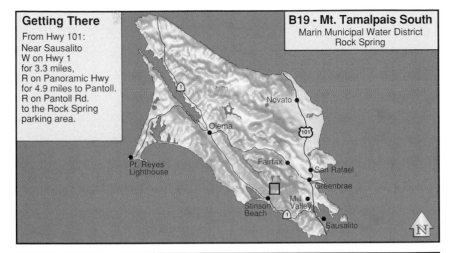

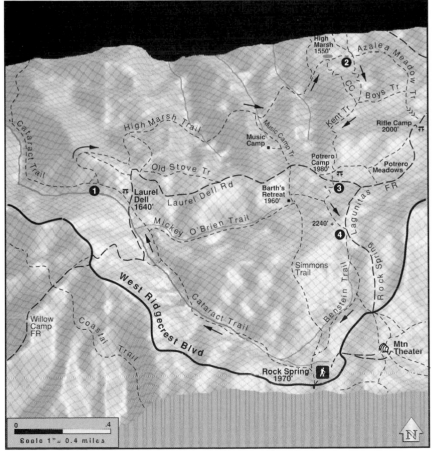

79

B20 East Peak Loop and Plankwalk Trails

Distance: 0.7 and 0.6 miles   Shaded: 20%
Elevation Change: 50' and 300'   The Plankwalk trail is steep.
Rating: Hiking - 10   Difficulty - 1 and 7
When to Go: Great anytime on a clear, windless day.

One hike loops around the East Peak on a paved path. The other hike climbs to the top of Mt. Tamalpais. Both offer incomparable views.

Verna Dunshee Trail - 0.7 miles and 50' Change

0.0 From the East Peak parking lot, go east towards the restroom and take the signed Verna Dunshee trail to circle the peak counterclockwise. The concrete picnic area is all that remains of the Tamalpais Tavern, a restaurant and inn built by the railroad in the 1890s. It suffered serious damage in a forest fire in 1913 and again in a kitchen fire in 1923. Each time, it was quickly rebuilt and, because of its remote location, thrived during prohibition. In 1942, the tavern was leased to the army for barracks. After the war, it fell into disrepair and was destroyed.

Tamalpais Tavern 1922

0.1 View. Look down at Mesa Junction. Here you can see the Old Railroad Grade make its famous Double Bowknot, laying claim to the "Crookedest Railroad in the World."

0.2 Sunrise Point. On a clear day, this point offers one of the finest views in the world! Watch for turkey vultures soaring below you.

0.7 Parking area with tables, water and restrooms. A small visitor center and snackbar is usually open on weekends from 12-4 pm.

Plankwalk Trail - 0.6 miles and 300' Change

0.0 From the East Peak snack bar, head east and left to take the signed Plankwalk trail uphill. The trail is rocky at the bottom and steeper at the top.

0.3 East Peak and the Gardner Lookout Station at 2571'. You can scramble around the rocks to find panoramic views in all directions. Landmarks include Mt. St. Helena 51 miles north, Mt. Diablo 37 miles east, San Bruno Mtn. 18 miles south and Pt. Reyes 25 miles west.

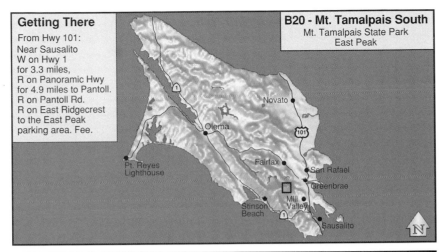

Getting There

From Hwy 101:
Near Sausalito
W on Hwy 1
for 3.3 miles,
R on Panoramic Hwy
for 4.9 miles to Pantoll.
R on Pantoll Rd.
R on East Ridgecrest
to the East Peak
parking area. Fee.

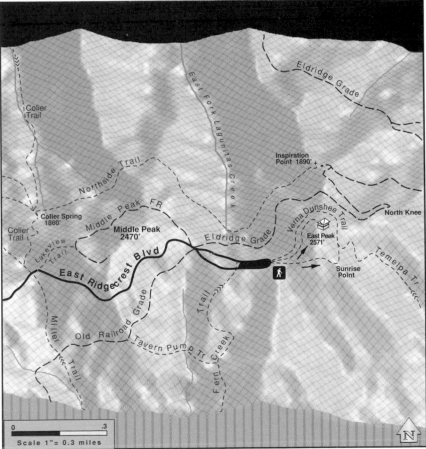

B21 Northside - Colier - Lakeview Trails

Distance: 4.3 miles   Shaded: 70%
Elevation Change: 500'
Rating: Hiking - 8   Difficulty - 7   Very rocky in places.
When to Go: Good anytime, best March to May after rain.
Wear sturdy boots to hike the rocky north slopes below East Peak.
Good chaparral, some redwoods and lots of oak and nutmeg.

0.0 From the East Peak parking lot, take the one-way paved road west, away from the restrooms.

0.3 Junction #1 with Eldridge Grade. Go through the gate and downhill past oak, chamise, manzanita, ceanothus, yerba santa and occasional chaparral pea. Spring wildflowers along the road include white milkmaids, modesty, yellow monkeyflower, red Indian warrior, Indian paintbrush and iris.

Look for California nutmeg, a California endemic with flat, one-inch, sharp, green needles. This 20' evergreen tree is common on this hike.

1.0 Hairpin turn. Continue around the hairpin turn. Up ahead, more moisture and better soil produce more luxuriant growth.

1.3 Junction #2. Take the Northside trail left toward Colier Spring.

1.4 Inspiration Point and great views. The hike leaves the road here and follows the narrow Northside trail, which starts out level and heads southwest into a canyon below East Peak.

3.1 Colier Spring and junction #3. Pause at the bench just below the spring to enjoy the large redwood grove. Alice Eastwood called this area "Butterfly Spring" because of the many specimens she found here. To continue the hike, take the Colier trail, which starts 30' east of the Colier Spring sign, and climb uphill along the winter streambed.

3.4 Two junctions #4. Go left up to Ridgecrest Blvd., then head east 100' to pick up the Lakeview trail which climbs toward Middle Peak.

3.6 Junction. Continue downhill on the Middle Peak FR. Back in 1905, two 300' wooden towers, placed on Middle Peak, were reported to be the tallest, wireless telegraph towers in the world. They blew over in a storm in December, 1905 and were not replaced. The current relay towers date from the 1950s. The Water District hopes that someday they can be removed for aesthetic reasons.

4.0 Junction #1. Follow the highway left up to the parking area.

4.3 Back at the parking area with water, tables and restrooms.

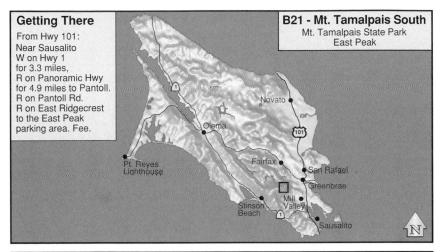

Getting There

From Hwy 101:
Near Sausalito
W on Hwy 1
for 3.3 miles,
R on Panoramic Hwy
for 4.9 miles to Pantoll.
R on Pantoll Rd.
R on East Ridgecrest
to the East Peak
parking area. Fee.

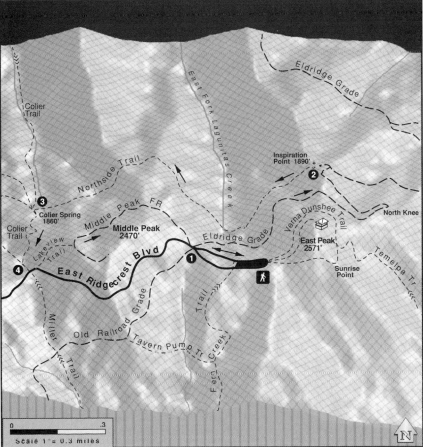

C - Mt. Tamalpais North - 19 Hikes

Starting from below Phoenix Lake in Ross at 80'
C1..... Phoenix Lake Trail 2.8
C2..... Tucker - Bill Williams Trails 2.9
C3..... Worn Springs Road to Bald Hill 3.9
C4..... Hidden Meadow - Yolanda Trails 3.9
C5..... Eldridge Grade - Tucker Trails 4.9

Starting from Deer Park in Fairfax at 200'
C6..... Deer Park Road - Yolanda Trail 3.3
C7..... Deer Park Road - Canyon - Six Points Trail 3.7

Starting from along Fairfax-Bolinas Rd.
C8..... Carson Falls, Pine Mountain and Oat Hill 3.2, 4.4, 7.4
C9..... Meadow Club Area to Carson Falls 4.8
C10... Lily Gulch Trail - Kent Pump Road 5.8*
C11... Cataract - High Marsh - Kent Trails 7.7

Starting from Sky Oaks Road at 700'
C12... Taylor - Concrete Pipe - Bullfrog Road 3.2

Starting from below Bon Tempe Lake at 660'
C13... Bon Tempe Lake Trail 4.1
C14... Kent Trail - Rocky Ridge Road 5.2

Starting from below Lake Lagunitas at 730'
C15... Lake Lagunitas Road 1.8
C16... Lakeview Road to Pilot Knob 2.2
C17... Pumpkin Ridge - Bon Tempe Trails 2.8
C18... Colier Spring - Northside - Lagoon Extension Trails 5.7
C19... Lake Lagunitas to East Peak 10.1

* Shuttle Hike

Pets allowed on all hikes except 19.

Region C Trailheads

Hikes 1-19 start in Marin
Municipal Water District,
phone 459-5267.

Region C
Mt. Tamalpais North

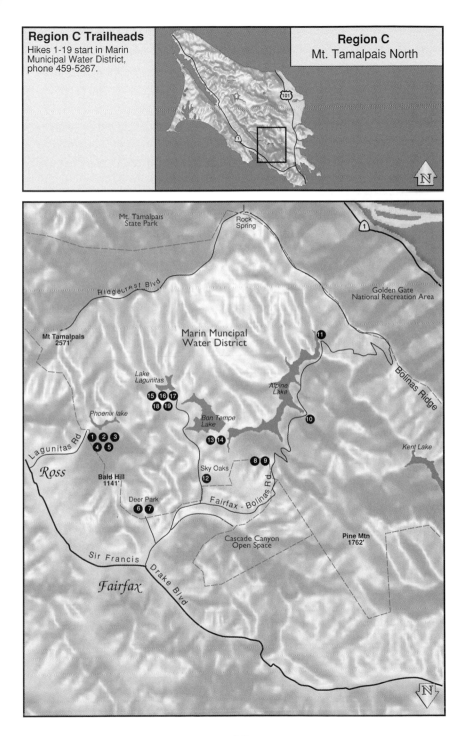

C1 Phoenix Lake Trail

Distance: 2.8 miles   Shaded: 70%
Elevation Change: 200'   Bicycle traffic on roads.
Rating: Hiking - 8   Difficulty - 5   One moderately steep area.
When to Go: Best in March and April for water runoff and flowers.

This heavily traveled trail around the lake passes through a mixture of oak, bay and redwood trees with wildflowers and good views.

0.0 Start at Natalie Greene Park in Ross. Notice the massive slide that occurred in 1986. Slide debris has raised this area by 3' as can be seen by the partially buried telephone booth in the center of the parking area. Take the trail up the left side of the creek to the dam.

0.2 Dam. Go left to circle the lake clockwise. The milky-green color of the water is due to algae and sediment, which are removed when the water is treated. However, this lake is so small that its water is only used for drinking during drought years.

0.8 Junction #1. Turn right and take the signed Gertrude Ord trail up the stairs. The trail passes through a mixture of tall oak, bay, Douglas fir and madrone trees shading low-growing tanoak and fuzzy-leaved hazel. Pink trillium, white milkmaids and blue hound's tongue can be found in February and March.

1.3 Junction. The stairs down to the right can be used as a shortcut in dry times. For a more interesting route, follow the trail left into the redwood ravine. The storm of 1986 scoured the creek bottom lowering the channel by three feet. Upstream, previous mudslides have left much debris including several large trees.

2.0 Junction #2. Turn right at the small bridge to take the Phoenix Lake Rd. east towards the dam. Up ahead, Phoenix Log Cabin, built in 1893 for the Porteous Ranch foreman, has been restored. Notice the octagonal turret and natural window frames. The cabin is not open to the public. Please do not enter the area, as it is also a ranger residence.

*Phoenix Log Cabin
Originally Built in 1893*

2.5 Dam. Go left down the road.

2.8 Parking area with water, tables and restroom facilities.

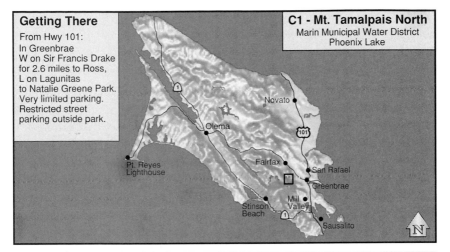

Getting There

From Hwy 101:
In Greenbrae
W on Sir Francis Drake
for 2.6 miles to Ross,
L on Lagunitas
to Natalie Greene Park.
Very limited parking.
Restricted street
parking outside park.

C1 - Mt. Tamalpais North
Marin Municipal Water District
Phoenix Lake

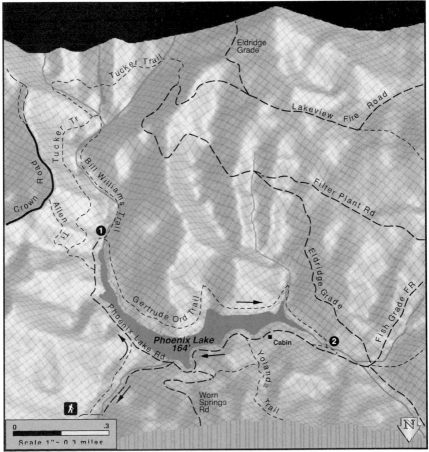

C2 Tucker - Bill Williams Trails

Distance: 2.9 miles   Shaded: 80%

Elevation Change: 400'   Creek not fordable during heavy runoff.

Rating: Hiking - 8   Difficulty - 8   Steep downhill.

When to Go: Good anytime, best after rain.

This is a fine hike that explores two small canyons offering enchanting oak-bay woods, redwoods, ferns and mosses in a creekside setting.

0.0 Start at Natalie Greene Park in Ross. From the parking lot, take the trail up the left side of the creek to the stairs and dam.

0.2 Dam. Go left to circle the lake clockwise. Ahead, look for seasonal wildflowers: red Indian warrior in March, white iris in April, blue brodiaea in May and pink clarkia in June.

0.6 Junction #1. Turn left on the signed Harry Allen trail and head into a small ravine with oak, bay and buckeye trees. Early flowers include pink shooting star, blue hound's tongue, and white zigadene. Later flowers include white modesty, blue dicks and wood rose.

0.8 Junction. The Harry Allen trail goes left uphill. Stay right and follow the Tucker trail past mosses, lichens and maidenhair ferns. Several small deer paths cross the trail before the next junction.

1.1 Main canyon. Redwoods grow along the north slope of Bill Williams canyon. Oaks and bays grow here along the south side. Up ahead, a small dam is just visible down the steep hillside.

Maidenhair Fern

1.5 Two junctions #2. An unmaintained trail comes down from the left. At the second junction, 100' ahead, turn right and go steeply down to the creek on the Bill Williams trail.

1.6 Two bridges. The trail makes three crossings of the creek, two by bridge and one by foot. (The creek may not be fordable in high water.) Cross the first bridge, go uphill 100' to a junction, turn right and go down to the creek for the second crossing over rocks. Continue along the creek past the dam to the second bridge. This dam was built in 1886 as part of a local water supply before Phoenix Lake was created in 1906. Cross the creek and continue through the redwoods.

2.1 Phoenix Lake Rd. Continue along the lake to the dam.

2.6 Dam and junction. Cross the dam and take the road downhill.

2.9 Back at the parking area with water, tables and restrooms.

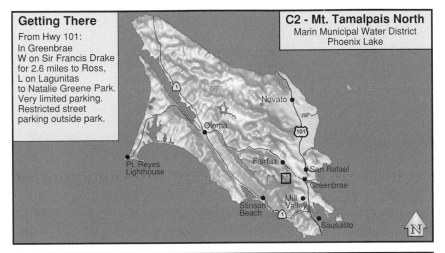

Getting There

From Hwy 101:
In Greenbrae
W on Sir Francis Drake
for 2.6 miles to Ross,
L on Lagunitas
to Natalie Greene Park.
Very limited parking.
Restricted street
parking outside park.

C2 - Mt. Tamalpais North
Marin Municipal Water District
Phoenix Lake

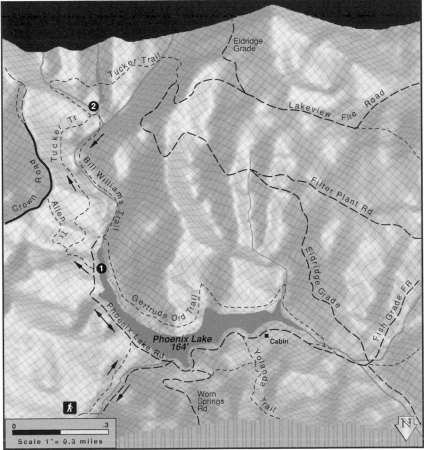

89

C3 Worn Springs Road to Bald Hill

Distance: 3.9 miles   Shaded: 50%
Elevation Change: 1100'   Some bicycles.
Rating: Hiking - 7   Difficulty - 5   Moderately steep in places.
When to Go: Good any cool, clear, calm day; best in spring.

Take binoculars and water to make the long climb up the road to Bald Hill. Spectacular views and lovely wildflowers in spring.

0.0 Start at Natalie Greene Park in Ross. From the parking lot, take the road uphill past oak, bay and madrone. Look for white wild onion and iris along the road in spring.

0.3 Dam. Take the Phoenix Lake Rd. to the right.

0.4 Junction #1. Take the signed Worn Springs Rd. right toward Bald Hill. This road was named after George Austin Worn, descendant of the family that founded the town of Ross.

0.7 Reservoir and junction. The small Ross Reservoir can hold one million gallons and is used only during drought. Take the left road and climb steeply.

1.4 Views. Good views south and east. Yellow buttercup, poppy, white popcorn flower, blue-eyed grass, blue dicks, lupine, and pink checkerbloom grow along the road from March to May.

2.1 Junction #2. The road left is the way down. For now, turn right and walk 150' to the top of the hill.

2.2 Bald Hill. Spectacular 360 degree views. Explore the hilltop to discover the best wildflower display, often yellow gold fields. To continue the hike, backtrack to junction #2 and bear right.

2.4 Junction #3. Bear right to head east. There is a good selection of wildflowers 100' uphill from this junction. Down the road, coyote brush and poison oak indicate the coastal scrub community.

2.5 Oaks. Look for two different oaks nearby. The deciduous California black oak has deeply lobed leaves, 3-4 inches long. The evergreen, coast live oak has one inch oval leaves with sharp edges.

2.9 Gate. Take the paved road downhill past large estates.

3.2 Junction. Take Upper Rd. right to Glenwood then right again.

3.6 Junction #4. Take Lagunitas Rd. right towards the park. Once past the park gate, look for blue forget-me-nots, white milkmaids, modesty, woodland star and mission bells in early spring.

3.9 Back at the parking area with water, tables and restrooms.

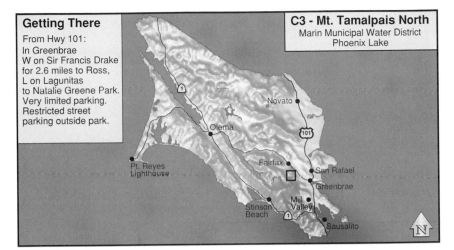

Getting There

From Hwy 101:
In Greenbrae
W on Sir Francis Drake
for 2.6 miles to Ross,
L on Lagunitas
to Natalie Greene Park.
Very limited parking.
Restricted street
parking outside park.

C3 - Mt. Tamalpais North
Marin Municipal Water District
Phoenix Lake

Novato

Olema

Fairfax

San Rafael

Greenbrae

Pt. Reyes
Lighthouse

Mill
Valley

Stinson
Beach

Sausalito

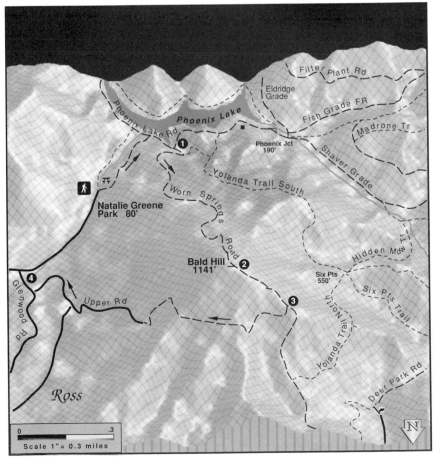

Filter Plant Rd

Eldridge
Grade

Fish Grade FR

Phoenix Lake Rd

Phoenix Lake

Madrone Tr

1

Phoenix Jct
190'

Shaver Grade

Yolanda Trail South

Worn Springs Road

Natalie Greene
Park 80'

Bald Hill
1141' **2**

Hidden Mdw

Six Pts
550'

Six Pts Trail

3

Yolanda Trail North

4

Upper Rd

Glenwood Rd

Deer Park Rd

Ross

0   .3

Scale 1" = 0.3 miles

C4 Hidden Meadow - Yolanda Trails

Distance: 3.9 miles   Shaded: 70%
Elevation Change: 600'   Trail may be overgrown.
Rating: Hiking - 9   Difficulty - 7   One steep uphill section.
When to Go: Good in spring, best in April and May.

The hike explores a small hidden meadow, then climbs steeply to skirt a south-facing hillside with great views and fine wildflowers.

0.0 From the Natalie Greene Park in Ross, start out on the left side of the creek. The trail passes through the picnic area, then climbs steeply up to the dam under a dense canopy of bay trees.

0.2 Stairs, dam and lake. Go right on the road across the spillway. Watch for osprey, cormorants and ducks. The cormorants are skillful fish catchers and are unwelcome by fishermen.

0.6 Junction and cabin. Continue around the lake. Two hundred feet ahead, Phoenix Log Cabin, built in 1893, has been recently restored.

0.9 Phoenix Jct #1. Take signed Shaver Grade to the right up towards Five Corners. Shaver Grade was originally a logging road built by Isaac Shaver in the 1890s to haul lumber from near Alpine Dam to Ross Landing (now the site of College of Marin, Kentfield).

1.2 Junction #2. Take the Hidden Meadow trail right along the creek.

1.4 Creek bed, junction and meadow. A large oak, backed by a buckeye welcomes visitors to Hidden Meadow. Stay to the right and continue along a small seasonal creek. Ahead, the trail climbs more steeply on the grassy hillside. Look for yellow buttercups, blue dicks and white popcorn flower in April.

1.9 Six Points Jct #3. Take the signed Yolanda trail south towards Phoenix Lake. Colorful wildflowers and spectacular views lie ahead as the trail winds along the south-facing canyon hillside.

2.3 Rock slide. A small rock slide was started by one of many winter storms. Two hundred feet above the slide is Rocky View Point.

2.4 Wildflowers. Pink shooting stars, blue dicks, yellow poppies, red larkspur and iris stand guard on small rocky outcroppings.

2.7 Spectacular views of Mt. Tamalpais!

3.0 Downhill. The trail tumbles downhill past several fallen trees. Stay right at the small Y-junction ahead.

3.2 Junction. Go left on Phoenix Lake Rd. towards the dam.

3.9 Back at the parking lot with tables, water and restrooms.

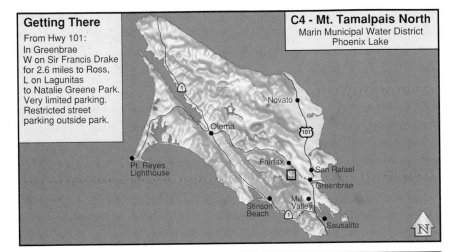

Getting There

From Hwy 101:
In Greenbrae
W on Sir Francis Drake
for 2.6 miles to Ross,
L on Lagunitas
to Natalie Greene Park.
Very limited parking.
Restricted street
parking outside park.

C4 - Mt. Tamalpais North
Marin Municipal Water District
Phoenix Lake

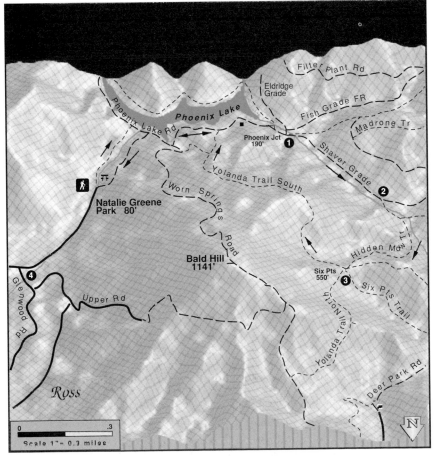

93

C5 Eldridge Grade - Tucker Trails

Distance: 4.9 miles   Shaded: 60%
Elevation Change: 600'   Bicycles on weekends.
Rating: Hiking - 9   Difficulty - 8   Steep downhill in places.
When to Go: Best in late winter and early spring.

Lots of water, views and wildflowers make this a great hike on the steep north slope of Mt. Tam. May be impassable after heavy rain.

0.0 Start at Natalie Greene Park in Ross. From the parking lot, take the road uphill past oak, bay and madrone. Watch out for poison oak.

0.3 Dam. Go right. In April, look for pink Chinese houses.

0.9 Phoenix Jct #1. Take the first left road, signed Eldridge Grade, for a steady climb through an interesting combination of redwood, big-leaf maple, oak, bay and madrone.

This road was built as a toll road by John C. Eldridge in the 1880s as the first wagon road to the summit. It has suffered many slides and is now being maintained as a trail. It is a heavily traveled bicycle route.

1.6 Rock garden. In an open ravine, water streams down large rocks to nourish mosses, lichens and spring flowers including red larkspur.

1.7 Junction with Filter Plant Rd. Continue left uphill.

2.1 Hairpin junction. Take either road as they merge ahead.

2.5 Junction #2 with the Tucker trail. As the road curves right, take the signed Tucker trail left towards Phoenix Lake.

3.0 Creek. The trail makes a steep descent down the north slope of Mt. Tam past tumbling creeks, cascading waterfalls, western azalea, redwood and iris. This is a magnificent section of trail.

3.4 Bill Williams Creek. Cross the creek to head uphill.

3.5 Junction #3. Take the signed Bill Williams trail left, steeply downhill to the bridge.

3.6 Two bridges. The trail makes three crossings of the creek: two by bridge and one by foot. Cross the first bridge, go uphill 100 feet to a junction, turn right and go down to the creek for the second crossing by rocks. Walk along the creek past the dam to the second bridge. Cross the creek again, continue on the trail through the redwoods.

4.1 Phoenix Lake Rd. Continue right around the lake.

4.6 Dam. Before the dam, go right on the trail, then down the stairs.

4.9 Back at the parking lot with tables, water and restrooms.

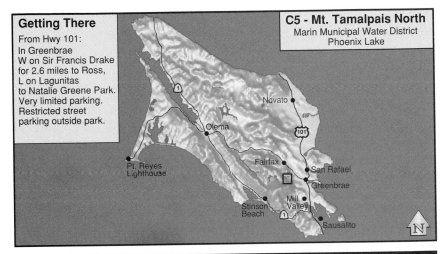

Getting There

From Hwy 101:
In Greenbrae
W on Sir Francis Drake
for 2.6 miles to Ross,
L on Lagunitas
to Natalie Greene Park.
Very limited parking.
Restricted street
parking outside park.

C5 - Mt. Tamalpais North
Marin Municipal Water District
Phoenix Lake

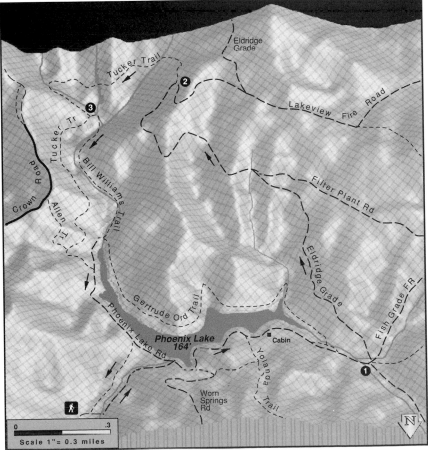

Scale 1" = 0.3 miles

C6 Deer Park Road - Yolanda Trail

Distance: 3.3 miles   Shaded: 70%
Elevation Change: 400'   Some bicycle traffic.
Rating: Hiking - 9   Difficulty - 6   Moderately steep in places.
When to Go: Good November to May, best in April for iris.

This is a good wildflower hike that begins in a canyon, then climbs the north slopes of Bald Hill. Great views of Mt. Tam and Bolinas Ridge.

0.0 Start at Deer Park in Fairfax. From the parking area, go left around the school and cross the field. Deer Park Rd. begins at the gate just past a magnificent bay tree and heads into a canyon.

0.5 Oak Tree Jct #1. Take the narrow Junction trail right past French broom. Then cross a small bridge and climb up an open hillside. Look for blue dicks, buttercup, filaree, paintbrush, clover, lupine, monkeyflower and popcorn flower scattered on the hillside in spring.

0.9 Boy Scout Jct. Take the Bald Hill trail which starts up on a steep, rutted path. About 100' up from the junction, at the end of the rutted section, look for a view west, framed by trees, to Bolinas Ridge. Below the ridge, you can see the Bolinas-Fairfax Rd. In 1884, it was a stagecoach road to Bolinas, once Marin's largest town as loggers provided lumber for San Francisco.

1.3 Junction. Continue left on the Bald Hill trail. Up ahead, the trail skirts above Hidden Meadow and offers great views to Mt. Tam.

1.6 Six Points Jct #2. Take the signed Yolanda trail (Yolanda North), towards Worn Springs Rd. The narrow trail follows the hillside contour through wooded stands of oak, bay and madrone.

2.1 Knoll. A spur trail heads 100' onto an oak-covered knoll. Lots of lichen on the trunks.

2.3 Wildflowers. Another open hillside displays spring flowers including white woodland star, baby blue-eyes and in late April, Chinese houses.

Chinese Houses

2.5 Junction with Worn Springs Rd. Turn left and head downhill. Good views east to the bay.

2.9 Junction #3. Follow the signed Deer Park trail left as it descends in switchbacks down the hillside. Lots of wildflowers bloom here in early spring, followed later by the sweet-smelling buckeye tree in May. At the bottom of the hill, bear right towards the schoolyard.

3.3 Parking area with water, picnic tables and restrooms.

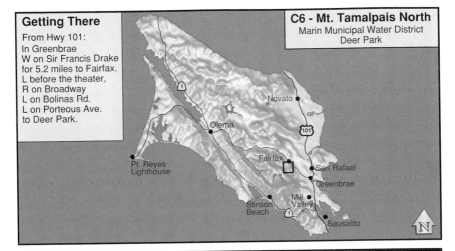

Getting There

From Hwy 101:
In Greenbrae
W on Sir Francis Drake
for 5.2 miles to Fairfax.
L before the theater,
R on Broadway
L on Bolinas Rd.
L on Porteous Ave.
to Deer Park.

C6 - Mt. Tamalpais North

Marin Municipal Water District
Deer Park

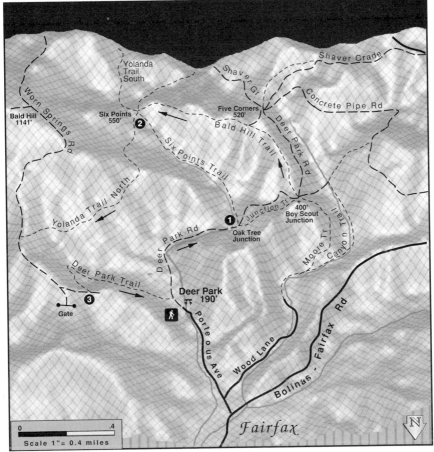

97

C7 Deer Park Rd. - Canyon - Six Points

Distance: 3.7 miles   Shaded: 90%
Elevation Change: 550'   Can be muddy or dusty. Bicycle traffic.
Rating: Hiking - 9   Difficulty - 6   Steep in places.
When to Go: Good November to May, best February through April.

This hike along roads and trails explores the hills and canyons west of Bald Hill offering great views, dark forests and lovely wildflowers.

0.0 Start at Deer Park in Fairfax. From the parking area, go left around the school and through the field. Deer Park Rd. begins at the gate just past a large bay tree and heads into a broad, shaded canyon with majestic oaks, madrone and buckeye trees. Spring wildflowers along the road include white milkmaids, Solomon's seal, yellow buttercup, blue hound's tongue, forget-me-nots, lupine and iris.

0.5 Oak Tree Jct. #1. Just before the road heads uphill, take the Junction trail right past a large oak and cross a small bridge. The trail climbs above a ravine on an open hillside. In late April, look for a small, white flower called jewel flower, *Streptanthus*.

0.9 Boy Scout Jct. Take the spur road downhill to the right towards the signed Canyon trail. The road can be muddy in winter.

1.0 Junction. At the bottom of the hill, cross the creek and go left on the Canyon trail. The trail enters a dark forest of mostly bay trees covered with moss. Up ahead, the trail makes a steep zig-zag climb.

1.3 Junction #2. Take the Concrete Pipe Rd. left. This road was originally a service road for a concrete water pipe built in 1918 to carry water from Alpine Lake to a pump station. A second steel pipe was added in 1926. The concrete pipe can be seen at the bend up the road. There is an excellent display of wildflowers along the roadbank in April, including iris, blue larkspur, Chinese houses and woodland star.

Blue Larkspur

2.0 Five Corners Jct. Take the second left, a spur road, that climbs steeply up towards Six Pts. At the top of the hill, the trail levels out and provides great views southeast to Mt. Tam. Look for iris in April.

2.6 Six Points Jct #3. Take the first left, Six Pts trail, down a narrow path marked by wooden erosion barriers. This trail is also known as the "dark trail", as it descends into a forest of bay trees.

3.2 Oak Tree Jct. Turn right and backtrack along Deer Park Rd.

3.7 Parking area with water, tables and restroom facilities.

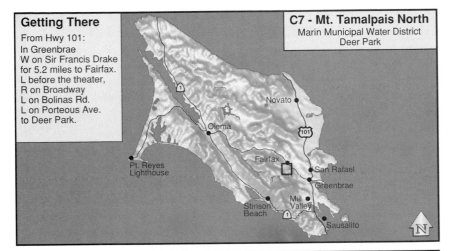

Getting There

From Hwy 101:
In Greenbrae
W on Sir Francis Drake
for 5.2 miles to Fairfax.
L before the theater,
R on Broadway
L on Bolinas Rd.
L on Porteous Ave.
to Deer Park.

C7 - Mt. Tamalpais North
Marin Municipal Water District
Deer Park

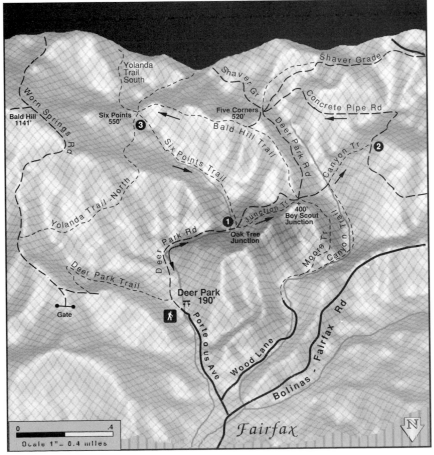

99

C8 Carson Falls, Pine Mtn. and Oat Hill

Distance: 3.2, 4.4 and 7.4 miles   Shaded: 0 - 30%
Elevation Change: 700' to 1200'   Lots of bicycles likely.
Rating: Hiking - 7   Difficulty - 5, 4, 8   Very steep by Oat Hill.
When to Go: Save these hikes for clear, cool winter days.

These three out-and-back hikes explore the Pine Mountain area south of Fairfax. They offer interesting chaparral and great views.

To Carson Falls at 1000' and Back - 3.2 miles and 800' Change

0.0 From the parking area at 1078', head west on Pine Mtn. Rd.

1.0 Ridgetop and two junctions. Head left on Oat Hill Rd.

1.3 Junction. Head right down the open hillside under the power line.

1.6 Top of Carson Falls and turnaround point #1. A trail to the right drops steeply down loose rock to viewpoint at the middle of the falls.

To Pine Mtn. at 1762' and Back - 4.4 miles and 700' Change

0.0 From the parking area, head west through the gate on Pine Mtn. Rd, which starts out in low-growing chaparral.

1.0 Ridgetop and two junctions. Bear right at both junctions. As you head downhill, you may be able to see the jutting profile of Mt. St. Helena 45 miles due north in Sonoma County.

1.4 Junction. Head left on the signed Pine Mtn. Rd. Up ahead, notice the Sargent cypress trees that only grow on serpentine soil.

2.2 Pine Mtn. and turnaround point #2. The road doesn't quite reach the top, which is marked by a small metal pole. Great views.

To Oat Hill at 1220' and Back - 7.4 miles and 1200' Change

0.0 From the parking area, head west on Pine Mtn. Rd.

1.0 Ridgetop and two junctions. Head left on Oat Hill Rd.

1.8 Junction. A utility road leads to Liberty Peak. However, the peak is overgrown with chaparral and doesn't provide any better views.

2.8 Junction with Old Vee Rd. Continue straight.

3.5 Junction. The road right deadends on another hilltop where the views are blocked by trees. Head left for the best views.

3.6 Trail to Oat Hill. The road ends in a saddle where a short, very steep trail climbs to the top of Oat Hill at 1200'.

3.7 Oat Hill and turnaround point #3. The hilltop offers great views of the Kent Lake watershed and of Alpine Lake and its dam.

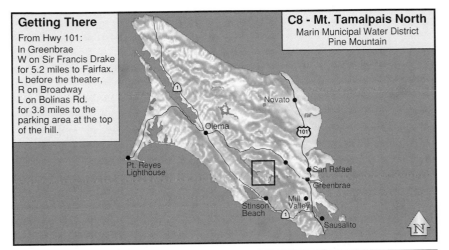

Getting There

From Hwy 101:
In Greenbrae
W on Sir Francis Drake
for 5.2 miles to Fairfax.
L before the theater,
R on Broadway
L on Bolinas Rd.
for 3.8 miles to the
parking area at the top
of the hill.

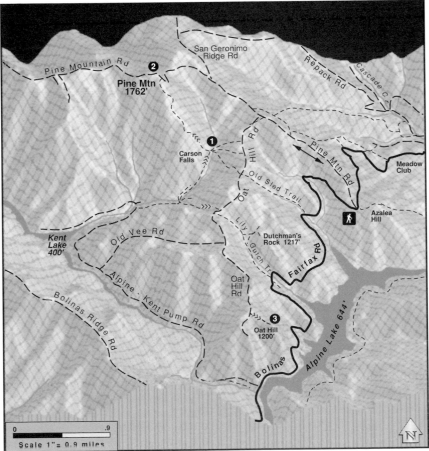

C9 Meadow Club Area to Carson Falls

Distance: 4.8 miles   Shaded: 50%
Elevation Change: 1500'   Poison oak crowds the trail.
Rating: Hiking - 9   Difficulty - 10   Very steep and slippery.
When to Go: Best during winter rain runoff and in spring.

This difficult, but rewarding, hike climbs to a ridge offering great views, then drops down to Carson Creek to follow it up to Carson Falls.

0.0 Park at a bend in the road near county mile marker 2.95. Step over the log and avoid the poison oak. Take the left trail uphill.

0.1 Ridgetop and junction. Head left. More poison oak.

0.6 Y-junction #1 at the top of a grassy hillside. Take the left trail.

0.7 Junction with road. Take Pine Mtn. Rd. right uphill.

0.9 Junction #2. Take the signed Oat Hill Rd. left along the ridge.

2.2 Junction #3 with Lily Gulch trail. To the left, you can see down a broad, grassy hillside to Dutchman's Rock and Alpine Lake. The trailhead is located over a bank on the right just before a rock outcrop with bay trees. Look for the sign (No bicycles) and head steeply down the open hillside. Down 200 yds., the footing gets better as the trail enters an unusual grove of bay trees, each with multiple trunks.

2.8 Junction and meadow. Head right on the road into the redwood grove, then bear left to cross the creek on a redwood log. The trail now climbs steeply, passing a small waterfall on the left. Cross this small creek and continue uphill along the left side of the main creek.

3.2 Little Carson Falls. The trail leaves the creek to circle up to a rocky outcropping at the middle of the 100' falls. From this viewpoint, the hike continues on a very steep, dirt path to the left of the falls and climbs to a grassy meadow above the falls. You can circle around to the top of the falls for some more views. Caution: Loose rocks.

Continue the hike by taking the main trail up along the power poles.

3.5 Junction with Oat Hill Rd. Head left uphill.

3.7 Junction #2 with Pine Mtn. Rd. Head left downhill for 200 yds.

3.8 Junction. Head right on an old road through the grass.

4.1 Junction. A trail comes up the chamise-covered ridge. Stay right.

4.3 Junction #1. Head left down the grassy hillside.

4.7 Junction. Head right down to the cars.

4.8 Back at the parking area. No facilities.

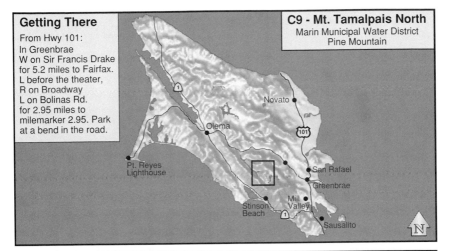

Getting There

From Hwy 101:
In Greenbrae
W on Sir Francis Drake
for 5.2 miles to Fairfax.
L before the theater,
R on Broadway
L on Bolinas Rd.
for 2.95 miles to
milemarker 2.95. Park
at a bend in the road.

C9 - Mt. Tamalpais North
Marin Municipal Water District
Pine Mountain

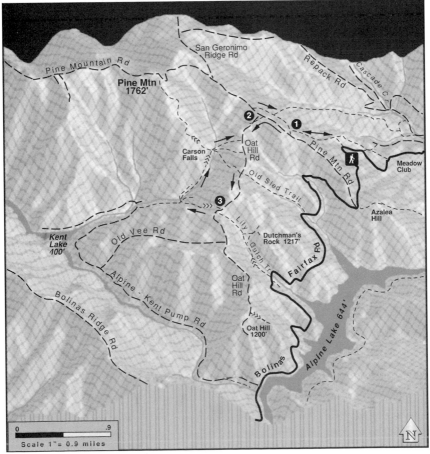

C10 Lily Gulch Trail - Kent Pump Road*

Distance: 5.8 miles   Shaded: 80%
Elevation Change: 1000'   Trail can be hard to follow.
Rating: Hiking - 9   Difficulty - 10   Very steep and slippery.
When to Go: Best late winter and early spring for water runoff.

The first part of this one-way hike involves some difficult climbing up and down, but offers great views and lots of creeks and waterfalls.

*Shuttle Hike. Leave pickup cars at mile marker 7.8 next to Alpine Dam. Shuttle all hikers to the bend in the road at mile marker 5.88.

0.0 Start up the left side of the ravine. The trail stays to the left of each ravine, but follows the far right ravine up to a large 30' rock.

0.4 Rock and junction #1. A small, hard-to-follow, spur trail heads north away from the main trail, again following the right-most ravine. Ahead, it finally crosses the ravine and makes a steep, switchback climb up the back side of Dutchman's Rock.

0.6 Dutchman's Rock at 1217'. Great views east to Mt. Diablo.

0.8 Above junction #1. Continue straight across the ravine to avoid backtracking downhill. The trail may be overgrown up ahead.

0.9 Small knoll and junction. In open grassland, pick up the main trail which now heads south over to another small ravine. Follow this ravine up through a small sloping meadow to Oat Hill Rd.

1.2 Junction #2. Go right on the road 120 yds. to the bay trees.

1.3 Junction. Just past the bay trees, climb 10' to take the signed trail down the very steep hill. It may help to zig-zag to keep from slipping.

1.9 Junction #3 and meadow. Head right on the road into the redwood grove, then bear left to cross the creek on a redwood log. The trail climbs 100 yds. up to a small waterfall on the left.

2.0 Seasonal waterfall. **Option:** Little Carson Falls is another 0.4 miles further up a very steep trail. Return to junction #3.

2.1 Junction #3. Take the road west towards Kent Lake.

2.3 Two junctions and pump station. Go right, then right again up a short spur road to view the start of the Pine Mtn. Tunnel. Then take the Alpine - Kent Pump Rd. out of the canyon and head south.

5.1 Junction #4. Take the road right to view the bottom of Alpine Dam, then return and head uphill. This 140' dam was built in 1918.

5.8 Parking area with no facilities.

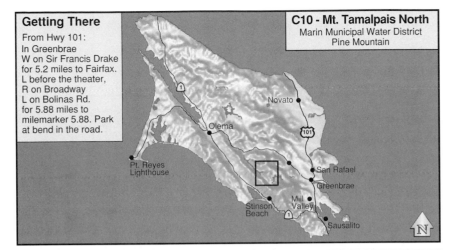

Getting There

From Hwy 101:
In Greenbrae
W on Sir Francis Drake
for 5.2 miles to Fairfax.
L before the theater,
R on Broadway
L on Bolinas Rd.
for 5.88 miles to
milemarker 5.88. Park
at bend in the road.

C10 - Mt. Tamalpais North

Marin Municipal Water District
Pine Mountain

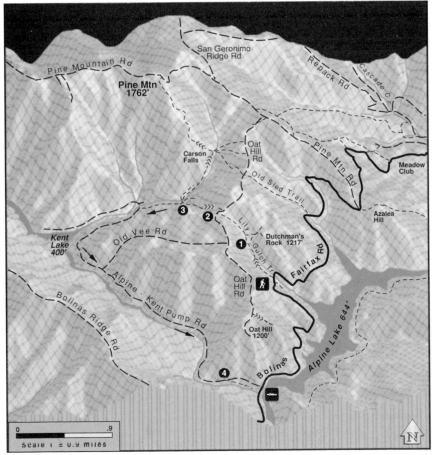

C11 Cataract - High Marsh - Kent Trails

Distance: 7.7 miles   Shaded: 90%
Elevation Change: 2100'
Rating: Hiking - 10   Difficulty - 8   Steep and rocky in places.
When to Go: Best during rainy season and in spring for flowers.

This is a strenuous but spectacular hike in the most remote section of Mt. Tamalpais. Wonderful pools, waterfalls and conifer forests.

0.0 Park anywhere south of Alpine Dam and walk to the signed trailhead 0.2 miles from the dam. The trail starts along the lake in a conifer forest with some bay, oak and big-leaf maple trees.

0.3 Cataract Creek. The trail begins a steep climb up the right side of the creek past refreshing views of pools and waterfalls.

0.6 Bridge and junction. Above the bridge, bear right past a spectacular creekside setting. Ahead, the trail levels somewhat.

1.0 Sunlight. A small open hillside lets in light to grow yellow buttercups and baby blue-eyes. Up ahead, scenery typical of Hawaii.

1.3 Bench and junction #1 with the High Marsh trail. A large, flat bench provides a welcome rest stop. Continue uphill along the creek.

1.5 Laurel Dell picnic area. Tables and restrooms. Backtrack down the trail to junction #1 and take High Marsh trail right, which climbs past a fallen oak tree. Up ahead, on the open hillside, look for woodland star, popcorn flower, fiddleneck, poppy and blue dicks.

3.5 Junction. The Willow Mdw. trail goes left downhill. Continue right.

3.7 Junction and High Marsh. The CC Boys trail heads right. Stay left to skirt the marsh, which is a drainage pond created by a landslide.

3.8 Junction #2. Take the signed Kent trail left downhill.

3.9 Junction near Serpentine Knoll. Bear left and head downhill.

4.3 Junction #3 with the Stocking trail. Take the Kent trail left towards Alpine Lake. The trail descends through an enchanting redwood forest, then past a large slide on a fork of Swede George Creek.

5.1 Junction #4 with Alpine Lake. Go left as the trail leaves the lake and traverses several ridges. Up ahead, the trail crosses Swede George Creek on a bridge built from lumber floated across the lake.

7.1 Junction and bridge. After a long climb, bear right at this junction to retrace your steps down alongside Cataract Creek.

7.7 Back at the trailhead. No facilities.

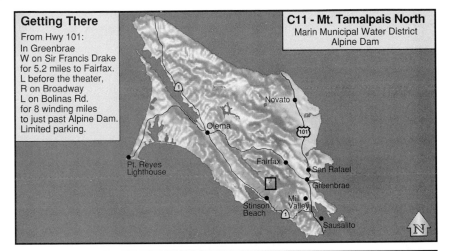

Getting There

From Hwy 101:
In Greenbrae
W on Sir Francis Drake
for 5.2 miles to Fairfax.
L before the theater,
R on Broadway
L on Bolinas Rd.
for 8 winding miles
to just past Alpine Dam.
Limited parking.

C11 - Mt. Tamalpais North
Marin Municipal Water District
Alpine Dam

Novato

Olema

Fairfax

Pt. Reyes
Lighthouse

San Rafael

Greenbrae

Stinson
Beach

Mill
Valley

Sausalito

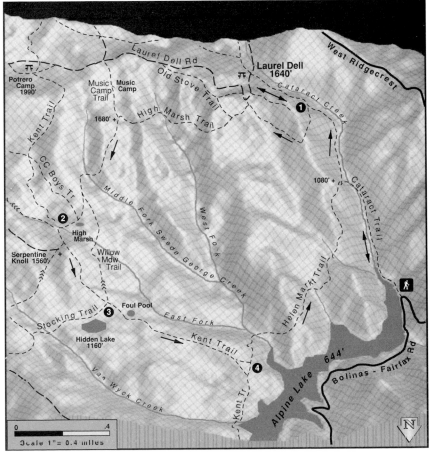

Laurel Dell Rd

Old Stove Trail

West Ridgecrest

Laurel Dell
1640'

Cataract Creek

Potrero
Camp
1990'

Music
Camp
Trail

Music
Camp

Kent Trail

1680' +

High Marsh Trail

❶

CC Boys Tr

Middle Fork Swade George Creek

West Fork

1080' +

Cataract Trail

❷

High
Marsh

Serpentine
Knoll 1560'

Willow
Mdw
Trail

Helen Markt Trail

Stocking Trail

❸

Foul Pool

East Fork

Kent Trail

Hidden Lake
1160'

❹

Alpine Lake 644'

Van Wyck Creek

Kent Tr

Bolinas - Fairfax Rd

0   .4

Scale 1"= 0.4 miles

C12 Taylor - Concrete Pipe - Bullfrog Rd.

Distance: 3.2 miles   Shaded: 60%
Elevation Change: 250'   Bullfrog Rd. can be boggy.
Rating: Hiking - 6   Difficulty - 6   One short steep section.
When to Go: Good mosses when wet, flowers in April.
This is a good hike, mostly along fire roads, through open and wooded areas offering a wide selection of wildflowers and local views.

0.0 Start at the parking area just past the Sky Oaks toll booth and walk back towards the toll booth. Notice the large oaks on the right. In the early morning, look for grey foxes that have a den nearby.

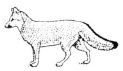

Grey Fox

0.1 Junction. The Taylor trail begins at a gate to the left (north) of the ranger station and starts down parallel to the main road.

0.6 Junction #1 with Concrete Pipe Rd. Bear right and watch for some great spring wildflowers including iris, modesty, blue dicks, Chinese houses, baby-blue eyes, lupine, blue larkspur and pink shooting star. The best display is in late April.

1.3 Five Corners Jct. Take the Elliott trail right to climb the steps and parallel Shaver Grade. The trail gets steep here.

1.6 Junction #2. Go left on Shaver Grade. Watch for bicycles.

1.9 Junction. Go straight across Sky Oaks Rd. and take the trail.

2.0 Junction. Take either the dirt road or the parallel trail down towards Alpine Lake. This road was part of the Bolinas - Fairfax - San Rafael stage route that started service around 1890. Look for deer on the open hillside to the right.

2.4 Junction with road to Bon Tempe dam. Continue right.

2.5 Alpine Lake and picnic spot. When full, the scenic lake lives up to its name. To continue the hike, go past the gate along Bullfrog Rd.

2.9 Rock quarry. Red-brown sandstone and blue-green serpentine mark the site of an old quarry along the road. Rock from the quarry was used to build Bon Tempe dam in 1949.

3.0 Junction #3 with golf course road. Keep right. Look for moss and lichen growing on the serpentine rocks breaking through the thin hillside soil. Up ahead, the road may have standing water. If so, you can try to detour to the right towards Sky Oaks Rd.

3.2 Parking area with restrooms and water near the ranger station.

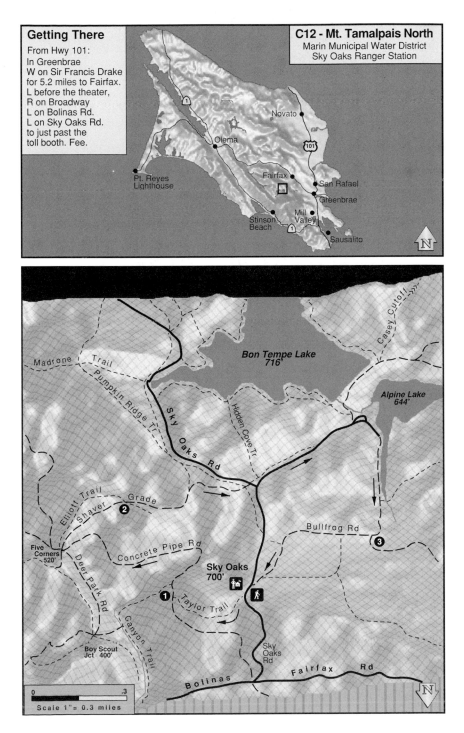

Getting There

From Hwy 101:
In Greenbrae
W on Sir Francis Drake
for 5.2 miles to Fairfax.
L before the theater,
R on Broadway
L on Bolinas Rd.
L on Sky Oaks Rd.
to just past the
toll booth. Fee.

C12 - Mt. Tamalpais North
Marin Municipal Water District
Sky Oaks Ranger Station

Novato

Olema

101

Pt. Reyes
Lighthouse

Fairfax

San Rafael

Greenbrae

Stinson
Beach

Mill
Valley

Sausalito

N

Madrone Trail

Pumpkin Ridge Tr

Bon Tempe Lake
716'

Casey Cutoff

Alpine Lake
644'

Sky Oaks Rd

Hidden Cove Tr

Elliott Trail

Shaver Grade

②

Five
Corners
520'

Concrete Pipe Rd

Bullfrog Rd

③

Deer Park Rd

Sky Oaks
700'

Taylor Trail

①

Ganyon Trail

Boy Scout
Jct 400'

Sky
Oaks
Rd

Bolinas

Fairfax Rd

0   .3
Scale 1"= 0.3 miles

N

109

C13 Bon Tempe Lake Trail

Distance: 4.1 miles   Shaded: 50%
Elevation Change: 50'   Some mud after heavy rains.
Rating: Hiking - 9   Difficulty - 3
When to Go: Good anytime, best in spring.

This is the best of the three lake hikes. It passes through wooded and open hillsides that provide good wildflowers and great views.

0.0 From the parking area below Bon Tempe dam, head up the dirt road towards the dam, which was built in 1949. At the dam, go right to circle the lake counter-clockwise. Stop and enjoy some great views across Bon Tempe to Mt. Tamalpais and also down to Alpine Lake.

0.3 Junction #1 and restroom. At dam's end, take the signed Bon Tempe trail into oak-bay woodland. March flowers include white milkmaids, woodland star, blue hound's tongue and iris.

0.8 Bridge. The first of 3 bridges along the "dark side" of Bon Tempe. Up ahead, many of the taller trees are black oak, too tall to clearly see their distinctive leaves, which are 4-6 inches long with deep lobes. Look for fallen leaves on the path.

1.3 Grassland. Yellow gold fields, buttercup, sun cups, blue lupine and pink shooting star grow among the grasses here.

1.6 Junction #2 and Lagunitas picnic area. Just past the redwood grove, go left across the bridge into the picnic area. Skirt the Lagunitas parking area and continue on around the lake.

2.0 Junction #3. The dirt road heads inland here. Go up 50', then take the trail left. Thirty feet to the right of the junction, notice the large oak and madrone trees locked together in a struggle for sunlight.

2.5 Oaks. Large oaks stand majestically on Pine Point peninsula overlooking the lake. Occasionally, osprey and great blue heron are seen here. Cormorants, gulls and wintering ducks are common.

2.8 Junction with the paved Sky Oaks Road. Go left. Ahead, the paved ramp provides fishing access for wheelchairs.

3.1 Junction #4. Leave the paved road to follow the trail around the "sunny side" of the lake. Watch for yellow sun cups, buttercup, poppy, white popcorn flower, iris and blue lupine in spring.

3.9 Pumphouse. Follow the road past the pumphouse and up the hill, then head downhill towards the parking area.

4.1 Back at the parking area. Restrooms only.

Getting There

From Hwy 101:
In Greenbrae
W on Sir Francis Drake
for 5.2 miles to Fairfax.
L before the theater,
R on Broadway
L on Bolinas Rd.
L on Sky Oaks Rd.
R on road to Bon
Tempe Dam. Fee.

C13 - Mt. Tamalpais North
Marin Municipal Water District
Bon Tempe Dam

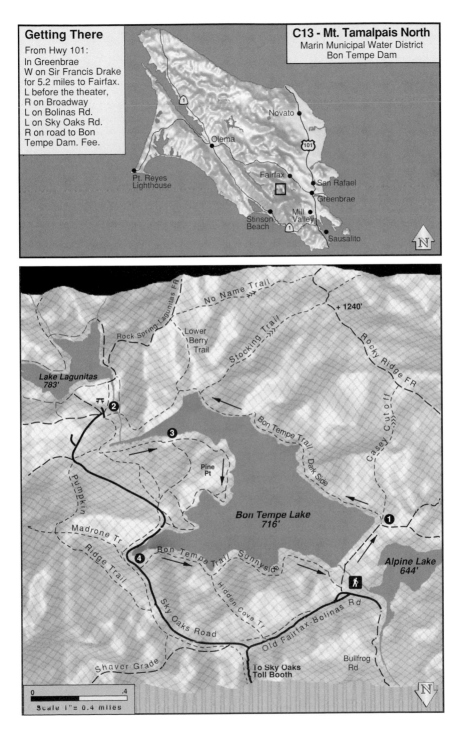

111

C14 Kent Trail - Rocky Ridge Road

Distance: 5.2 miles   Shaded: 70%
Elevation Change: 500'   Very steep, rutted in places.
Rating: Hiking - 10   Difficulty - 10   (See option below)
When to Go: Good anytime, best in spring.
This is an exhilarating hike along the conifer shores of Alpine Lake, up through a redwood forest, emerging onto a ridge with good views.

0.0 Start at the parking area below Bon Tempe dam and head uphill to the spillway. Go across the dam and enjoy the views.

0.3 Junction #1. At dam's end, continue right above Alpine Lake and past lichen-covered oaks. In February, look for white milkmaids, yellow buttercup, pink shooting star and blue hound's tongue among the ferns and mosses along the road bank.

0.8 Pumphouse and Kent trail. The road ends at a pumphouse where water from Alpine Lake is pumped to Bon Tempe Lake and on to a treatment plant. Follow the narrow trail as it winds along the lake.

1.8 Views. The trail offers great views of conifer forest across the lake, just like the high Sierra. Just ahead, the trail enters Van Wyck canyon, a gorgeous canyon of tall redwood, bay, ferns and mosses.

2.1 Big fir. A giant Douglas fir stands on a small knoll watching over skinny madrones; its side trunk is as big as the main trunk. Up ahead, the trail enters into a silted canyon with a narrow stream bed.

2.3 Junction #2. Just opposite the sign, Helen Markt Tr, take the Kent trail left uphill past exposed waterpipe. This trail was originally called the Swede George trail after an oldtimer who had a cabin in the area around 1870. Huckleberries can be picked here in early fall.

2.6 Canyon and forest. The trail enters a large canyon covered with tall oaks, bay and redwood. Up past a slide, the trail skirts Foul Pool, then follows the creek through a magnificent redwood forest.

3.1 Junction #3. Take the signed Stocking trail left. The trail heads downhill skirting secluded Hidden Lake, then uphill along a creek bed.

3.8 Junction with Rocky Ridge FR. Turn left and go up the road 200' for great views south and east. Continue on the road.

4.4 Junction #4. At the far edge of a stand of Douglas fir, look for the Casey Cutoff trail heading to Bon Tempe. This trail is very steep.
Option: For an easier route, continue down the Rocky Ridge FR.

5.2 Back at the parking area. Restroom facilities only.

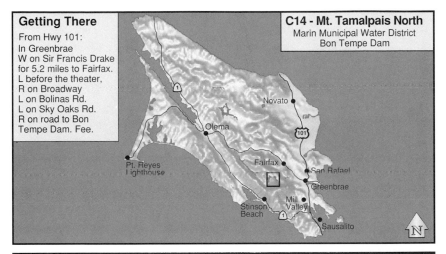

Getting There

From Hwy 101:
In Greenbrae
W on Sir Francis Drake
for 5.2 miles to Fairfax.
L before the theater,
R on Broadway
L on Bolinas Rd.
L on Sky Oaks Rd.
R on road to Bon
Tempe Dam. Fee.

C14 - Mt. Tamalpais North
Marin Municipal Water District
Bon Tempe Dam

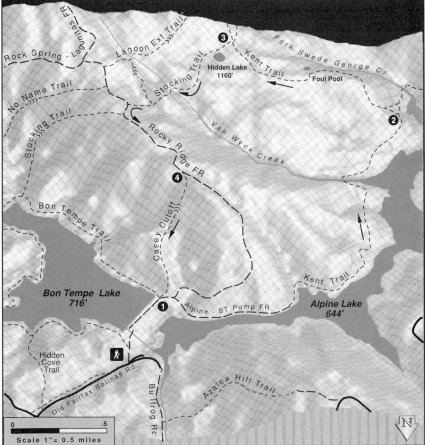

Rock Spring - Lagunitas FR

No Name Trail

Stocking Trail

Lagoon Ext Trail

Stocking Trail

Hidden Lake
1160'

3

Kent Trail

Fork Swede George Cr

Foul Pool

2

Rocky Ridge FR

Van Wyck Creek

4

Bon Tempe Trail

Casey Cutoff

Kent Trail

Bon Tempe Lake
716'

1

Alpine - BT Pump FR

Alpine Lake
644'

Hidden
Cove
Trail

Old Fairfax-Bolinas Rd

Bullfrog Rd

Azalea Hill Trail

0   .5

Scale 1"= 0.5 miles

C15 Lake Lagunitas Road

Distance: 1.8 miles   Shaded: 70%
Elevation Change: 50'   Some standing water after heavy rains.
Rating: Hiking - 9   Difficulty - 3   Some bicycle traffic.
When to Go: Good November to May, best February to April.

This is a level hike on roads around the lake with mosses, redwoods, oaks and great views across the lake to Mt. Tamalpais. Good birding.

0.0 Start at the Lagunitas parking lot. If you're fortunate, you might hear or see the pileated woodpecker nearby. It is a large 15" woodpecker with a black body, partly white neck and red tufted head. There are many other birds around the lake area, including wintering water birds. Often, you can see osprey flying over the treetops. To start the hike, go into the picnic area and pick up the trail next to the spillway. Climb up to the dam, which was built in 1873.

0.1 Dam. See if you can spot the rare Pacific pond turtles sunning on the floating logs by the dam. Go right over the spillway to circle the lake counter-clockwise. In February, look for white milkmaids, red Indian warrior and blue hound's tongue.

Lagunitas Lake

0.3 Junction #1 with Rock Spring - Lagunitas Road. Continue left.

0.5 Bridge and redwoods. This first of 3 bridges crosses a creek that provides water for a grove of redwoods. You rarely see moss on redwoods, but often can find a grey-green lichen on the bark.

0.9 Mosses. In winter, look for a fine display of mosses, lichens, ferns, succulents and other moisture lovers along the rocky bank.

1.2 Bridge and junction #2. Under a canopy of tall oaks and madrones, the road crosses the East Fork of Lagunitas Creek. Go straight past the bridge and left on Lakeview Rd.

1.4 Junction. The road uphill leads to the Pilot Knob trail. Continue left past the large moss-covered oak at the junction.

1.5 Junction. The road veers right up to the ranger's residence. Stay left on the trail as it passes through French broom and down the stairs to the dam. Cross the dam to head down the stairs to the picnic area.

1.8 Parking area. Water, picnic tables and restroom facilities.

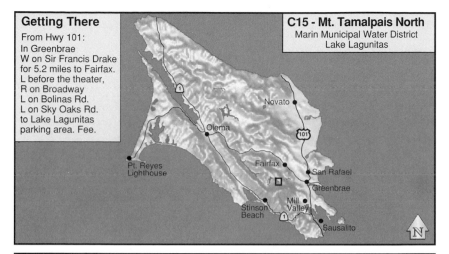

Getting There

From Hwy 101:
In Greenbrae
W on Sir Francis Drake
for 5.2 miles to Fairfax.
L before the theater,
R on Broadway
L on Bolinas Rd.
L on Sky Oaks Rd.
to Lake Lagunitas
parking area. Fee.

C15 - Mt. Tamalpais North

Marin Municipal Water District
Lake Lagunitas

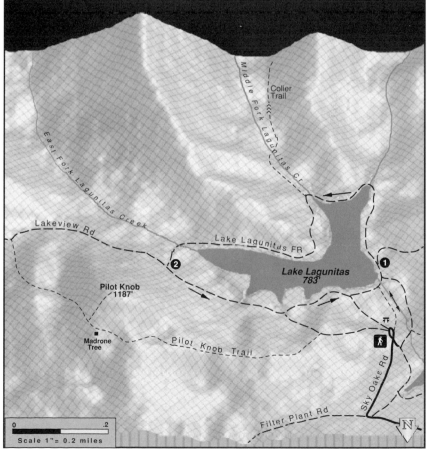

115

C16 Lakeview Road to Pilot Knob

Distance: 2.2 miles   Shaded: 70%
Elevation Change: 500'   Some bicycles.
Rating: Hiking - 8   Difficulty - 5   Moderately steep.
When to Go: Good November to May, best February to April.

This is a good hike through mixed forest, climbing to Pilot Knob for great views, then passing the largest madrone tree seen anywhere.

0.0 Start at the Lagunitas parking lot. Take the road overlooking the picnic area up to the dam. February flowers include white milkmaids and blue hound's tongue under the oak, bay and madrone trees.

0.2 Dam. Look for the rare and endangered Pacific pond turtles that often sun themselves on the floating logs by the dam. Go left up the stairs past the ranger residence and on to Lakeview Rd.

0.6 Junction #1. The road right goes around the lake. Stay left and enjoy great views to Mt. Tam on the right and Pilot Knob on the left.

1.1 Junction #2. Take the signed trail to Pilot Knob left up the hill. The trail climbs steeply through tall madrone, oak, Douglas fir and redwood trees with an understory of tanoak and huckleberry.

1.4 Junction #3. At a knoll, next to a large bay tree, take the spur trail left uphill to Pilot Knob. Ahead, notice the grove of young redwoods that will someday overgrow the tall madrones nearby.

1.5 Pilot Knob at 1187'. Enjoy great views south to Mt. Tam, west to Bon Tempe lake, and to Mt. Diablo in the east bay. To continue the hike, return down the spur trail and bear left along the main trail.

1.8 Madrone. The grandfather of madrones! An incredible madrone tree with six main trunks, each the size of a single madrone. The tree has limited foliage and may not live many more years. The trail continues along the ridgetop past lichen-covered oaks and more normal-sized madrone trees.

Giant Madrone Tree

2.1 Junction. The road left returns along the lake. Head right past redwood, Douglas fir, oak and madrone trees and follow the steep downhill road back to the parking lot.

2.2 Parking lot. Water, tables, barbecue, map and restrooms.

Getting There

From Hwy 101:
In Greenbrae
W on Sir Francis Drake
for 5.2 miles to Fairfax.
L before the theater,
R on Broadway
L on Bolinas Rd.
L on Sky Oaks Rd.
to Lake Lagunitas
parking area. Fee.

C16 - Mt. Tamalpais North
Marin Municipal Water District
Lake Lagunitas

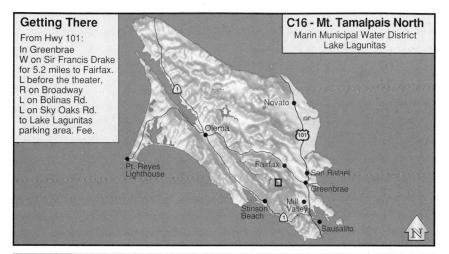

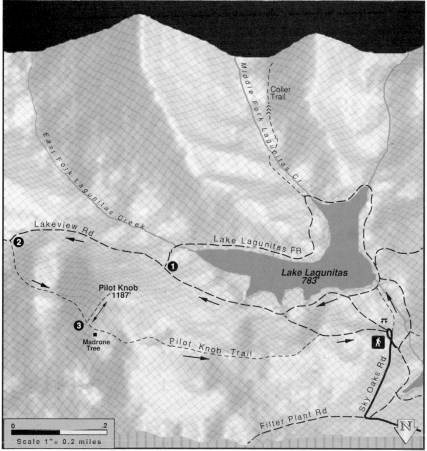

117

C17 Pumpkin Ridge - Bon Tempe Trails

Distance: 2.8 miles   Shaded: 50%
Elevation Change: 400'   Trail can be crowded with grasses.
Rating: Hiking - 9   Difficulty - 4
When to Go: Best around mid-April for spectacular iris.

This hike explores the rolling hills north of Bon Tempe Lake. Good views, oaks and wildflowers along the open and wooded ridges.

0.0 Start at the Lagunitas parking lot and head west to the edge of Bon Tempe Lake. Follow the dirt road past the large valves out to Sky Oaks Rd. In spring, look for yellow sun cups, buttercups and a pale purple lily, *Calochortus*, in the meadow along the road.

0.2 Junction #1 with Sky Oaks Rd. Cross the paved road and head up the open hillside dotted with lichen-covered oaks. This is classic oak-woodland country with occasional madrones and firs mixed in.
The Pumpkin Ridge trail follows the ridgetop providing fine vistas of Mt. Tam. In April, the ridgetop displays a glorious selection of iris with delicate hues of cream, gold, violet and blue.

Douglas Iris

0.9 Junction #2. Just before the Sky Oaks Rd., take the Sky Oaks-Lagunitas trail right as it parallels the road heading north.

1.2 Junction with Shaver Grade and Sky Oaks Rd. Continue on the trail directly across the paved road.

1.3 Junction #3 with the gravel road to Bon Tempe dam. Go down the road a few feet, then take the Hidden Cove trail left which heads towards a saddle between two tree-covered hilltops. (Power line poles also head for the same saddle.) At the top of the saddle, there is a huge madrone tree 50' to the left (or northeast) of the trail. There are also many non-native Coulter pines, which produce large, dense cones. These trees were planted in the 1930s, but will be removed.

1.6 Junction with the lake. Take the Bon Tempe Lake trail to the left.

1.9 Junction with Sky Oaks Rd. Head right on the paved road.

2.2 Junction. A power pole and garbage can mark this junction. Take the dirt road up and over the small knoll, which offers good views.

2.6 Junction #4. Just before the lake, 50' to the left of the trail, look for a large oak and madrone with trunks entwined. Go left at the lake.

2.8 Parking area with water, tables, barbecue and restrooms.

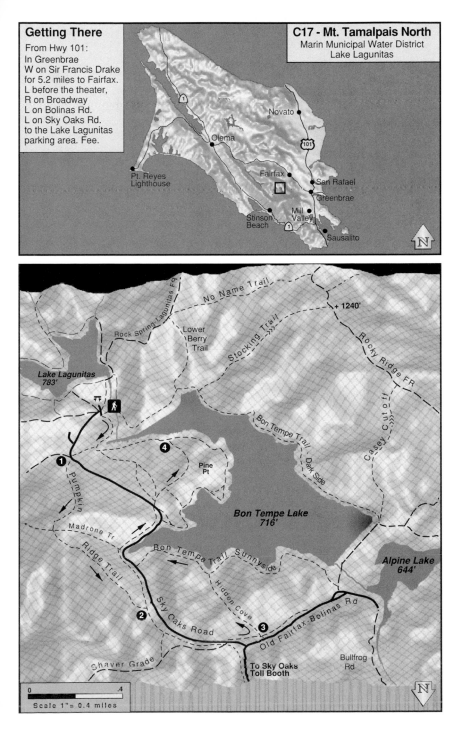

Getting There

From Hwy 101:
In Greenbrae
W on Sir Francis Drake
for 5.2 miles to Fairfax.
L before the theater,
R on Broadway
L on Bolinas Rd.
L on Sky Oaks Rd.
to the Lake Lagunitas
parking area. Fee.

C17 - Mt. Tamalpais North
Marin Municipal Water District
Lake Lagunitas

Novato
Olema
Pt. Reyes
Lighthouse
Fairfax
San Rafael
Greenbrae
Stinson
Beach
Mill
Valley
Sausalito

No Name Trail
+ 1240'
Rock Spring Lagunitas FR
Lower
Berry
Trail
Stocking Trail
Rocky Ridge FR
Lake Lagunitas
783'
Casey Cut off
❶
❹
Bon Tempe Trail Dark Side
Pine
Pt
Pumpkin
Bon Tempe Lake
716'
Madrone Tr
Alpine Lake
644'
Ridge Trail
Bon Tempe Trail Sunnyside
Hidden Cove
❷
Sky Oaks Road
❸
Old Fairfax Bolinas Rd
Shaver Grade
To Sky Oaks
Toll Booth
Bullfrog
Rd

0 .4
Scale 1" = 0.4 miles

119

C18 Colier - Northside - Lagoon Ext.

Distance: 5.7 miles   Shaded: 80%
Elevation Change: 1200'   Several uncertain junctions.
Rating: Hiking - 9   Difficulty - 10   Very steep and rocky.
When to Go: Best in winter for creek flow and in May for flowers.

This strenuous hike, best for experienced hikers, offers cascading creeks, redwoods, views north and a challenge not to get lost.

0.0 Start at the Lagunitas parking lot. Head into the picnic area and along the spillway to the dam. Head right, to circle the lake.

0.5 Bridge and junction #1. Turn right and follow the signed Colier trail up the left side of the creek. Up ahead, the trail crosses the creek twice. Downed trees can make the trail difficult to follow at times.

1.2 Creek junction and crossing. Two creeks come tumbling together here. Fifty yds. upstream, cross the creek again and follow the steep trail up and over to the next ridgetop to parallel another creek.

1.6 Colier Spring, resting bench and junction #2. To continue the hike, take the second trail on the right, the Upper Northside trail.

2.1 Two junctions. The International trail enters from the left and 100 yds. ahead, the trail crosses the Rocky Ridge Fire trail. Good views.

2.7 Rifle Camp and two junctions #3. Go through the camp to the road and take the Azalea Meadow trail downhill. This trail follows a small creek steeply down the hillside.

3.0 Two junctions. Continue downhill past Cross Country Boys trail.

3.6 Junction #4. Take the Kent trail, cross the creek and bear right.

3.8 Creek crossing and two junctions. Head right for 50 yds. up through chaparral to a viewpoint on Serpentine Knoll. Head left down the Lagoon Ext. trail which soon becomes narrow, steep and rutted.

4.3 Creek and junction #5. After crossing a small creek, the trail enters chaparral and an uncertain junction. Head straight uphill 50', then through overgrown manzanita to the Rocky Ridge FR.

4.4 Junction. Take the Rocky Ridge FR left downhill for 100 yds.

4.5 Clearing and junction. Head right into a large, level clearing on the No Name trail that enters the woods and gets steep and rocky.

5.0 Junction #6. Take the signed Berry trail downhill.

5.4 Junction with Bon Tempe Lake. Head right along the lake.

5.7 Parking area. Water, picnic tables and restroom facilities.

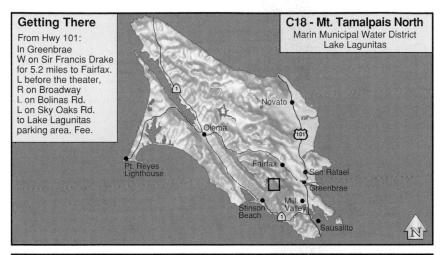

Getting There

From Hwy 101:
In Greenbrae
W on Sir Francis Drake
for 5.2 miles to Fairfax.
L before the theater,
R on Broadway
L on Bolinas Rd.
L on Sky Oaks Rd.
to Lake Lagunitas
parking area. Fee.

C18 - Mt. Tamalpais North
Marin Municipal Water District
Lake Lagunitas

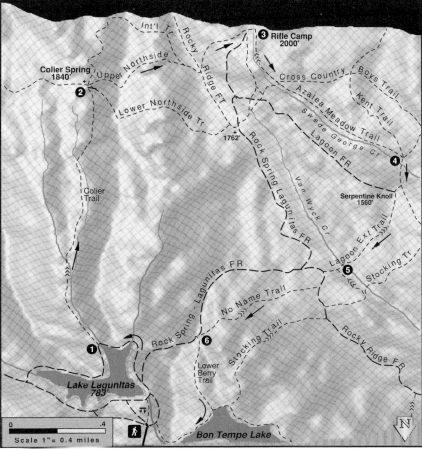

121

C19 Lake Lagunitas to East Peak

Distance: 10.1 miles   Shaded: 70%
Elevation Change: 1700'   Lots of bicycle traffic on the roads.
Rating: Hiking - 9   Difficulty - 10   Downhill steep and rocky.
When to Go: Best when cool and clear.
This hike climbs to the top of Mt. Tam, then loops back offering great views, streams and secluded forests. Best for experienced hikers.

0.0 Start at the Lake Lagunitas parking lot. Take the road overlooking the picnic area up to the dam. Then head left up the stairs.

0.5 Junction. Continue straight on the Lakeview Rd.

1.3 Junction #1. Take Eldridge Grade right. This road, built for wagon traffic in the late 1880s, makes a long gradual climb up Mt. Tam.

4.8 Ridgecrest Blvd. and junction #2. Take the paved road east.

5.1 East Peak viewpoint, Visitor Center and snackbar. **Option:** Take the Plankwalk trail to climb to the top of Tam (see Hike B20).

5.4 Junction #2. Go 200' past Eldridge Grade to take the Middle Peak FR right. The road circles the peak, heading for the antennas.

6.0 Junction. At a hairpin turn, take the Lakeview trail right which heads east tunneling through low-growing oaks and tall manzanita.

6.7 Three junctions. Head 50' along E. Ridgecrest Blvd., then take the International trail right. About 100' downhill, go right again.

7.1 Colier Spring and junction #3. A bench and chain ferns mark the spring, which was named after John Monroe Colier, a wealthy but eccentric Scotsman who worked on various trails in the early 1900s. To continue the hike, take the second trail on the left, the Lower Northside trail, which heads gradually downhill.

8.0 Junction #4. Take the Rocky Ridge FT right downhill 100 yds.

8.1 Junction. Head right, down the Rock Spring - Lagunitas FR. Stay to the right and watch out for bicycles as this is a major bike route.

8.6 Junction. Take the Rocky Ridge FR left. **Option:** For a much easier downhill, continue on the Rock Spring - Lagunitas FR.

8.9 Junction #5. Take the No Name trail right, which starts out on open serpentine soil, then enters a forest. The trail is steep and rocky.

9.4 Junction. Take the signed Berry trail downhill.

9.8 Junction. Head right along the Bon Tempe Lake trail.

10.1 Back at the parking area with restrooms and water.

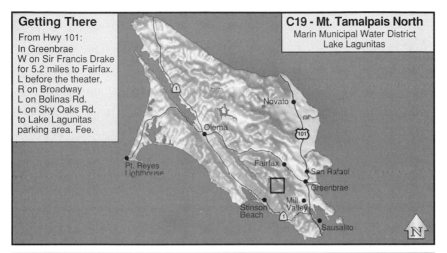

Getting There

From Hwy 101:
In Greenbrae
W on Sir Francis Drake
for 5.2 miles to Fairfax.
L before the theater,
R on Broadway
L on Bolinas Rd.
L on Sky Oaks Rd.
to Lake Lagunitas
parking area. Fee.

C19 - Mt. Tamalpais North
Marin Municipal Water District
Lake Lagunitas

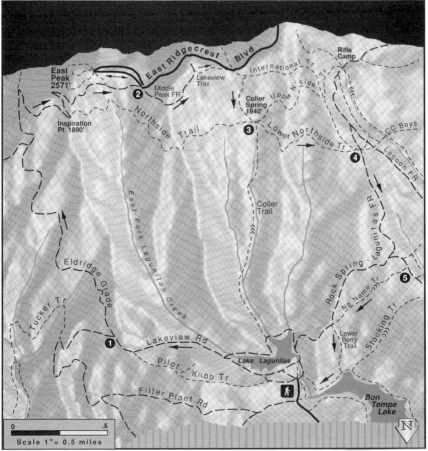

123

D - Central Marin - 15 Hikes

Starting from Kent Woodlands at 640'
D1..... King Mountain Loop - Dawn Falls 5.3

Starting from Cascade Canyon in Fairfax
D2..... Cascade Canyon Trail to Cascade Falls 1.9
D3..... Cascade Canyon to Cascade Peak 3.5
D4..... Toyon Fire Road to Cascade Peak 3.7

Starting from Fairfax at 240'
D5..... Loma Alta Open Space Loop 4.7

Starting from Woodacre at 200'
D6..... Roy's Redwoods Trails 2.6

Starting from Samuel P. Taylor State Park
D7..... Creek and Ox Trails History Loop 2.5
D8..... Pioneer Tree - Riding & Hiking Trails 2.8
D9..... Ridge Trail to Mt. Barnabe 4.6
D10... Devil's Gulch - Stairstep Falls Trails 3.9
D11... Devil's Gulch to Mt. Barnabe 6.3

Starting from near the Marin Civic Center at 100'
D12... Marin Civic Center to China Camp 5.7*

Starting from China Camp State Park at 20'
D13... Miwok - Bay View - Shoreline Trails 5.5
D14... Bayview - Miwok Fire Trails 5.8
D15... Turtle Back Island - Shoreline Trails 3.8

* Shuttle Hike

Pets allowed on hikes 1-6.

Region D Trailheads

Hikes 1-6 and 12 start in Marin County Open Space, phone 499-6405.

Hikes 7-11 start in Samuel P. Taylor State Park, phone 488-9897.

Hikes 13-15 start in China Camp State Park, phone 456-0766.

Region D
Central Marin

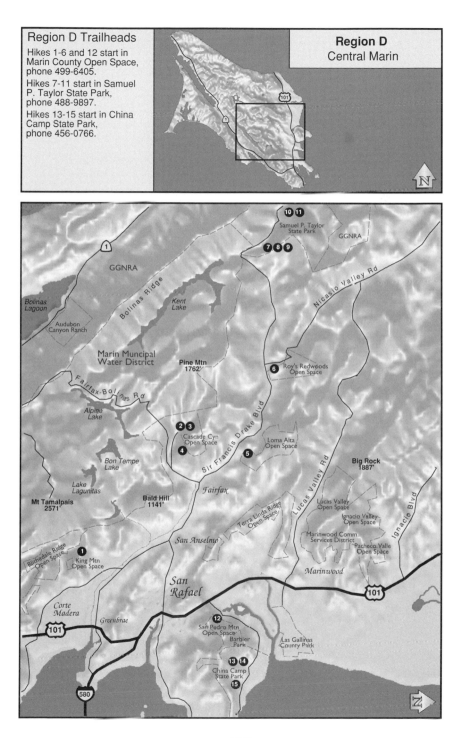

D1 King Mountain Loop - Dawn Falls

Distance: 5.3 miles   Shaded: 60%
Elevation Change: 900'   One steep section. Can be muddy.
Rating: Hiking - 8   Difficulty - 9   Shortcut possible. See note.
When to Go: Best in late winter for falls and flowers.
This hike explores the trails on King Mountain, then descends to Dawn Falls in Baltimore Canyon. Good views. Trillium in March.

0.0 Head up the dirt fire road that starts with an easy climb past oak, and non-native acacia and eucalyptus trees.

0.1 Gate. Continue past the King Mountain open space sign.

0.5 Junction. A road heads right towards private property. Continue straight towards the fence.

0.6 Gate, fence and paved road. Head left up the dirt road.

0.8 Junction #1. Leave the road and take the signed trail left. Portions of this trail pass through easements on private land, part of the agreement that allows four luxury homes on top of the mountain.

1.6 Junction with the trail to Wilson Way. Continue straight.

1.7 Junction #2. Take the connector trail down towards Dawn Falls.

Note: This trail is very steep at the bottom. It also requires fording Larkspur Creek, which can be a foot deep or more during heavy runoff. There are plans to reroute the trail and build a bridge across the creek. **Option**: For an easier shortcut, continue straight.

About half-way down into the canyon, there are still signs of an old hippie camp on a small madrone-covered knoll.

2.2 Creek and junction #3. Cross the creek and take the Dawn Falls trail right up into the canyon. The original redwoods were logged here in the 1860s. Look for trillium along the creek in March. Ahead, the trail climbs to a vantage point next to lovely Dawn Falls.

2.7 Junction. Take Southern Marin Line FR right. Good views ahead.

3.0 Gate and junction. Continue on the paved street, Crown Rd.

3.2 Stop sign and junction #4. Take Evergreen down to the right, then right again on Ridgecrest Rd.

3.8 Gate. Continue past the gate and up the gravel road.

3.9 Junction #5. Take the trail to the left, down into redwoods.

4.5 Junction #1. Head left down the road.

5.3 Back at the parking area. No facilities.

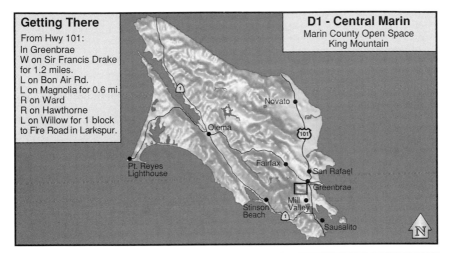

Getting There

From Hwy 101:
In Greenbrae
W on Sir Francis Drake
for 1.2 miles.
L on Bon Air Rd.
L on Magnolia for 0.6 mi.
R on Ward
R on Hawthorne
L on Willow for 1 block
to Fire Road in Larkspur.

D1 - Central Marin
Marin County Open Space
King Mountain

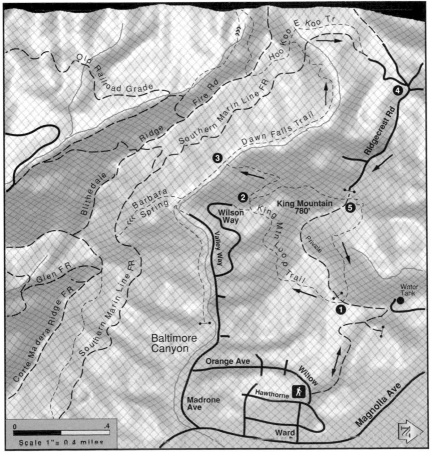

127

D2 Cascade Canyon and Falls

Distance: 1.9 miles   Shaded: 70%
Elevation Change: 400'   Cascade Creek may be impassable.
Rating: Hiking - 9   Difficulty - 6   One steep section.
When to Go: Good two weeks after heavy rains. Best in March.

This hike explores Cascade Canyon and Cascade Falls west of Fairfax. Most of the hike is along creeks. Great flowers in spring.

Note: Fairfax requires 12' of pavement clearance when parking.

0.0 Start at the Cascade open space gate at the end of Cascade Dr. Head through the gate and stay right on the trail all the way to the bridge. Look for wildflowers: milkmaid, shooting star, hounds tongue, Indian warrior and mission bells, starting in late February.

0.2 Junction. The trail joins a road and both head right uphill.

0.3 Bridge and junction #1. Cross the bridge and head up the left side of the creek. Look for trillium hidden along the bank in March.

0.5 Refreshing Cascade Falls. Continue by returning to the bridge.

0.7 Bridge and junction #1. Take the rocky road left uphill. After a short climb, the road levels out and crosses a ravine. Good views.

0.9 Junction #2. At the signed post, take the short trail right downhill.

1.0 Junction. Head left along the creek.

1.1 Junction. Leave the trail and, if possible, follow the road across Cascade creek. In winter, it takes one to two weeks after heavy rain for the creek to subside enough to ford. Continue downstream on the other side. (If the creek is too deep to cross, retrace your steps.)

1.2 Bridge and junction #3. Just before the bridge, take the trail up the right edge of a side creek. Up ahead at a Y, stay along the creek.

1.3 Tree and spur trail. Pass around a downed tree to follow a short spur trail upstream to a dramatic setting of moss-covered rocks.

Return to the tree to continue the hike, which now moves away from the creek slightly. Up ahead at a Y and at a junction, stay left. After crossing a knoll, the trail drops back down to the creek.

1.5 Creek crossing. The trail passes through abundant spring wildflowers, then climbs to a knoll, offering views across the canyon.

1.7 Two bridges and junction #4. Continue downhill.

1.8 Junction with Cascade Creek. Cross the creek and head right.

1.9 Back at the parking area. No facilities.

Getting There

From Hwy 101:
In Greenbrae
W on Sir Francis Drake
for 5.4 miles to Fairfax.
L before the theater,
R on Broadway
L on Bolinas Rd.
R on Cascade Dr. to
the end. Very limited
parking.

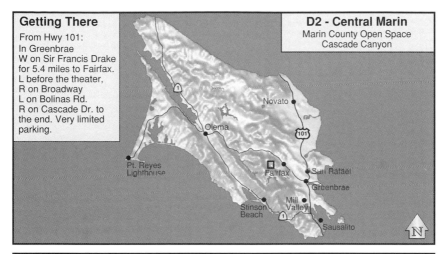

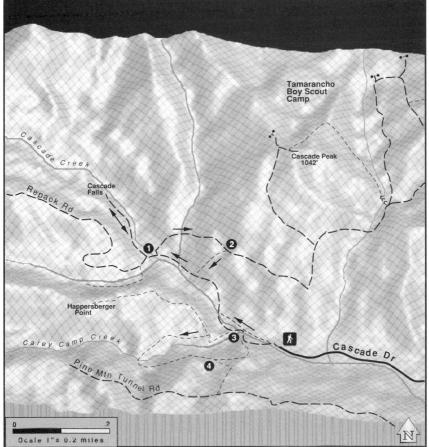

D3 Cascade Canyon to Cascade Peak

Distance: 3.5 miles   Shaded: 70%
Elevation Change: 900'   Can be muddy. Some bicycle traffic.
Rating: Hiking - 8   Difficulty - 7   Steep in places.
When to Go: Good after rain. Best in March.

This hike explores Cascade Canyon west of Fairfax. It offers great views, waterfalls and abundant wildflowers in March.

Note: Fairfax requires 12' of pavement clearance when parking.

0.0 Start at the Cascade open space gate at the end of Cascade Dr. Head through the gate and stay right on the trail. March wildflowers include milkmaids, shooting star, hound's tongue, Indian warrior and an abundance of mission bells.

0.2 Junction. The road joins the trail and both head right uphill.

0.3 Bridge and junction #1. Cross the bridge and bear right along the creek. This is a nice shady forest of oaks and bays.

0.5 Beautiful Cascade Falls. Cascade Creek only drains a small canyon east of White Hill as can be seen on the topographic map on page 6. Consequently, water flow is best during heavy rains.

0.7 Bridge and junction #1. Take the road left uphill.

0.9 Junction with trail. Continue straight on the road, which rolls in and out of clearings providing good views across the canyon.

1.3 Junction #2. Continue straight to enter a small canyon. Up ahead, a creek crossing can be tricky during heavy runoff.

1.6 Creeks and junction #3. Head left across the creek to take the trail which starts out very steep. Bays, oaks, madrones and fir provide welcome shade. Look for lots of iris here in April.

2.1 Junction #4 with road. Head left for a short climb to the top.

2.2 Cascade Peak at 1042'. Great views. Notice that there are two peaks, both of which are worth exploring.

2.3 Junction #4. Continue straight down the road.

2.4 Junction. Go left to start a steep downhill section. Ahead, the open chaparral area provides great views of Cascade Canyon.

2.8 Junction #2. The hike heads right back down the road.

3.2 Junction. Take the trail left, then left again along Cascade Creek.

3.5 Back at the parking area with no facilities.

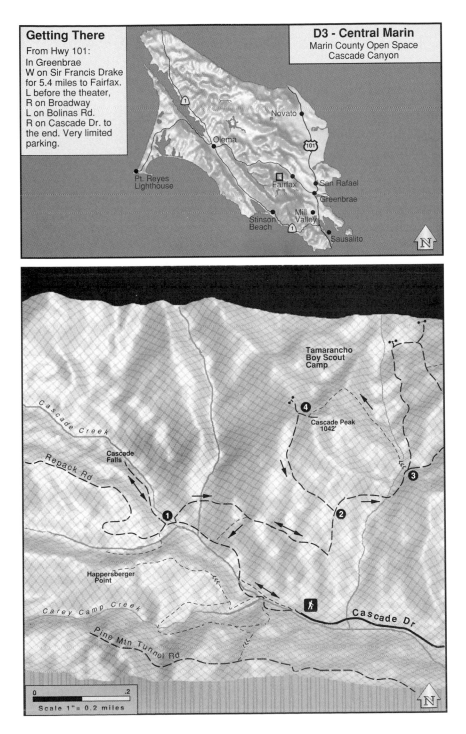

Getting There

From Hwy 101:
In Greenbrae
W on Sir Francis Drake
for 5.4 miles to Fairfax.
L before the theater,
R on Broadway
L on Bolinas Rd.
R on Cascade Dr. to
the end. Very limited
parking.

D3 - Central Marin
Marin County Open Space
Cascade Canyon

Novato

Olema

Pt. Reyes
Lighthouse

Fairfax

San Rafael

Greenbrae

Mill
Valley

Stinson
Beach

Sausalito

N

Cascade Creek

Repack Rd

Cascade
Falls

Tamarancho
Boy Scout
Camp

4

Cascade Peak
1042'

3

1

2

Happersberger
Point

Carey Camp Creek

Pine Mtn Tunnel Rd

Cascade Dr

0   .2
Scale 1"= 0.2 miles

N

131

D4 Toyon Fire Road to Cascade Peak

Distance: 3.7 miles   Shaded: 70%
Elevation Change: 1400'   Poison oak crowds trail in one area.
Rating: Hiking - 9   Difficulty - 8   Several very steep sections.
When to Go: Good on clear, cool days, best in March.

This hike explores the ridges above Fairfax. It offers good wildflowers in spring, an interesting oak-bay-madrone forest and great views.

Note: Fairfax requires 12' of pavement clearance when parking.

0.0 From Toyon Dr., go through the open space gate uphill. Ahead, Spanish broom, with fragrant yellow flowers, is invading the area.

0.5 Junction #1. Head right uphill on the dirt road.

0.7 Peak. The road ends on a small peak. Continue downhill on the trail. In spring, look for milkmaids, hound's tongue, iris and lots of Indian warrior under the oak and madrone trees. Poison oak crowds the trail in several areas here.

1.0 Junction #2. The trail joins a road. Go right on the road.

1.1 Junction. The hike heads left here. However, it's worth a short 100 yds. detour on the road right to view the open hills, most of which are part of the Tamarancho Boy Scout Camp.

1.5 Creek and junction #3. Take the signed trail uphill to the right and start a steep climb through dense vegetation.

2.0 Junction #4 with road. Head left for a short climb to the top.

2.1 Cascade peak at 1042'. Great views. Notice that there are two peaks, both of which are worth exploring.

2.2 Junction #4. Continue straight down the road.

2.3 Junction. Go left to start a steep downhill section on a fire road. The southern exposure offers good views across the canyon.

2.8 Junction #5. The hike heads left back up into the canyon.

3.1 Junction #3 and creek crossing. Head right uphill.

3.2 Junction #1. Head right along the ridge to a knoll and viewpoint.

3.4 Junction. A short spur trail heads left uphill to a small plaque commemorating Pam Ettinger, who died in an accident in 1974. This ridge was named for her after her family purchased the ridge and donated it to open space. Return to junction #1.

3.6 Junction #1. Head right along the road.

3.7 Back at the parking area on Toyon Dr. No facilities.

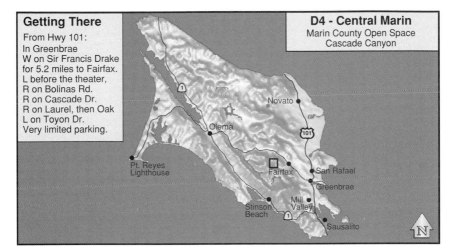

Getting There

From Hwy 101:
In Greenbrae
W on Sir Francis Drake
for 5.2 miles to Fairfax.
L before the theater,
R on Bolinas Rd.
R on Cascade Dr.
R on Laurel, then Oak
L on Toyon Dr.
Very limited parking.

D4 - Central Marin
Marin County Open Space
Cascade Canyon

Novato

Olema

Pt. Reyes
Lighthouse

Fairfax

San Rafael

Greenbrae

Mill
Valley

Stinson
Beach

Sausalito

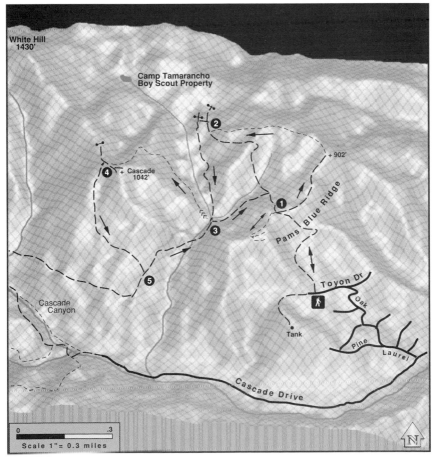

White Hill
1430'

Camp Tamarancho
Boy Scout Property

② + 902'

④ + Cascade
1042'

①

③

Pams Blue Ridge

⑤

Toyon Dr

Oak

Cascade
Canyon

Tank

Pine

Laurel

Cascade Drive

0   .3
Scale 1" = 0.3 miles

D5 Loma Alta Open Space Loop

Distance: 4.7 miles   Shaded: 20%
Elevation Change: 1200'   Can be muddy. Bicycle traffic possible.
Rating: Hiking - 7   Difficulty - 7   Steep in places.
When to Go: Best on clear, cool days in winter and spring.

This hike explores the Loma Alta open space just west of Fairfax. It offers great views and an unexpected 30' waterfall.

0.0 Park at the end of Glen Drive just past White Hill School in Fairfax. The hike starts by passing through an open space gate along Glen FR, then enters a woodsy canyon.

0.5 Water tanks and junction. Go left on Smith Ridge FR.

0.8 Junction #1. Stay on the road. **Option:** A trail climbs the ridgeline almost to the top of Loma Alta. This alternate route offers much better views east and north. However, the trail is very steep in places.

1.7 Junction #2. Continue uphill to a lookout point.

1.9 Gate and viewpoint. The open space land ends here at 1345' elevation. Loma Alta at 1592' lies another 0.5 miles uphill on private property. Fortunately, this knoll offers outstanding views west to Mt. Barnabe, east to the the bay and Mt. Diablo and south to Mt. Tamalpais. This vantage point offers a good view of the profile of the "sleeping maiden" along the ridge of Mt. Tamalpais. Legend has it that a young Miwok maiden was saved from the devil Diablo tribe by a great shuddering of the mountain. Afterwards, her profile could be seen on the ridgetop. The hike continues back down the road.

2.1 Junction #2. Head right down the ridge, which is steep in places.

2.8 Gate and junction #3. Turn sharp left and continue downhill.

3.2 Junction and hidden waterfall. It's surprising to find a picturesque 30' waterfall here. The hike heads back uphill along the road.

3.5 Junction #4. The road narrows to a trail and drops down steeply into a ravine to a junction. Continue straight uphill out of the ravine. Ahead, the trail enters a narrow pass that can be wet and muddy after rains. Also, watch out for poison oak on the banks. This road was once the railroad route over White's Hill to West Marin.

4.1 Junction #5 with road to school. Continue left into the canyon.

4.5 Canyon, fence and junction. Head right down the road, which crosses the creek, then go right again at the road.

4.7 Back at the parking area.

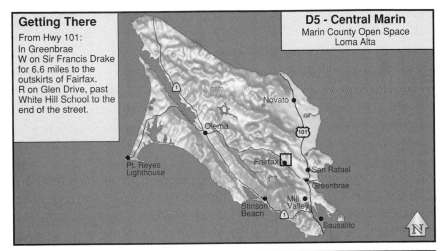

Getting There

From Hwy 101:
In Greenbrae
W on Sir Francis Drake
for 6.6 miles to the
outskirts of Fairfax.
R on Glen Drive, past
White Hill School to the
end of the street.

D5 - Central Marin
Marin County Open Space
Loma Alta

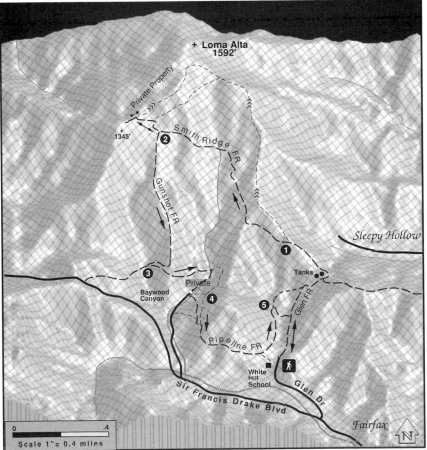

135

D6 Roy's Redwoods Trails

Distance: 2.6 miles   Shaded: 90%
Elevation Change: 650'   Can be muddy. Some poison oak.
Rating: Hiking - 9   Difficulty - 5   Moderately steep downhill.
When to Go: Good in fall and winter. Best in spring for green hills.
This short hike explores the hill area around an interesting grove of
redwoods, offering good wildflowers and local views.

0.0 Pass through the open space gate and head left into a
picturesque meadow ringed by tall bays and stately redwoods. This
area is named after the Roy brothers who owned the property for 80
years and operated a dairy ranch nearby.

0.1 At the far end of the meadow, angle to the right to pass between
two small redwood groves. The right grove consists of a large 30'
diameter ring of second generation redwoods. The original tree must
have been huge. Look for the trail sign about 100' further on and take
the signed trail left. Up ahead, the trail climbs to an open area and at
another Y, bear left again.

0.3 Junction #1. Take the horse trail to the right.

0.5 Saddle and junction #2. Take the trail to the left for about 100' to
a notched rock for good views east. Return to junction #2 and
continue left. The trail winds down off the hill passing through a large
ravine darkened by dense stands of oaks, bays and redwoods.

1.0 Junction #3. **Option:** At the bottom of the hill, next to a creek, you
can continue out towards Sir Francis Drake Blvd. to loop back to the
starting point. However, the route can be noisy, windy and overgrown
with grass. Otherwise, retrace your steps back up the hill.

1.5 Junction #2. Take the trail left uphill. Lots of poison oak off trail.

1.7 Junction. Take the trail right which climbs the hill, then loops back
to this point. Up ahead, the trail crests the hilltop and offers glimpses
south to the golf course, Pine Mountain and Mt. Tamalpais.

2.0 Junction #2 again. Head left. Watch closely for the next junction.

2.1 Junction. Take the trail left downhill past the sign (No Horses). At
the bottom of the hill, keep left and look for the trail which follows the
creek and skirts the hillside. This main redwood grove is a great area
to just wander about and explore. The trail, which may be overgrown
or blocked in places, stays to the left near the hillside.

2.6 Back at the parking area with restrooms.

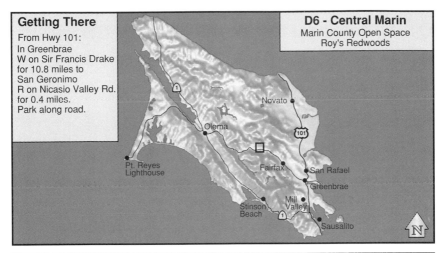

Getting There

From Hwy 101:
In Greenbrae
W on Sir Francis Drake
for 10.8 miles to
San Geronimo
R on Nicasio Valley Rd.
for 0.4 miles.
Park along road.

D6 - Central Marin
Marin County Open Space
Roy's Redwoods

Novato

Olema

Pt. Reyes
Lighthouse

Fairfax

San Rafael

Greenbrae

Stinson
Beach

Mill
Valley

Sausalito

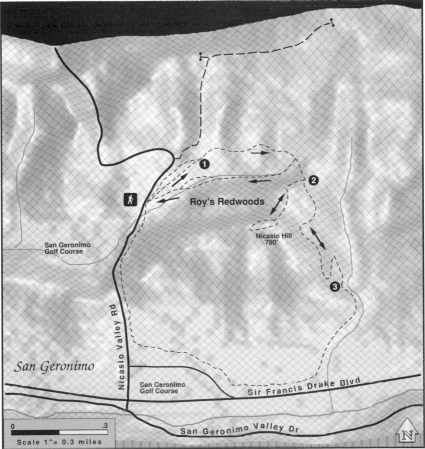

1

2

Roy's Redwoods

Nicasio Hill
780'

3

San Geronimo
Golf Course

Nicasio Valley Rd

San Geronimo

San Geronimo
Golf Course

Sir Francis Drake Blvd

San Geronimo Valley Dr

0   .3

Scale 1"= 0.3 miles

D7 Creek and Ox Trails History Loop

Distance: 2.5 miles   Shaded: 80%
Elevation Change: 200'   Bicycles likely. Traffic noise.
Rating: Hiking - 9   Difficulty - 2   Can be muddy in places.
When to Go: Best in summer for weather and winter for quiet.

This is an easy hike along Papermill Creek that features redwoods, a riparian setting and a glimpse of the history of Samuel P. Taylor Park.

0.0 Park in the main picnic area. The hike starts at the museum and ranger station where you can pick up a brochure that describes the history of the park at numbered posts. At the large redwood stump, take the paved road left through the picnic area.

0.1 Post 2. A billboard displays some great historical photos. Continue along the road and across the bridge, then take a right on the bike path. This path is part of the old railroad bed that ran from Sausalito to the coast and up to the Russian River town of Cazadero.

0.3 Junction #1. Leave the bike path and take the signed Creek trail right. The trail passes by a large redwood, then past bays and alders.

0.5 Junction. The trail climbs back up to the bike path for 100' then drops back down towards the creek. By taking the Creek trail, you'll miss historical posts 5, 6 and 7, but you can still read the brochure.

0.6 Junction. At the Y in the trail, a wooden post points the way to the right.

0.7 Creek junction #2. A large boulder stands opposite the creek at Devil's Gulch. Head uphill into a storage area and continue right.

1.1 Junction. A rock and plaque mark the site of the first papermill built on the west coast by Samuel P. Taylor. Continue on the trail.

Artist Sketch of the New Papermill

1.2 Bridge, swimming hole and restroom. After exploring the area, head back along the bike path.

1.3 Junction #3. Take the Ox trail right uphill. This was the original trail used to bring supplies to the mill by oxen.

2.2 Junction. The trail ends on the camp road. Head left downhill.

2.5 Back at the picnic area with full facilities.

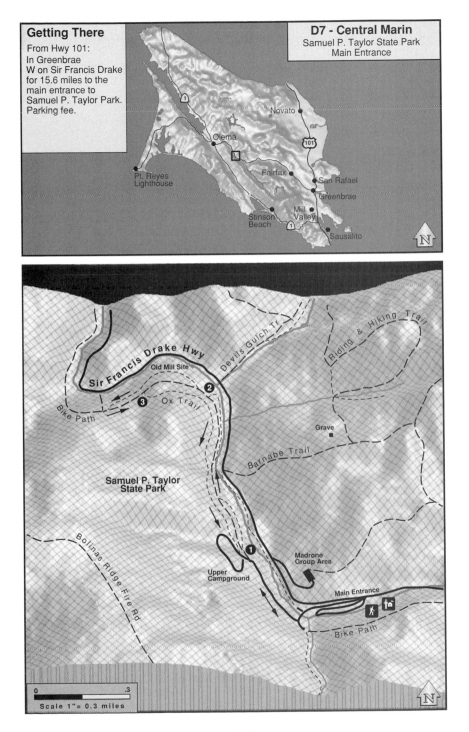

Getting There

From Hwy 101:
In Greenbrae
W on Sir Francis Drake
for 15.6 miles to the
main entrance to
Samuel P. Taylor Park.
Parking fee.

D7 - Central Marin
Samuel P. Taylor State Park
Main Entrance

Novato

101

Olema

Pt. Reyes
Lighthouse

Fairfax

San Rafael

Greenbrae

Mill
Valley

Stinson
Beach

1

Sausalito

N

Sir Francis Drake Hwy

Old Mill Site

Devils Gulch Tr

Riding & Hiking Trail

Bike Path

Ox Trail

③

②

Grave

Barnabe Trail

Samuel P. Taylor
State Park

Bolinas Ridge Fire Rd

①

Madrone
Group Area

Upper
Campground

Main Entrance

Bike Path

0   .3

Scale 1" = 0.3 miles

N

139

D8 Pioneer Tree - Riding & Hiking Trails

Distance: 2.8 miles   Shaded: 90%

Elevation Change: 700'   Some traffic noise.

Rating: Hiking - 9   Difficulty - 3   Can be muddy in winter.

When to Go: Best in February for trillium and late fall for colors.

This is a relatively easy hike that features the magnificent redwood forest of Samuel P. Taylor State Park and the Pioneer Tree.

0.0 Park in the main picnic area near the Visitor Center. This picnic area was the site of the Camp Taylor Hotel, which started out as a one-story hotel in 1874. Two stories were added later as shown in the picture. Passenger service on the North Pacific Coast Railroad began in 1875; by 1890 up to 3000 people came to Camp Taylor on weekends to picnic, swim, camp and hike. A large dance pavilion was an added attraction.

To start the hike, follow the road across the bridge on Lagunitas Creek, then bear left to go past the group picnic area.

Camp Taylor Hotel 1908

0.1 Junction #1. Take the signed Pioneer Tree trail right up Wildcat Canyon. This is a beautiful redwood forest with many lovely ferns. Ahead, stop at the bench to admire the view.

1.0 Pioneer Tree. A bench provides a place to rest and contemplate the large gnarled Pioneer Tree. Notice the ring of redwoods around the main trunk. Redwoods sprout new growth from roots and burls, especially after a tree has been damaged. Be sure to look inside the hollowed-out section of tree. It has a double cavity.

1.6 Junction #2. Take the bike path right across the bridge.

1.7 Junction. Take the signed Riding and Hiking trail left uphill.

2.0 Creek. The trail drops down a ravine alongside Barnabe Creek towards the road, then heads back up the other side of the creek.

2.2 Junction #3. Take the road left down towards Madrone Camp.

2.5 Madrone Group Camp. Continue down the paved road.

2.6 Highway. Carefully cross the road and take the trail left.

2.8 Back at the parking area with full facilities.

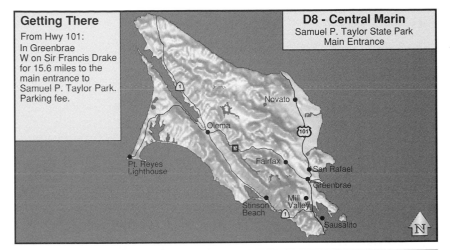

Getting There

From Hwy 101:
In Greenbrae
W on Sir Francis Drake
for 15.6 miles to the
main entrance to
Samuel P. Taylor Park.
Parking fee.

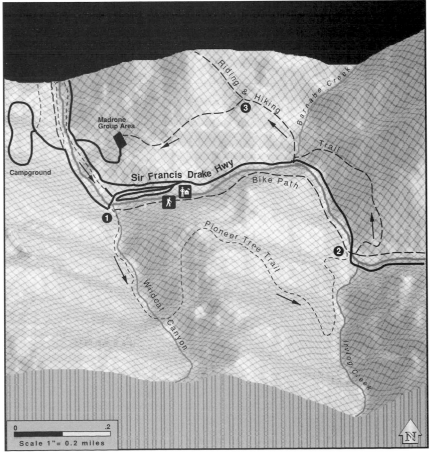

Scale 1"= 0.2 miles

D9 Ridge Trail to Mt. Barnabe

Distance: 4.6 miles   Shaded: 40%
Elevation Change: 1400'   Some bicycles. Traffic noise.
Rating: Hiking - 7   Difficulty - 7   Fire road is steep in places.
When to Go: Best on clear, cool, calm days.
This hike climbs out of the redwoods of Taylor park and up along the southern ridge of Mt. Barnabe to offer great views of central Marin.

0.0 The hike starts at the Irving picnic area. Take the Riding and Hiking trail east along the old railroad bed towards the Ridge trail and Mt. Barnabe. The North Pacific Coast Railroad was built in 1874 by James Shafter, who owned much of Point Reyes. He hoped to expand his fortune hauling lumber from the Russian River to Sausalito, then by ferry to San Francisco. The railroad also brought tourists in the other direction. This service ended when the 1250' tunnel through White Hill collapsed in the big earthquake of 1906. The coast section of the railroad continued operating until 1938, when it was abandoned.

0.6 Junction #1. Take the signed Ridge trail uphill. This trail is moderately steep for most of its two miles. Ahead, the trail enters a small canyon and circles out the other side.

1.6 Junction #2. The Ridge trail heads to the left to parallel the fire road. If the trail is overgrown with grasses, it's better to stay on the road. There are lots of ticks in these hills, so it's not a good idea to hike through grass, especially in winter and spring.

2.6 Mt. Barnabe and junction #3. This peak offers one of the great viewing spots of West Marin. On a clear day you can see Tomales Bay to the west, Mt. Diablo to the east and the jutting profile of Mt. St. Helena to the north. Also, Mt. Barnabe sits in a unique central position relative to the ridgeline running from the East Peak of Mt. Tamalpais to Bolinas Ridge. This ridgeline spans a full 180 degrees from southwest to northeast. (See the topographic map on page 6 for an overview.) When ready to continue, take the Barnabe trail downhill, which can be steep in places.

2.8 Junction with Bills trail. Continue downhill on the road.

3.8 Junction #4. Take the Riding and Hiking trail left.

4.1 Junction. The road right goes downhill to the Madrone group area. Continue on the Riding and Hiking trail left.

4.6 Back at the Irving picnic area. Water, tables and restrooms.

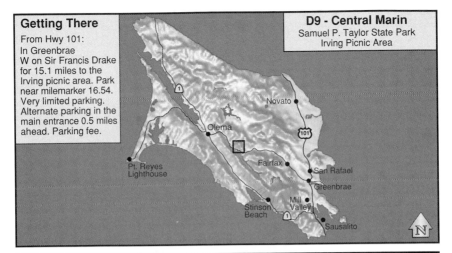

Getting There

From Hwy 101:
In Greenbrae
W on Sir Francis Drake
for 15.1 miles to the
Irving picnic area. Park
near milemarker 16.54.
Very limited parking.
Alternate parking in the
main entrance 0.5 miles
ahead. Parking fee.

D9 - Central Marin
Samuel P. Taylor State Park
Irving Picnic Area

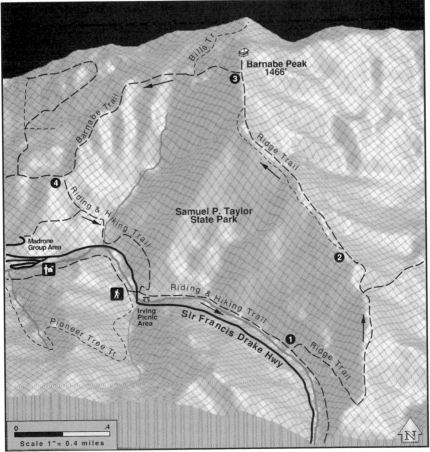

143

D10 Devil's Gulch - Stairstep Falls Trails

Distance: 3.9 miles   Shaded: 80%
Elevation Change: 200'
Rating: Hiking - 9   Difficulty - 3   Can be somewhat muddy.
When to Go: Best in November 2-3 weeks after the first heavy rains. In winter, this hike offers fall colors, a picturesque waterfall and spawning salmon. Wait a few days after rain for the water to clear.

0.0 Park off the highway near mile marker 18.05. Cross the highway and hike up the paved road into Devil's Gulch.

0.1 Junction. Take the trail along the creek. Bay trees and sword fern dominate the riparian setting. Big-leaf maple provides fall color.

In November, watch for king salmon in the creek. It takes about 5" of rain before the salmon will enter Tomales Bay and head up Papermill Creek to spawn. Once in the creek, they stay in deep pools during low water flow and move upstream after rains and runoff. Spawning salmon are three years old and undergo major changes as they end their life-cycle. Males turn brick red and their upper jaws distort forming a hook-like shape. Females often turn a dull bronze.

0.2 Junction #1 and bridge. Cross the bridge and head left to take Bills trail towards Mt. Barnabe.

0.8 Junction #2. Take the left trail which heads down into a ravine.

0.9 Stairstep Falls. The trail ends here with great views of the 50' picturesque falls. The hike now backtracks downhill to the bridge.

1.6 Bridge and junction #1. Cross the bridge and head right up the narrow trail along the creek. Resume watching for salmon. In December, you may see salmon that have spawned and died, lying in the river and along the banks.

2.2 Junction #3 with road. Head right to explore the upper reaches of Devil's Gulch. Look for California nutmeg tree with flat, sharp needles.

2.4 Junction. An old road heads downhill. Continue straight.

2.6 Gate. This is the turn-around point. **Option:** Continue 0.3 miles to explore the next canyon located on GGNRA property.

3.0 Junction #3 with the creek trail. Continue along the road which now enters open grassland. Up ahead, stop to admire the large oaks that line the small streambeds that cross the road.

3.6 Paved road and horse camps. Restrooms and water nearby.

3.9 Highway and parking area. No facilities.

Getting There

From Hwy 101:
In Greenbrae
W on Sir Francis Drake
for 16.6 miles to the
Devil's Gulch area
(located 1.0 mile past
the main entrance to
Samuel P. Taylor
State Park.) Limited
parking.

D10 - Central Marin
Samuel P. Taylor State Park
Devil's Gulch

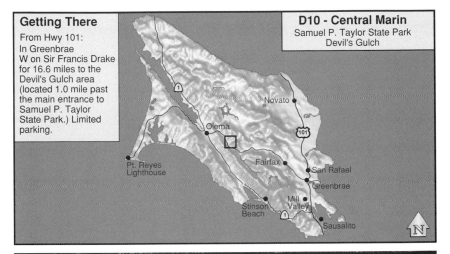

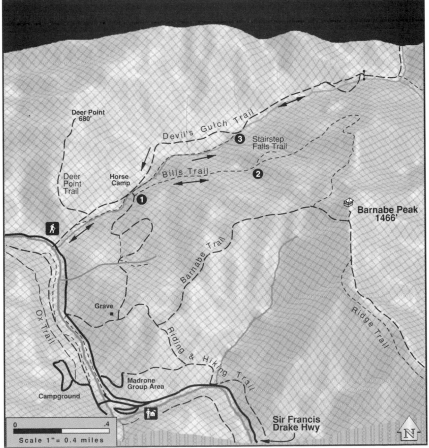

145

D11 Devil's Gulch to Mt. Barnabe

Distance: 6.3 miles   Shaded: 70%
Elevation Change: 1300'   Bicycle traffic possible.
Rating: Hiking - 9   Difficulty - 6   Moderately steep.
When to Go: Best in spring for views of green hills.

This hike climbs through forest up the backside of Mt. Barnabe, then descends the south-facing open hillsides. Great views.

0.0 Park off the highway near mile marker 18.05. Carefully cross the highway and hike up the paved road into Devil's Gulch.

0.1 Junction. Take the trail along the creek.

0.2 Junction #1 and bridge. Cross the bridge and head left to take Bills trail towards Mt. Barnabe.

0.8 Junction #2. Take the left trail for a short sidetrip.

0.9 Stairstep Falls. The trail ends here with great views of the 50' picturesque waterfalls. The hike now backtracks uphill.

1.0 Junction #2. Head left and continue uphill. This trail, built to state requirements of 5% incline or less, provides a long, easy climb through a magnificent forest of bay, fir and big-leaf maple.

4.0 Junction #3. Head left up the Barnabe trail.

4.2 Mt. Barnabe and junction #4. This peak was named after an old white mule purchased by Taylor from the army. "Barnabe" was the Taylor children's favorite pet. He often escaped from his corral and could be found grazing on these hillsides. The fire lookout station is run by the county. The hike now backtracks down the Barnabe trail.

4.4 Junction #3. Continue downhill to the left.

5.4 Junction with the Riding and Hiking trail. Keep right.

5.5 Junction #5 and grave site. The white picket fence encloses the grave site of Samuel Taylor and his daughter. Taylor, scouting for lumber, entered this area on horseback over Indian trails in 1854. He purchased 100 acres from Rafael Garcia and, two years later, constructed the first papermill on the Pacific Coast.

From the grave site, take the Riding and Hiking trail north.

5.8 Creek and junction. Cross the creek, then take the trail left to bypass a steep loop in the road.

6.1 Junction #1 and bridge. Head left.

6.3 Back at the parking area. No facilities.

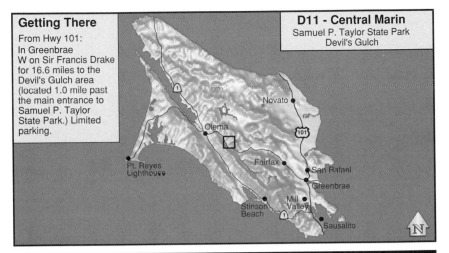

Getting There

From Hwy 101:
In Greenbrae
W on Sir Francis Drake
for 16.6 miles to the
Devil's Gulch area
(located 1.0 mile past
the main entrance to
Samuel P. Taylor
State Park.) Limited
parking.

D11 - Central Marin
Samuel P. Taylor State Park
Devil's Gulch

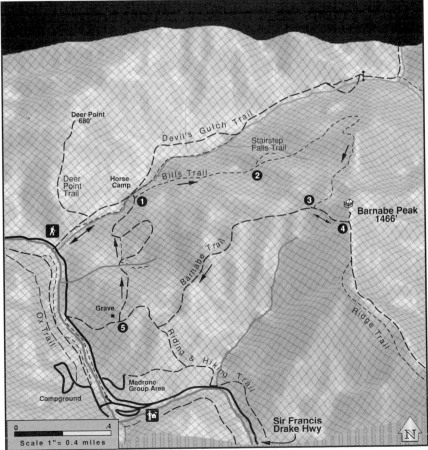

D12 Marin Civic Center to China Camp*

Distance: 5.7 miles   Shaded: 70%
Elevation Change: 1100'   Some bicycles possible.
Rating: Hiking - 8   Difficulty - 8   Steep in places.
When to Go: Good anytime, best when clear.

This one-way hike climbs to the Nike site on San Pedro Mountain to offer breathtaking views east, then winds down to China Camp.

*Shuttle Hike. Leave pickup cars along the road near Back Ranch campground. Shuttle hikers back on N. San Pedro Rd. to San Pablo Ave, then go left for one block and park near the trailhead.

0.0 Take the small, paved uphill path, which starts out in open grassland with some manzanita and oaks nearby.

0.1 Junction. Take the road right uphill.

0.3 Junction. At a switchback, take the unofficial trail right uphill.

0.4 Junction #1. The trail climbs to a road and viewpoint in a small saddle. Another road comes up from the south. Head left.

0.9 T-junction. Head left on the crossing road. Good views down the steep canyon on the right to the Dominican area. Up ahead, great views of the Civic Center and north.

1.3 Junction #2. Continue right on the dirt road.

2.1 Junction, Nike missile site, park and picnic area. At the gate, take the paved road right to the missile site. Be sure to visit the concrete platform farthest east. It offers tremendous views down to China Camp and the mudflats, and east across San Pablo Bay.

This hike passes through three jurisdictions. It starts on San Pedro Mtn. Open Space, then enters San Rafael's Harry Barbier Memorial Park, and ends in China Camp State Park. Over 700 acres of the open space land was donated by Frank Sinatra in the 1970s.

2.4 Junction #3. Take the dirt road left downhill into the state park.

2.7 Junction under powerlines. Head downhill to the left.

2.9 Junction under eucalyptus trees. Continue down to the left.

3.1 Junction #4. Take the Bay View trail left for a long gradual descent. **Option**: For a faster trip downhill, take the Back Ranch FT.

4.2 Wooden fence and junction. Take the switchback to the right. Down below, cross the road and continue on the Bay View trail.

5.7 Gate and parking area.

Getting There

From Hwy 101:
In San Rafael
N on San Pedro Rd.
for 3.1 miles to the
Back Ranch
Campground. Leave
car along the road.
Shuttle hikers back
to San Pablo Ave.

D12 - Central Marin
Marin County Open Space
San Pedro Mountain

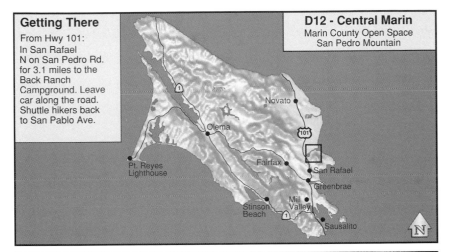

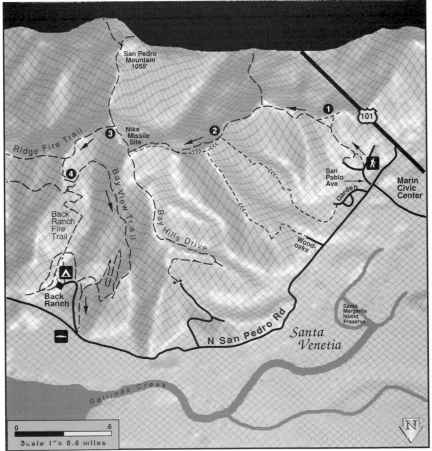

149

D13 Miwok - Oak Ridge - Shoreline Trails

Distance: 5.5 miles   Shaded: 70%

Elevation Change: 500'   Bicycles likely. Poison oak possible.

Rating: Hiking - 9   Difficulty - 4   Moderately steep uphill.

When to Go: Good anytime. Best early morning in winter and spring.

This is the best hike for exploring China Camp State Park and the historic village area. It also provides good views and spring flowers.

0.0 Park along the main road near the gate to Miwok Meadows. Head through the gate 100 yds. and take the Miwok FT uphill. Spring flowers include iris, suncups, buttercups and blue-eyed grass.

0.6 Junction #1. Take the Oak Ridge trail left.

0.9 Junction with McNear FR. Head down the road 50', then go right.

1.1 Viewpoint! A grassy hillside overlooking a MMWD water tank provides views south. The view is unusual because Pt. San Pablo in the east bay lies much closer than many familiar Marin landmarks.

1.5 Junction #2. Cross the McNear FT and take the trail downhill.

2.1 Junction. The trail right goes to Peacock Gap. Continue straight.

2.2 Junction. Take the Shoreline trail right. Look out for poison oak.

2.4 Ranger Station. Continue across the road on the Shoreline trail.

2.7 Junction #3. Take the Village trail left, which passes through a lush ravine. Down below, cross N. San Pedro Rd. to the parking area. Then take the paved road down to China Camp Village.

3.0 China Camp Village and Museum. During the 1880s, nearly 500 people, Chinese fishermen and their families, lived in this village. Many originally came for the gold rush, then stayed to fish for grass shrimp. At one time, there were three general stores, a boat store and a barber shop here. Part of their story is described in the museum.

To continue the hike, head back up the paved road.

3.2 Junction. Take the signed Rat Rock Cove trail to the right which parallels the main road. If the trail is overgrown, check yourself for ticks on the other side. Stay on the trail as far as it's possible.

3.5 Junction with N. San Pedro Rd. Walk along the side of the road.

3.6 Junction #4. Head left towards the Ranger Station.

3.7 Junction. Take the signed Shoreline trail right and stay on it. Up ahead, watch your footing. The trail surface is uneven in places.

5.5 Junction with Miwok Fire trail and the parking area. No facilities.

Getting There

From Hwy 101:
In San Rafael,
N on San Pedro Rd.
for 3.7 miles to the
Miwok Meadows
Group Area. Park
along the road.

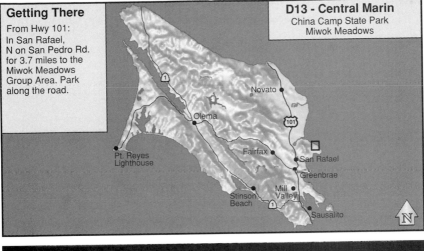

151

D14 Bay View - Miwok Fire Trails

Distance: 5.8 miles   Shaded: 70%
Elevation Change: 700'   Part of hike along road. Bicycle traffic.
Rating: Hiking - 9   Difficulty - 5   Moderate downhill.
When to Go: Good anytime. Best early winter mornings.

This pleasant hike circles above the campground and picnic area in China Camp visiting small forested ravines. Good views.

0.0 Park anywhere along the road near the Back Ranch Meadows campground. At the campground kiosk, take the signed Shoreline trail right as it parallels the road into the campground. The start of this hike provides an opportunity to compare madrones and manzanitas. Both have dense, smooth trunks. The madrone, a tree, is larger with big glossy leaves and orange-brown peeling bark, while the manzanita, a shrub, has smaller leaves and deep red bark.

0.2 Junction. Take the signed Bay View trail right and start a long, gradual climb. This ranch, China Camp and all of San Pedro Mtn. was purchased by John McNear in the late 1860s.

0.4 Junction #1. Head uphill on the road for 50', then take the new trail left to continue the gradual climb. Up ahead, see if you can find a large bay tree that has been cut to the ground. Notice the new sprouts around the circumference.

1.0 Wooden fence and junction #2. Continue right for a short loop.

1.1 Junction. A road comes up from the right. Take the trail left out to a small knoll with two power towers. Good views. Head back and take the right trail along the ridgetop. Lots of red Indian warrior here in March.

1.2 Junction #2. Continue straight.

Indian Warrior

2.8 Powerline and junction #3. Take the Back Ranch FT left downhill for 50', then continue on the Bay View trail to the right. This section of the Bay View trail was built in 1995.

4.0 Saddle and jct #4. At a large intersection, take the Ridge FT left.

4.3 Junction. Take the signed Miwok Fire trail left downhill.

4.8 Junction. Head north along N. San Pedro Rd.

4.9 Junction. Cross the road and take a small trail to Bullet Hill for some nice views of the bay. Continue down the other side.

5.2 Junction. Take the nature trail around Turtle Back Island.

5.8 Back at the parking area. No facilities here.

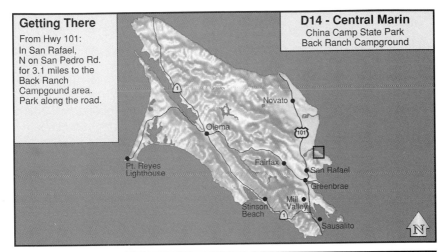

Getting There

From Hwy 101:
In San Rafael,
N on San Pedro Rd.
for 3.1 miles to the
Back Ranch
Campgound area.
Park along the road.

D14 - Central Marin
China Camp State Park
Back Ranch Campground

Novato

Olema

101

Pt. Reyes
Lighthouse

Fairfax

San Rafael

Greenbrae

Stinson
Beach

Mill
Valley

Sausalito

N

Ridge Fire Trail

Nike
Missile
Site

Bay View Trail

④

③

Bay View Trail

China Camp
State Park

Back
Ranch
Fire
Trail

Miwok Fire Trail

Shoreline Trail

Group
Area

Miwok
Meadows

Shoreline Trail

①

②

Chicken
Coop Hill

Bullet
Hill

Turtle
Back
Island

Back Ranch
Meadows
Campground

N San Pedro Road

Duck
Blinds

Duck
Blinds

Jake's
Island

San Francisco Bay

Gallinas Creek

N

0   .4
Scale 1"= 0.4 miles

153

D15 Turtle Back Island - Shoreline Trail

Distance: 3.8 miles   Shaded: 50%
Elevation Change: 200'   Traffic noise. Bicycles allowed.
Rating: Hiking - 9   Difficulty - 3   Some uneven footing.
When to Go: Good anytime. Best early winter and spring mornings.
This mostly level hike explores the northern part of China Camp, including Turtle Back Island. Good wildflowers from February-May.

0.0 Park along the road north of the Miwok Meadows gate. The hike starts by heading north along the main road.

0.1 Bullet Hill. Take the short path to the top of the hill for great views east out to the bay. The hike continues down the other side of the hill.

0.2 Main road. Continue north along the road. Pickleweed is the primary plant in the salt marsh, which also harbors the rare salt marsh harvest mouse and the clapper rail, a shy, brown 15" hen-like bird.

0.3 Turtle Back Island and junction #1. Take the dirt road through the gate and on around the island. Nature signs describe the area. Up ahead, the trail to Jake's Island may be closed because too many people have been trapped on the island by high tide. Jake was a notorious poacher who built a cabin and lived on the island from the 1920s to the 1940s.

0.9 North San Pedro Rd. Head north toward the campground.

1.1 Kiosk and junction. At the campground kiosk, take the signed Shoreline trail right as it parallels the road into the campground. Notice the tall, 15' manzanita shrubs along the way.

1.3 Junction #2. The Bay View trail climbs uphill to the right. Continue left. Ahead, the trail crosses the upper edge of the meadow, then enters into an oak-bay canyon. Look for Indian warrior in February.

1.7 Bridge and junction. Keep to the left.

1.9 Junction #3. Continue straight across the broad fire road.

2.4 Junction with North San Pedro Rd. Stay on the Shoreline trail.

2.6 Junction. Continue straight up the open meadow. Much of the grass in the park is rattlesnake grass, a non-native introduced from Europe. The park conducts regular burns to remove non-native plants and help restore native perennial grasses and wildflowers.

3.5 Group area and junction #4. The trail follows a split-rail fence to enter the group picnic area. Continue along the road.

3.8 Main road and parking area.

Getting There

From Hwy 101:
In San Rafael,
N on San Pedro Rd.
for 3.7 miles to the
Miwok Meadows
Group Area. Park
along the road.

D15 - Central Marin
China Camp State Park
Miwok Meadows Group Area

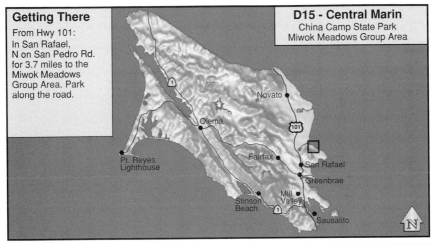

Novato

Olema

101

Pt. Reyes
Lighthouse

Fairfax

San Rafael

Greenbrae

Stinson
Beach

Mill
Valley

1

Sausalito

N

Ridge Fire Trail

Nike
Missile
Site

Bay View Trail

Bay View Trail

Back
Ranch
Fire
Trail

Miwok Fire Trail

3

Shore line Trail

Group
Area **4**

Miwok
Meadows

Shoreline Trail

A

Shoreline Trail

Back Ranch
Meadows
Campground

2

Chicken
Coop Hill

1

Bullet
Hill

Turtle
Back
Island

N San Pedro Road

Duck
Blinds

Duck
Blinds

Jake's
Island

San Francisco Bay

Gallinas Creek

N

0   .4

Scale 1"= 0.4 miles

E - North Marin - 14 Hikes

Starting from Terra Linda at 280'
E1 .... Terra Linda - Sleepy Hollow Ridge Trails 3.4*

Starting from Smith Ranch Road at 10'
E2 .... McInnis Park - Las Gallinas Wildlife Ponds 3.0

Starting from Marinwood
E3 .... Canyon Trail - Queenstone Fire Road 3.7*
E4 .... Big Rock Ridge - Luiz Fire Rds. 3.8*

Starting from Pacheco Valle at 120'
E5 .... Loma Verde - Pacheco Valle Ridge Trails 4.8

Starting from Indian Valley College at 200'
E6 .... Waterfall - High Meadow Trails 3.0
E7 .... Ab Schwindt - Wildcat Trails 3.7

Starting from Deer Island at 20'
E8 .... Deer Island Loop Trail 3.3

Starting from Vineyard Road in Novato at 280'
E9 .... Deer Camp - Big Trees Trails 5.5

Starting from Stafford Lake County Park at 200'
E10 .. Terwilliger Nature Trail 2.6

Starting from Mt. Burdell
E11 .. Fieldstone - Simmons Trails 2.7
E12 .. West Flank of Mt. Burdell 4.1
E13 .. Old Quarry Trail to Mt. Burdell 5.5

Starting from Olompali State Park at 40'
E14 .. Olompali State Park 4.5

* Shuttle Hike

Pets allowed on all hikes except 2, 10 and 14.

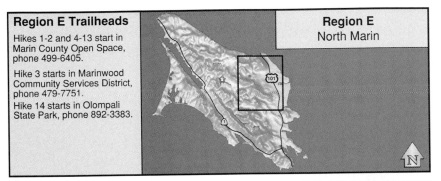

Region E Trailheads

Hikes 1-2 and 4-13 start in Marin County Open Space, phone 499-6405.

Hike 3 starts in Marinwood Community Services District, phone 479-7751.

Hike 14 starts in Olompali State Park, phone 892-3383.

Region E
North Marin

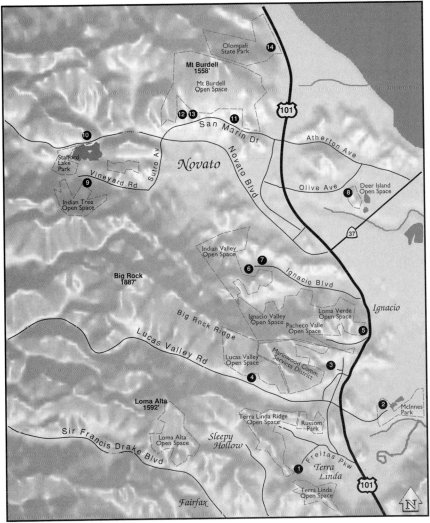

E1 Terra Linda - Sleepy Hollow Ridge*

Distance: 3.4 miles   Shaded: 10%
Elevation Change: 600'   Mostly dirt roads, bicycles possible.
Rating: Hiking - 7   Difficulty - 4   Grass crowds trail section.
When to Go: Best in winter and early spring before the grass dries.

This one-way hike follows a U-shaped ridge around Terra Linda and the Santa Margarita Valley. It offers lovely views of surrounding hills.

*Shuttle Hike. Leave pickup cars at the end of Wintergreen Terrace. Shuttle all hikers to the very end of Freitas Parkway.

0.0 Go through the open space gate and up the paved path.

0.1 Junction and saddle. Take a sharp right and continue climbing. Good views west to Sleepy Hollow and Loma Alta. During the 1970s, a road was planned here to connect Sleepy Hollow with Terra Linda.

0.2 Plateau. Continue on around to the right and follow the ridge.

0.6 Junction #1. Take the right road which offers shade and a change in vegetation from grass to trees. Ahead, great views down the valley.

This valley and hills were once part of a 22,000 acre rancho, an 1844 land grant to Timothy Murphy, a 300 pound Irishman. According to historian Jack Mason, Murphy, known as Don Timoteo, was well-liked and was the most legendary figure in early Marin. One day his horse threw him to the ground in front of a brown bear. He had no choice but to wrestle with the bear until both agreed to separate. When he died in 1853, much of his property went to his nephew, John Lucas.

0.9 Junction. Take the small trail to the right of the fire road.

1.4 Junction #2. Head downhill to the right. **Option:** The road left goes uphill on open space land for about a mile.

1.8 Junction and saddle. Continue downhill to the right.

1.9 Junction #3. Before reaching the street, head left on the trail.

2.1 Junction. Under a power line, take the trail left uphill.

2.2 Fence and junction. Head right on the trail, which may be overgrown. The fence is part of a private residence on a narrow strip of land that juts into county open Space.

2.8 Junction. A road comes up from the left. Continue straight.

3.2 Junction #4. Just below a level hilltop and before a fence, take the overgrown road right downhill, then continue right on the trail.

3.4 Back at the shuttle parking area. No facilities.

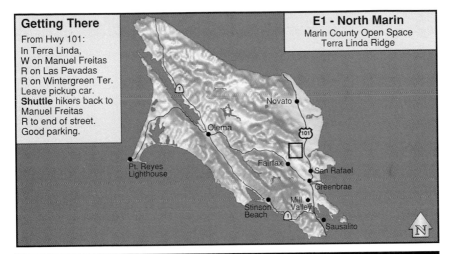

Getting There

From Hwy 101:
In Terra Linda,
W on Manuel Freitas
R on Las Pavadas
R on Wintergreen Ter.
Leave pickup car.
Shuttle hikers back to
Manuel Freitas
R to end of street.
Good parking.

E1 - North Marin
Marin County Open Space
Terra Linda Ridge

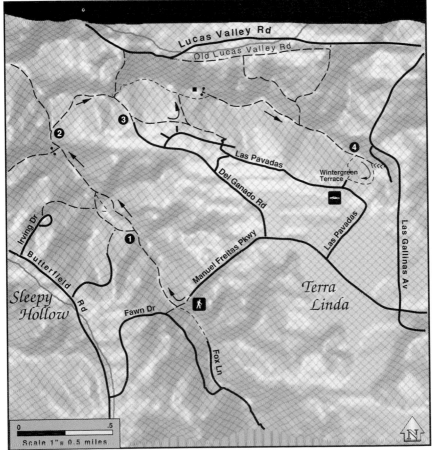

Scale 1" = 0.5 miles

159

E2 McInnis Park - Las Gallinas Ponds

Distance: 3.0 miles   Shaded: 0%
Elevation Change: 120'   Bring binoculars.
Rating: Hiking - 7   Difficulty - 2   Mostly levees.
When to Go: Best winter mornings for shorebirds.

This hike climbs a small hill in McInnis Park for great views, then skirts wildlife ponds in Las Gallinas Sanitary District. Good birding.

0.0 Head past the tennis courts and follow the trail to the top of the hill for great 360 degree views. Continue east on the paved path.

0.1 Junction. As you enter the broad, flat, Nike missile site, take the signed trail right as it skirts the hillside just above the golf course. When you reach the paved road, go downhill past the sanitation plant.

0.2 Junction #1. Cross the bridge and check the bulletin board for birding news. Head left to circle the inner pond clockwise. This 20 acre freshwater marsh holds treated water on its way to the bay. The small islands have been created to shelter birds. All of the ponds are required during summer months when treated water can not be dumped into the bay.

White Pelican with St. Vincents Church in the background

0.8 Junction #2. Head left out towards the bay.

1.4 Power tower, viewpoint and junction #3. One rare and endangered bird you might see is the California clapper rail, a drab-brown, hen-like bird that is found in bay area salt marshes. During twilight in the spring mating season, you can listen for pairs of birds exchanging a rapid clattering call.

1.7 Turnaround point #4. The gravel road changes to dirt, which can be muddy in winter. You can continue on the road which ends next to Hamilton Field, where you can see the old runway and hangers. The Coast Guard still operates helicopters there.

2.8 Junction #1. Go past the treatment plant and follow the paved road uphill to the missile site, which dates to the 1950s. Hippies occupied the underground storage areas in the 1960s until authorities flooded the holes. Now, the relined storage areas hold fresh water.

3.0 Back at the parking area. Restrooms and water.

Getting There

From Hwy 101:
In Terra Linda,
R on Smith Ranch Rd
to McInnis Park.
L on Smith Ranch Rd.
R to tennis courts.
Upper lot open
from 8am to 5:30pm.
Lower lot open later.

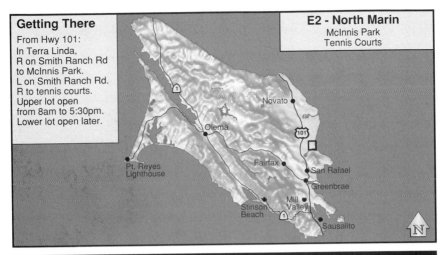

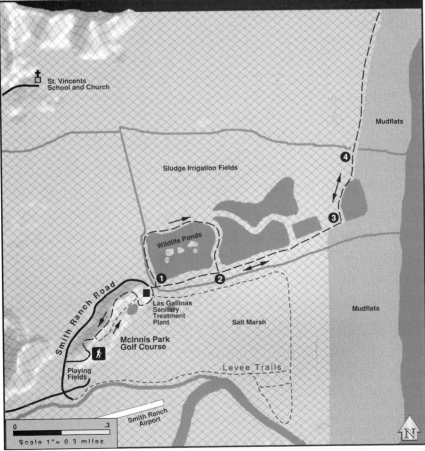

161

E3 Canyon Trail - Queenstone Fire Rd.*

Distance: 3.7 miles   Shaded: 30%
Elevation Change: 1300'   Trail hard to follow in places.
Rating: Hiking - 7   Difficulty - 8   Steep uphill. Poison oak.
When to Go: Good when cool and clear. Best in spring.
This strenuous hike climbs up a small lovely canyon to Big Rock Ridge offering great views, then returns down the ridge on a fire road.

*Shuttle Hike. Leave pickup cars on Queenstone Drive off Miller Creek Rd. Shuttle all hikers east on Miller Creek Rd., then left on Las Gallinas Rd. to Blackstone, then left on Valleystone Rd. **Note:** The shuttle distance is only 1.0 miles and can easily be walked.

0.0 At the end of the street, go past the open space gate and follow the trail up the left side of the creek. This delightful narrow canyon is shaded by oaks and bays with some buckeye and madrone trees.

0.7 Junction. At a Y in the trail, keep right and climb up to a small rocky overlook. Several trails cross the creek. Stay on the main trail.

0.8 Falls. The creek has cut to bedrock creating a small picturesque falls. Up ahead, at a Y and a post, keep to the right of the main creek.

1.0 Junction #1. Two old water pipes head left up into a small ravine. Continue right uphill to see a small dam, then return here.

1.1 Dam. This ten-foot dam was once used as a water supply.

1.2 Junction #1. Take the small trail right into the ravine. The trail quickly climbs right, out of the ravine, and on to a small narrow ridge to begin a long, very steep climb. Watch out for poison oak.

1.5 Knoll, oak tree and fire pit. The trail may be difficult to follow from here. It veers left to pass a small rock outcrop, then left a little more to cross the upper end of the canyon. If tall grass crowds the trail, check yourself for ticks once you're at the road.

1.7 Junction #2 with the Queenstone FR. Great views. Head left 100 yds. to a spur trail and viewpoint, then head downhill on the Queenstone FR. This road is used to access several antennas located on the top of Big Rock Ridge. Cars and trucks are possible.

Option: You can explore the ridgeline of Big Rock Ridge by heading west uphill. This dirt road can be taken for another 1.5 miles to a small knoll at 1640' offering great views in all directions. See Hike E4 for map details.

3.7 Back at the parking area.

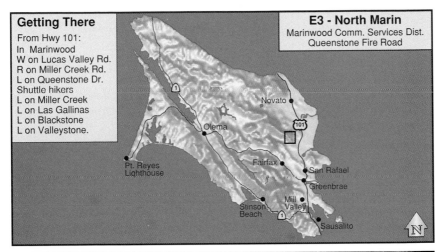

Getting There

From Hwy 101:
In Marinwood
W on Lucas Valley Rd.
R on Miller Creek Rd.
L on Queenstone Dr.
Shuttle hikers
L on Miller Creek
L on Las Gallinas
L on Blackstone
L on Valleystone.

E3 - North Marin
Marinwood Comm. Services Dist.
Queenstone Fire Road

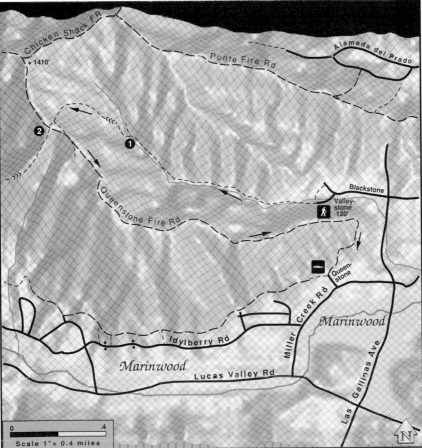

E4 Big Rock Ridge - Luiz Fire Roads*

Distance: 3.8 miles   Shaded: 20%
Elevation Change: 1400'   Can be windy. Some poison oak.
Rating: Hiking - 7   Difficulty - 7   Steep uphill and down.
When to Go: Save for winter and early spring.
Bring binoculars to climb up the south-facing slope of Big Rock Ridge to a hilltop offering magnificent views in all directions.

*Shuttle Hike. Leave pickup cars at the concrete bridge that spans the creek on Bridgegate Dr. Shuttle hikers back on Lucas Valley Rd., then left on Mt. McKinley, left on Idylberry and right on Rubicon Dr. **Note:** This hike was made a shuttle hike to avoid walking through local neighborhoods. However, the start of the hike is only 0.4 miles from the finish if you walk up Bridgegate Dr., then right down a paved fire road opposite Golden Iris.

0.0 Start at the fire road at the end of Rubicon Dr. One hundred yds. in, at a junction, continue straight to pass by a wooden corral.

0.3 Junction #1. Stay along the creek for a short detour to a small landing where three creeks join together, then return to junction #1.

0.5 Junction #1. Now head left to begin a long, steep climb to the ridge.

*Big Rock Ridge
as seen from San Pedro Mtn.*

0.9 Falls and ferns. A ten foot waterfall carved from bedrock and surrounded by chain ferns creates a pleasant grotto and rest stop.

1.2 Junction #2. Take the Big Rock Ridge FR left.

1.6 Junction #3. Continue uphill to a viewpoint.

1.7 Junction. Take the small trail right to the hilltop.

1.8 Knoll and great viewpoint! Big Rock Ridge gets its name from a large 30' boulder located at the upper end of Lucas Valley next to Lucas Valley Rd. It can just be seen from here.

Big Rock is also the name of the highest point on the ridge at 1887'. It's antenna-covered peak is the second tallest mountain in Marin.

2.0 Junction #3. Take the Luiz FR road right for a long descent.

3.5 Junction #4. Cross the street. Take the footpath along the creek.

3.8 Back at the bridge and parking area.

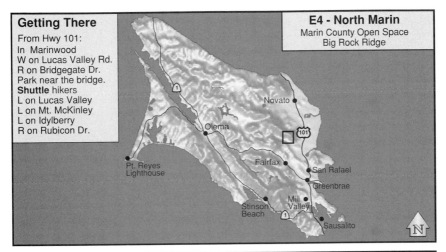

Getting There

From Hwy 101:
In Marinwood
W on Lucas Valley Rd.
R on Bridgegate Dr.
Park near the bridge.
Shuttle hikers
L on Lucas Valley
L on Mt. McKinley
L on Idylberry
R on Rubicon Dr.

E4 - North Marin
Marin County Open Space
Big Rock Ridge

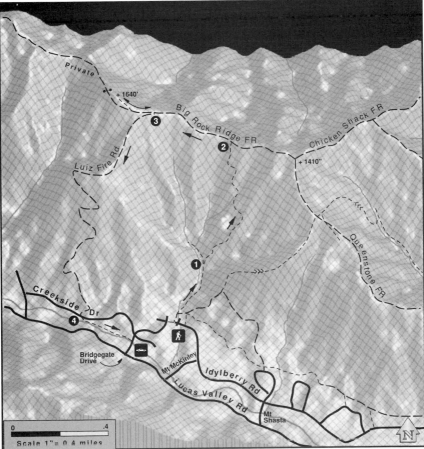

165

E5 Loma Verde - Pacheco Valle Ridge

Distance: 4.8 miles   Shaded: 50%
Elevation Change: 1300'   Part of hike on streets.
Rating: Hiking - 7   Difficulty - 6   Steep in places.
When to Go: Good fall to spring. Best when clear.

This hike climbs a ridge to circle Pacheco Valle. It offers oak woodland hills and great views north, south and east.

0.0 Park along Clay Ct. or in the Park and Ride lot across the street. Go through the open space gate and head uphill on the paved road.

0.3 Tennis court and gate. The tennis court sits atop a water reservoir supplying Pacheco Valley. Continue past the gate.

0.9 Junction. Take the small trail right to a hilltop with good views east to Hamilton Field and across the bay. From World War II to the early 1970s, the Air Force operated Hamilton Field and, from here, you could see bomber and fighter planes taking off and landing.

The area directly below is part of the original 6,600 acre historic Pacheco Ranch granted to Ignacio Pacheco in 1840. The ranch is still owned by descendants of the Pacheco family. About a half-mile north of the trailhead on Alameda del Prado, you can see a white Victorian house built by Ignacio's son in 1881. Continue on the trail.

1.0 Junction #1. As the trail circles to rejoin the main road, three trails enter from the right. Take the last trail, which parallels the main road. It is more interesting, offering oak trees and better views.

1.4 Junction. The trail rejoins the road in a saddle offering good views north to Mt. Burdell and south down Pacheco Valle.

1.5 Junction. Continue right uphill on the road marked Big Rock, which is also called Chicken Shack FR on some maps.

2.3 Viewpoint. A clearing offers great views to the north and to the slopes below Big Rock Ridge. Look for evidence of fires that periodically sweep up these hills to the ridgetops.

2.7 Junction #2. Take the Ponte FR left down the ridge.

3.7 Junction with road to street. Continue straight.

3.9 Junction with a crossing road. Continue straight.

4.3 Junction #3 and water tank. Head left down the trail.

4.5 Junction with the street. Head right to Alameda del Prado.

4.8 Back at the parking area. No facilities.

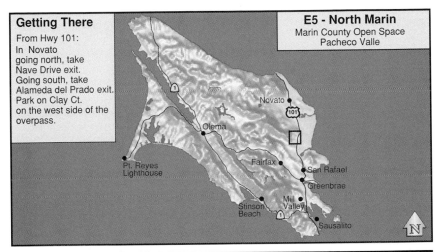

Getting There

From Hwy 101:
In Novato
going north, take
Nave Drive exit.
Going south, take
Alameda del Prado exit.
Park on Clay Ct.
on the west side of the
overpass.

E5 - North Marin
Marin County Open Space
Pacheco Valle

Novato

Olema

Pt. Reyes
Lighthouse

Fairfax

San Rafael

Greenbrae

Mill
Valley

Stinson
Beach

Sausalito

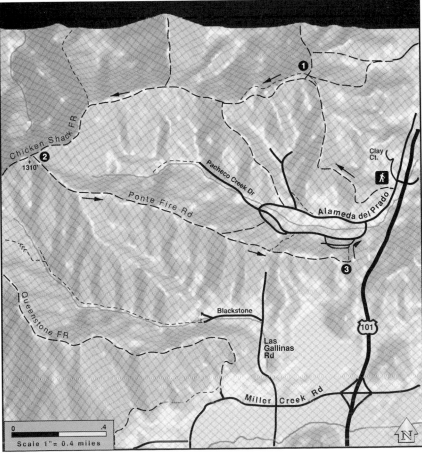

Chicken Shack FR

1310'

Ponte Fire Rd

Pacheco Creek Dr

Clay
Ct.

Alameda del Prado

Queenstone FR

Blackstone

Las
Gallinas
Rd

Miller Creek Rd

0 .4
Scale 1" = 0.4 miles

E6 Waterfall - High Meadow Trails

Distance: 3.0 miles   Shaded: 60%
Elevation Change: 700'
Rating: Hiking - 7   Difficulty - 8   One short, steep up and down.
When to Go: Good winter and spring. Best early March for flowers.

This is a pleasant hike that explores north-facing slopes near Big Rock Ridge. It offers oak-bay woods, pretty flowers and views.

0.0 From the parking area, head west on the street toward the turnaround circle, then right past the IVC corporation yard. Up in the large meadow, continue straight on the Indian Valley FR.

0.5 Bridge and junction #1. Take the Waterfall trail left across the bridge into oak-bay woodland and up the right side of the creek. This hike follows the largest trail, which winds up the ravine crossing the creek several times. Up ahead, a 15' seasonal waterfall provides a refreshing sight during heavy runoff.

March wildflowers include milkmaid, shooting star, mission bells and buttercups. Iris in the ravine bloom in April.

1.5 Junction #2. The Burgi trail heads left up to a knoll and an unofficial trail heads right up to private property on Big Rock Ridge. Continue straight and head downhill into a canyon. Good views.

2.0 Pacheco Pond and junction. Head right to skirt the reservoir, which was built for the Pacheco ranch in 1948. This valley was granted to Ignacio Pacheco, a sergeant in the Mexican army, in 1840.

2.1 Junction. At the far corner of the reservoir, take the High Meadow trail right, which is steep, narrow and rutted. The trail starts out under oaks, bay and madrone, but soon crests on a grassy knoll. Up ahead at another small knoll, keep to the left at a Y-junction.

2.4 Junction. The fire road on the ridge offers good views of Big Rock Ridge (with all its antennas) to the southwest. Now head left on the Montura FR which goes steeply downhill.

2.5 Junction #3. You can extend this hike by following a rollercoaster ridge road out for a mile and back. If you don't, it is still worth going down the ridge road 100' to a view point under a power pole. Then, retrace your steps and head downhill to the north.

2.8 Junction with the IVC campus loop road. Head left. Up ahead, the road passes the Olympic size swimming pool.

3.0 Back at the parking area. No facilities.

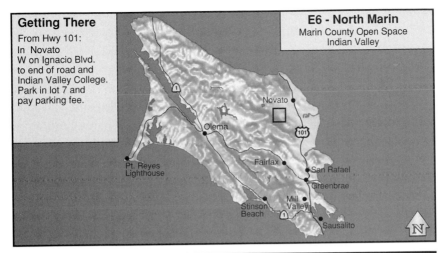

Getting There

From Hwy 101:
In Novato
W on Ignacio Blvd.
to end of road and
Indian Valley College.
Park in lot 7 and
pay parking fee.

E6 - North Marin
Marin County Open Space
Indian Valley

Novato

Olema

Fairfax

San Rafael

Greenbrae

Pt. Reyes
Lighthouse

Stinson
Beach

Mill
Valley

Sausalito

Big Rock Ridge

Private

Montura FR

+ 640'

❸

High
Meadow
Trail

❷

College of Marin
Indian Valley
Campus

Ignacio Blvd

Pacheco
Pond FR

Burgi Tr

Waterfall Trail

Private

Alexander
Trail

+ 600'

Hill Ranch Tr

Wildcat Tr

Indian   Valley

❶

Ad Schwindt Trail

Buzzard
Burn FR

Indian Valley Rd

0 _____ .5
Scale 1"= 0.5 miles

169

E7 Ad Schwindt - Wildcat Trails

Distance: 3.7 miles   Shaded: 70%
Elevation Change: 450'   Horseback riders likely.
Rating: Hiking - 8   Difficulty - 5   Grass crowds trail.
When to Go: Good in fall and winter. Best in early spring for flowers.
This woodsy hike tours the oak-bay hills around Indian Valley
Campus and open space areas. Many unofficial trails for exploring.

0.0 After entering Indian Valley Campus, take the 2nd left to park in lot #2. From the parking lot, cross Ignacio Blvd, head left on the sidewalk 70 yds. and then take the trail right up into the parcourse.

0.2 Junction #1. Go left up through the beautiful rolling hills. Up ahead, the trail joins an old road and continues west. Look for a large, stately oak tree that is missing a major branch.

0.4 Saddle. Good views southwest to Big Rock Ridge. Head downhill, and at each Y bear right towards the open space gate.

0.6 Open space gate. Take the Ad Schwindt trail into open space, then make a moderately steep descent through a grove of bay trees.

0.8 Junction. The road right leads to stables. Bear left.

1.1 Junction. The trail joins a gravel road. Head left on the road.

1.2 Junction #2. Take the Buzzard Burn FR right down into a creek bed, then up the ridge. Up ahead, notice the large, old manzanita shrubs struggling for sun under the taller oaks. Many are dying out.

1.5 Hilltop. You can go left 100' to get a view out to the bay. Up ahead, more dying manzanita. This progression of vegetation from shorter shrubs to taller trees is sometimes called "natural succession."

1.9 Junction #3. The Wildcat trail ends here. Take the Hill Ranch trail left. The trail right climbs steeply up to private property and a road.

2.0 Junction #4. One hundred yds. after crossing the creek, the Alexander trail climbs steeply uphill. Continue to the left. **Option**: You can lengthen the hike by heading right to the Waterfall trail. This optional route has a very steep up and down section.

2.8 Bridge and junction #5. Head right on the Indian Valley FR.

3.2 Open space gate and junction. Continue straight.

3.4 Police station and IVC campus. Go past the circle and take the path along side the creek. **Option**: Tour the IVC campus.

3.7 Back at the parking area with no facilities.

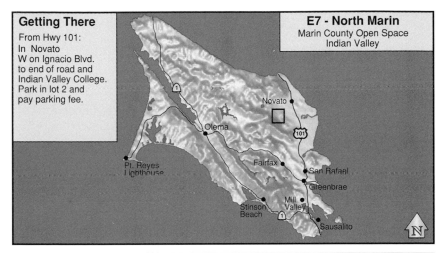

Getting There

From Hwy 101:
In Novato
W on Ignacio Blvd.
to end of road and
Indian Valley College.
Park in lot 2 and
pay parking fee.

E7 - North Marin
Marin County Open Space
Indian Valley

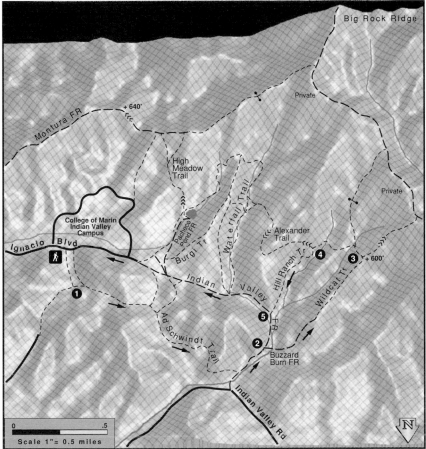

171

E8 Deer Island Loop Trail

Distance: 3.3 miles   Shaded: 50%
Elevation Change: 250'
Rating: Hiking - 7   Difficulty - 5   Moderately steep downhill.
When to Go: Good in winter for birds and spring for flowers.

This hike explores 135 acre Deer Island lying in a floodplain east of Novato. Good views in all directions. Good flowers in rainy years.

0.0 Park in the small parking area and go through the open space gate. Take the trail right for 30', then go left uphill. The trail starts out in open grassland with oaks dotting the low-lying hillside.

0.3 Ridgetop. Good views south and west. Big Rock Ridge at 1887' dominates the southwestern skyline.

0.7 Knoll and junction #1. A short, overgrown spur trail goes right. Take the main trail left downhill. The descent is moderately steep.

0.9 Junction #2. Keep right at a Y and follow the Deer Island Loop trail to the right. The large pond on the left stores treated effluent from the Novato Sanitary treatment plant and is used to irrigate pasturelands. The smaller pond was created to support wildlife.

1.2 Viewpoint #3. The view west of ponds, wetlands, creeks and shopping center represents a microcosm of the history of the bay. Deer Island was once a real island until the gold rush struck the Sierra and hydraulic mining washed million of tons of sediment into the bay, much of it deposited in the quieter areas of San Pablo Bay.

These shallow waters became mudflats and tidal marshes until 1890 when the railroad built a levee east of here. More dikes and fill turned some of the land into pasture, some into wetland. In 1990, more fill was added to create the Vintage Oaks shopping center due west.

2.1 Ranger residence and parking lot. The hike continues past the parking area to make a short loop that explores the eastern side of the island. Up ahead, the trail enters a small forest of dense, skinny bay trees. Watch out for poison oak crowding the trail.

2.4 Y-junction #4. Head left to drop down to the open road.

2.6 Fence and junction #5. The road veers inland to join the trail. Head right on the trail to loop back to the start. Look for some good displays of flowers here in spring, especially blue-eyed grass, buttercups and an unusually deep purple vetch.

3.3 Back at the parking area. No facilities.

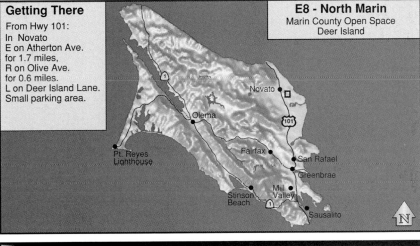

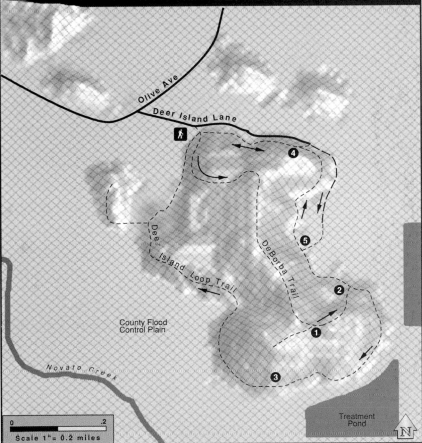

Getting There

From Hwy 101:
In Novato
E on Atherton Ave.
for 1.7 miles,
R on Olive Ave.
for 0.6 miles.
L on Deer Island Lane.
Small parking area.

E8 - North Marin
Marin County Open Space
Deer Island

Novato

Olema

Pt. Reyes
Lighthouse

Fairfax

San Rafael

Greenbrae

Stinson
Beach

Mill
Valley

Sausalito

Olive Ave

Deer Island Lane

4

Deer

Island Loop Trail

DeBorba Trail

5

2

1

County Flood
Control Plain

Novato Creek

3

Treatment
Pond

0   .2

Scale 1"= 0.2 miles

E9 Deer Camp - Big Trees Trails

Distance: 5.5 miles   Shaded: 60%
Elevation Change: 1300'   Horses likely.
Rating: Hiking - 8   Difficulty - 7   Steep in places.
When to Go: Good when cool, best when clear.

This hike climbs to one of the highest points in North Marin. It offers oaks, buckeyes and redwoods, and great views in all directions.

0.0 Park at the top of the hill just beyond the last house on Vineyard Rd. Head past the open space sign into grassland.

0.1 Junction #1 and gate. Go through the cow gate and take the Upper Meadow trail to the right. Continue on this trail as it skirts the hillside above the stables and enters a canyon shaded by redwoods.

Note: When the hillside is wet, this trail and the Deer Camp FR ahead can be muddy and very messy due to cow and horse hooves. Under these conditions, it may be best to stay on the Big Trees trail.

1.0 Junction #2. Take the Deer Camp FR left uphill. At the top of the canyon, bear left to follow the Deer Camp trail uphill.

1.5 Junction with Cut Off trail. Continue uphill on the Deer Camp trail.

2.2 Junction. Take the Big Trees trail right uphill.

2.7 Double junction #3. It's well worth exploring the surrounding area. Take the road right and head west uphill into a grove of redwoods.

2.8 Fence and gate. The open space ends at the fence. Backtrack 100' and take the narrow trail right onto a hilltop offering good views south. Look for an overgrown trail down towards junction #3.

2.9 Double junction #3. Continue to the Y in the road and head right to another viewpoint and small grove of redwoods. The largest tree in this grove is called Indian Tree or Ships' Mast. The tree has a secret compartment with a small opening on the north-facing side.

It may seem strange to find redwoods in the middle of hot, dry Novato. However, a look at the topographic map on page 6 shows that the canyon north of here drains to the ocean, thus gets foggy.

When done, backtrack down to the Y in the road and head right, on Indian Tree FR, which follows a fenceline down the ridge.

4.8 Paved road and house. Continue downhill, then take the trail.

5.2 Vineyard road. Head left on a small path along the road.

5.5 Back at the parking area with no facilities.

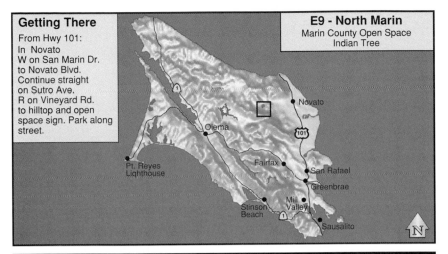

Getting There

From Hwy 101:
In Novato
W on San Marin Dr.
to Novato Blvd.
Continue straight
on Sutro Ave.
R on Vineyard Rd.
to hilltop and open
space sign. Park along
street.

E9 - North Marin
Marin County Open Space
Indian Tree

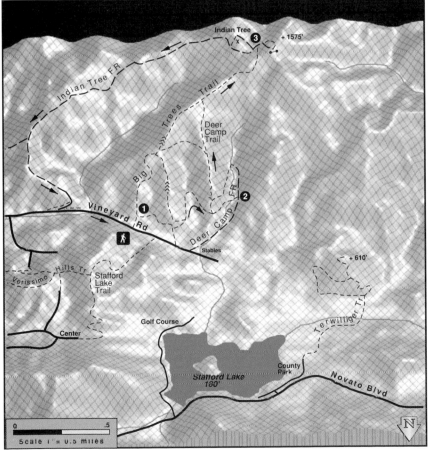

Scale 1" = 0.5 miles

E10 Stafford Lake County Park

Distance: 2.6 miles   Shaded: 30%
Elevation Change: 450'   Some poison oak crowds the trail.
Rating: Hiking - 8   Difficulty - 5
When to Go: Best in March and April for flowers and green hills.

Stafford Lake is a good place for a group or family hike followed by a picnic. The hike offers scenic views of the lake and local hills.

0.0 When you enter the park, ask for the nature trail handout at the toll booth, then head right. The hike begins at the far end of the parking area. Follow the trail sign that directs you down the paved path which circles a small pond. The hike starts out level on the signed Terwilliger trail heading west into pastureland.

0.3 Bridge and marsh. The hike crosses a marshy section of Novato creek. During the 1950s, water from this creek, stored in Stafford Lake, was the primary water source for Novato with enough water to supply about 15,000 people for a year. Now, Novato also requires Russian River water. The lake itself is owned by the North Marin Water District, while most of the park belongs to the County of Marin. Watch for redwing blackbirds among the tules.

0.4 Gate and junction #1. Head left to start the loop trail. Notice the moss-covered rocks on the hillside. Up ahead, yellow mimulus indicates that there is water here, seeping out of the hillside.

0.8 View. In wet years, abundant buttercups provide a yellow carpet on the green rolling hills. Recently, a half-dozen feral turkeys have made this area their new home.

1.3 Knoll. A bench on an interesting rocky knoll, provides views south to the lake and the surrounding hills.

1.4 Junction #2. Take the trail left uphill. Watch out for poison oak in the shady areas. Up ahead, it's a surprise to find redwoods. They need water in summer, usually provided by fog drip.

1.7 Hilltop and viewpoint. The tallest peak to the west is Black Mountain, which lies just east of Point Reyes Station. You can also see the bay by walking along the fence a few feet. This is the turnaround point. The hike continues back down the same trail.

1.9 Junction #2. Head left downhill on the loop trail.

2.2 Junction #1. Head left.

2.6 Back at the parking area with full picnic facilities.

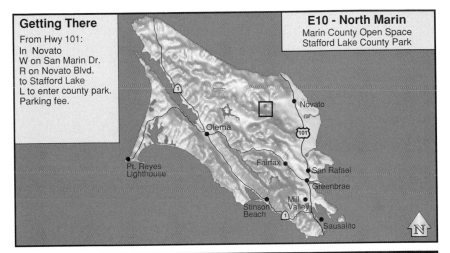

Getting There

From Hwy 101:
In Novato
W on San Marin Dr.
R on Novato Blvd.
to Stafford Lake
L to enter county park.
Parking fee.

Novato

Olema

Pt. Reyes
Lighthouse

Fairfax

San Rafael

Greenbrae

Stinson
Beach

Mill
Valley

Sausalito

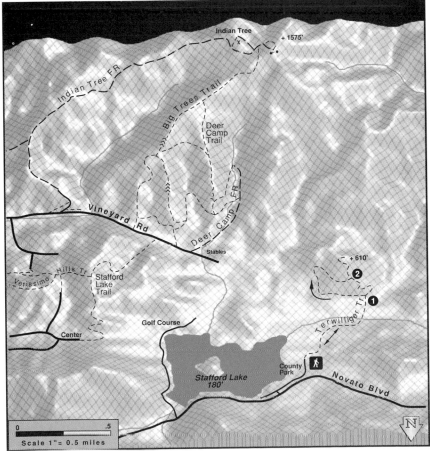

Indian Tree

+ 1575'

Indian Tree FR

Big Trees Trail

Deer
Camp
Trail

Deer Camp FR

Vineyard Rd

Stables

+ 610'

2

1

Verissimo

Hills Tr

Stafford
Lake
Trail

Terwilliger Tr

Golf Course

Center

County
Park

Novato Blvd

Stafford Lake
180'

0   .5

Scale 1" = 0.5 miles

177

E11 Fieldstone - Simmons Trails

Distance: 2.7 miles   Shaded: 40%
Elevation Change: 700'
Rating: Hiking - 7   Difficulty - 6   Moderately steep downhill.
When to Go: Good in late fall and winter, best in spring.

This hike climbs the south flank of Mt. Burdell into a fieldstone quarry. It offers great oaks, good views south and spring flowers.

0.0 Park at the end of Simmons Lane and go through the open space gate. Head right on the road, which starts out level. In April, look for blue dicks and purple vetch on the grassy hills.

0.2 Gate and street. Take Butterfield Drive for 100 yds., then go left on Fieldstone Drive.

0.3 Junction #1. Go through the open space gate and head uphill on the signed Fieldstone trail. Up ahead, the trail crosses a small wooden bridge, then zig-zags up the hill.

0.9 Junction. Although the trail right to the rock slide looks inviting, continue on the main trail. It offers a more interesting hike through the quarry. Up ahead, mosses, shrubs and oaks are slowly transforming the mining scars into a rock garden.

1.2 Junction #2. Take the road left.

1.3 Junction. Go through the gate and continue straight on the Middle Burdell FR. Five of California's nine species of tree oaks are found on Mt. Burdell. These include the coast live, valley, black, blue, and garry (or Oregon) oak. Coast live oak is the only evergreen oak on the list and dominates the rolling hills of Mt. Burdell. This abundance of oak trees

One of many oaks on Mt. Burdell

is one reason the Miwoks thrived at Olompali on the north side of the mountain. One large oak can provide hundreds of pounds of acorns.

1.7 Junction #3. Go through the gate and head left downhill.

2.0 Junction. Take the Salt Lick FR left. Good views south.

2.2 Junction #4. Take the road right, which drops down steeply.

2.5 Junction. Take the Simmons trail left down through the gate.

2.7 Back at the parking area. No facilities.

Getting There

From Hwy 101:
In Novato
W on San Marin Dr.
for 1.4 miles.
R on Simmons Ln.
Park at end of street.

E11 - North Marin
Marin County Open Space
Mt. Burdell

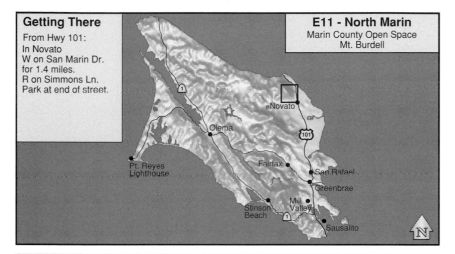

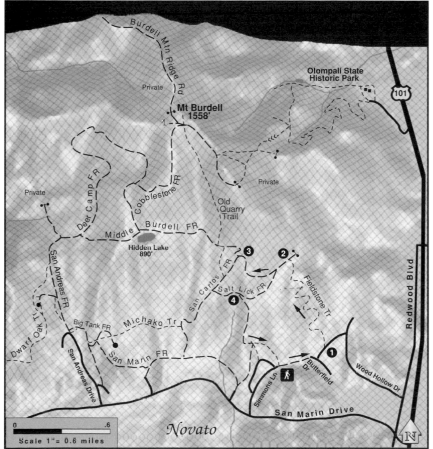

179

E12 West Flank of Mt. Burdell

Distance: 4.1 miles   Shaded: 20%
Elevation Change: 800'   Bicycles possible.
Rating: Hiking - 7   Difficulty - 5   Rocky in places.
When to Go: Best when the hills are green.

This hike explores the west flank of Mt. Burdell. It offers fine specimens of oak and buckeye trees. Good views south and west.

0.0 Park near the end of San Andreas Drive. Go through the open space gate and take the road uphill.

0.1 Junction. Take the trail left through the fence gate. The trail, shaded by magnificent oak trees, parallels the San Andreas FR.

0.2 Junction. Take the road left towards a water tank.

0.3 Junction and water tank. Continue past the junction and take the small trail to the left of the water tank.

0.4 Lookout point and junction #1. An open area provides good views down to Novato. Make a sharp right to take the Dwarf Oak trail back past the water tank. Watch out for poison oak.

0.6 Cowgate and junction. Take the San Andreas FR left to the north. See if you can spot 3-4 small birdhouses built for bluebirds.

0.8 Junction. Continue straight on the Middle Burdell FR.

0.9 Junction #2. Take the Deer Camp FR left. Up ahead, look for three grand old buckeye trees with gnarled, twisted trunks.

1.8 Slopes of Mt. Burdell. The smooth, grassy slopes of Mt. Burdell rise above the trail, providing a peaceful calm. Mt. Burdell was named after Dr. Galen Burdell, San Francisco's first dentist, who arrived during the gold rush in 1849. Later, he married Mary Black and the couple received Olompali ranch, 800 cattle and Mt. Burdell as a wedding present from the Black family. Parts of the Burdell adobe mansion can be seen at Olompali. See Hike E14.

2.5 Junction #3. This is the highest point of the hike at 1080'. Head right downhill. **Option:** The energetic hiker can continue to the top of the mountain by taking the road left, climbing 500' in 0.8 mile.

2.8 Junction and Hidden Lake. At one time, local residents used to come here to swim in the lake. Now, it has become a marsh. Head right towards the west. At the end of the lake, you can go through the fence gate and get to the marsh edge.

4.1 Back at the parking area. No facilities.

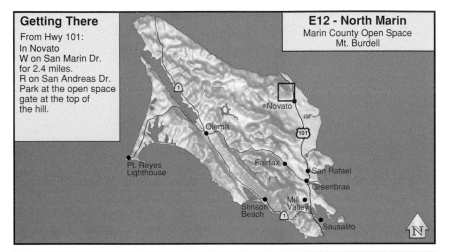

Getting There

From Hwy 101:
In Novato
W on San Marin Dr.
for 2.4 miles.
R on San Andreas Dr.
Park at the open space
gate at the top of
the hill.

E12 - North Marin
Marin County Open Space
Mt. Burdell

Novato
Olema
Pt. Reyes
Lighthouse
Fairfax
San Rafael
Greenbrae
Stinson
Beach
Mill
Valley
Sausalito

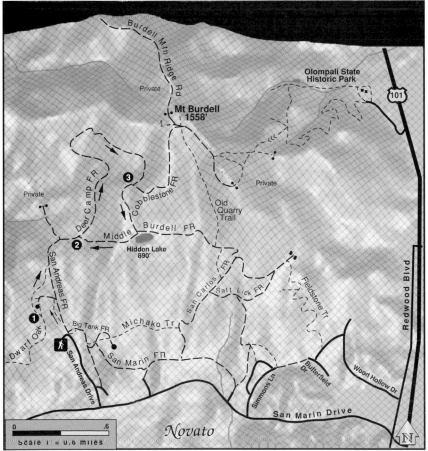

Burdell Mtn Ridge Rd

Olompali State
Historic Park

Private

Mt Burdell
1558'

Deer Camp FR

3

Cobblestone FR

Private

Private

Old
Quarry
Trail

Middle Burdell FR

2

Hidden Lake
890'

San Carlos FR

Salt Lick FR

Fieldstone Tr

San Andreas FR

1

Dwarf Oak

Big Tank FR

Michako Tr

San Marin FR

San Andreas Drive

Simmons Ln

Butterfield
Dr

Wood Hollow Dr

Redwood Blvd

San Marin Drive

Novato

0 .6
Scale 1" = 0.6 miles

181

E13 Old Quarry Trail to Mt. Burdell

Distance: 5.5 miles   Shaded: 10%
Elevation Change: 1400'   Bicycles possible.
Rating: Hiking - 8   Difficulty - 8   Steep and rocky in places.
When to Go: In spring when the hills are green. Dusty in fall.

This is the best hike for exploring Mt. Burdell. It offers magnificent oak trees, good wildflowers, great views and a visit to a rock quarry.

0.0 Park near the end of San Andreas Drive. Go through the open space gate and take the trail right, which starts out level and soon joins the Big Tank FR. Ahead, a trail parallels the road, which can be muddy when wet. In spring, look for a display of blue dicks.

0.4 Junction. Take the signed Michako trail left. Good views south.

0.9 Junction #1. Take the San Carlos FR left. Notice the large oaks.

1.3 Junction. Take the signed Old Quarry trail left towards the gate.

1.5 Junction #2. Take the road left 100' and then continue uphill on the Old Quarry trail, which climbs steeply into a large ravine.

Option: You can cut the hike short by 2.3 miles and save 700' of climbing by staying on Middle Burdell FR towards junction #5.

2.4 Junction #3. Head right on the Burdell Mtn. Ridge Rd. to explore the mountain top and enjoy some well-earned views.

2.6 Junction with dirt road. Continue on the Burdell Mtn. Ridge Rd.

2.7 Quarry, view and turnaround point. A small lookout point offers great views south and west. Opposite the viewpoint, a short, narrow spur trail leads 100' into a quarry, where cobblestones were mined to pave the streets of San Francisco in the 1870s. Return to junction #4.

2.8 Junction #4 and power pole. Take the dirt road right 200 yds. up past a rock wall and the Olompali State Park boundary. This hilltop offers good views east to the Petaluma River, the bay and Mt. Diablo.

3.0 Junction #3. Head right uphill on the trail. The rock walls were built in the 1870s by Chinese laborers who came here after completing work on the transcontinental railroad.

3.1 Mt. Burdell at 1558'. This is the highest point in north Marin.

3.2 Junction #3. Take the rocky Cobblestone FR downhill.

4.3 Junction and Hidden Lake. Head right on the Middle Burdell FR.

4.9 Junction #5. Take the San Andreas FR left.

5.5 Back at the parking area. No facilities.

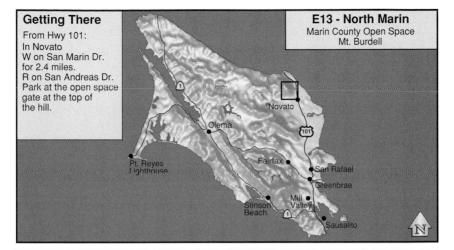

Getting There

From Hwy 101:
In Novato
W on San Marin Dr.
for 2.4 miles.
R on San Andreas Dr.
Park at the open space
gate at the top of
the hill.

E13 - North Marin
Marin County Open Space
Mt. Burdell

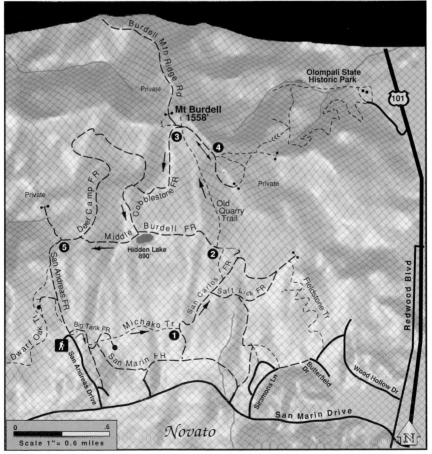

183

E14 Olompali State Park

Distance: 4.5 miles   Shaded: 70%
Elevation Change: 1600'   A less strenuous loop is possible.
Rating: Hiking - 9   Difficulty - 8   Steep upper half of the hike.
When to Go: Best in early March for wildflowers. Open 10am-6pm.

This hike on the north slopes of Mt. Burdell offers great views, spectacular wildflowers and a glimpse of California history.

0.0 From the parking area, go north towards the buildings. A signpost offers historical information describing Olompali, which was an important Miwok trading village for hundreds of years. The trail then passes by the remains of the Burdell mansion, which is enclosed in a structure to protect its adobe walls. The hike starts on a dirt road just north of the buildings and heads west towards the barn.

0.2 Junction #1 and barn. A sign marks the start of the Loop trail. Continue straight up the oak-bay covered hills. Ahead, the hike crosses a creek, then bears right at a Y in the road.

0.5 Fence and pond. Continue up the ravine.

0.6 Junction. The road right deadends. Continue left. Watch out for poison oak alongside the trail.

0.9 Bench and junction #2. Go straight past the bench and start a long, steep climb up the mountain. Look for lots of milkmaids and shooting stars in March. **Option**: You can cut the hike short by heading left on the loop trail.

1.3 Grassy slope, rock wall and two junctions #3. Bear left across the grassy slope and pass over the rock wall built by Chinese. Go right up to the asphalt road for a few yds., then take the trail right uphill.

1.6 Two junctions #4. Head left on the Burdell Mtn. Ridge Rd.

1.7 Rock quarry and view site. Opposite a splendid view, a short spur trail enters a quarry, where cobblestones were mined in the 1870s. Now head back on the Burdell Mtn. Ridge Rd.

2.0. Junction with Cobblestone Rd. Take the trail right uphill.

2.1 Mt. Burdell at 1558' and good views to the north. Retrace your steps all the way back to junction #2.

3.1 Bench and junction #2. Take the Loop trail right.

3.5 Wildflowers. These north-facing hills offer more great flowers, shooting star, milkmaids and buttercup.

4.5 Back at the parking lot. Restroom available.

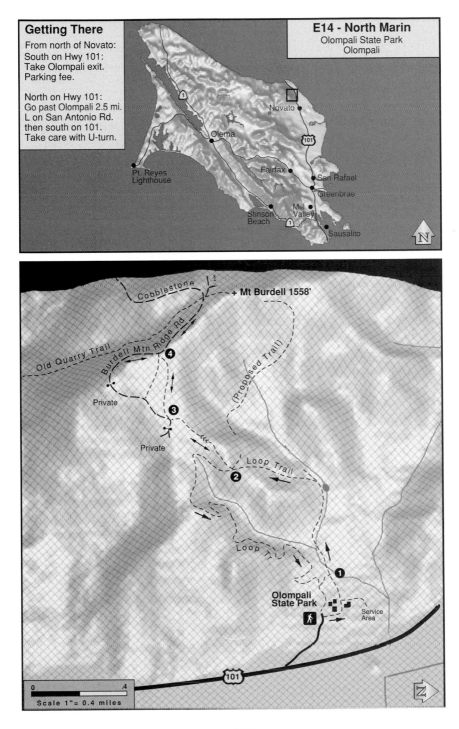

Getting There

From north of Novato:
South on Hwy 101:
Take Olompali exit.
Parking fee.

North on Hwy 101:
Go past Olompali 2.5 mi.
L on San Antonio Rd.
then south on 101.
Take care with U-turn.

E14 - North Marin
Olompali State Park
Olompali

Novato

1

101

Olema

Pt. Reyes
Lighthouse

Fairfax

San Rafael

Greenbrae

Stinson
Beach

Mill
Valley

Sausalito

1

N

Cobblestone

1

+ Mt Burdell 1558'

Old Quarry Trail

Burdell Mtn Ridge Rd

4

(Proposed Trail)

Private

3

Private

Loop Trail

2

Loop Tr

1

**Olompali
State Park**

Service
Area

0   .4

Scale 1" = 0.4 miles

101

N

185

F - Point Reyes South - 18 Hikes

Starting from Bear Valley at 105'
F1 ..... Bear Valley Interpretive Trails 0.6, 0.7 and 0.8
F2 ..... Bear Valley - Meadow - Horse Trails 6.1
F3 ..... Bear Valley - Old Pine - Mt. Wittenberg Trails 6.9
F4 ..... Bear Valley Trail to Arch Rock 8.2
F5 ..... Bear Valley - Mt. Wittenberg - Sky Trails 10.5
F6 ..... Bear Valley - Glen Camp Loop - Coast Trails 11.6
F7 ..... Bear Valley - Sky - Woodward Valley - Coast 11.6

Starting from Five Brooks at 240'
F8 ..... Five Brooks Trailhead to Bear Valley 4.6*
F9 ..... Olema Valley - Bolema - Stewart Trails 6.2
F10 ... Stewart - Greenpicker Trails 6.9
F11 ... Greenpicker - Glen - Coast - Stewart Trails 10.3

Starting from along Highway 1 in Olema Valley
F12 ... Randall - Olema Valley - Bolema - Ridge Trails 9.8
F13 ... Olema Valley Trailhead to Five Brooks 5.5*

Starting from Palomarin Trailhead at 260'
F14 ... PRBO and Palomarin Beach Trails 0.5 and 0.8
F15 ... Coast Trail to Double Point 8.0
F16 ... Ridge - Lake Ranch - Coast Trails 11.2
F17 ... Coast Trail to Wildcat Camp 11.6

Starting from Audubon Canyon Ranch at 30'
F18 ... Griffin Loop - Bird Overlook Trails 2.9

* Shuttle Hike

Pets are not allowed on any hikes.

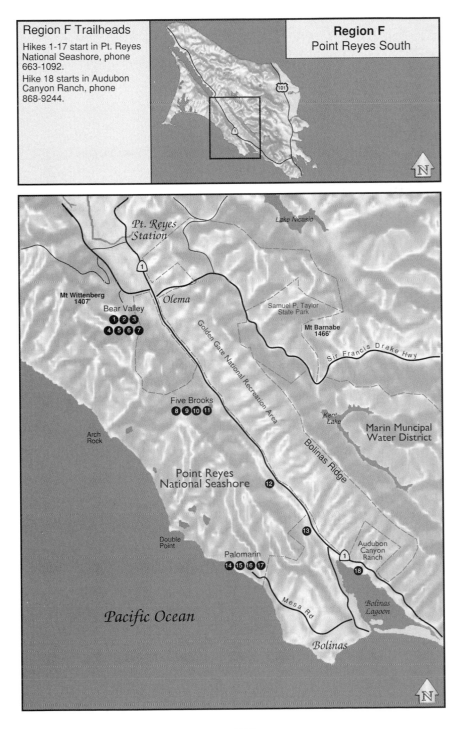

Region F Trailheads

Hikes 1-17 start in Pt. Reyes National Seashore, phone 663-1092.

Hike 18 starts in Audubon Canyon Ranch, phone 868-9244.

Pt. Reyes Station

Lake Nicasio

1

Mt Wittenberg
1407'

Bear Valley

Olema

Samuel P. Taylor
State Park

Mt Barnabe
1466'

Sir Francis Drake Hwy

Golden Gate National Recreation Area

Five Brooks

Kent
Lake

Arch
Rock

Marin Muncipal
Water District

Bolinas Ridge

Point Reyes
National Seashore

Double
Point

Palomarin

Audubon
Canyon
Ranch

1

Mesa Rd

Bolinas
Lagoon

Pacific Ocean

Bolinas

N

F1 Bear Valley Interpretive Trails

Distance: 0.6, 0.7 and 0.8 miles   Shaded: 70%
Elevation Change: No more than 150'
Rating: Hiking - 10   Difficulty - 2
When to Go: Excellent anytime, best in spring.

These three interpretive trails all have information signs explaining the geology, natural history, or Miwok culture.

Earthquake Trail - 0.6 miles and 100' Change

0.0 This trailhead is located east of the Visitor Center next to the picnic area. The trail is paved the entire way and wheelchair accessible. The trail has signs and exhibits explaining the great earthquake of 1906.

0.3 Earthquake motion. The Pacific plate jumped 20 feet northward relative to the North American plate as shown by the fence display.

0.6 Back at the trailhead next to the restroom.

*Acorn Woodpecker
Found on all
three hikes.*

Kule Loklo Trail - 0.7 miles and 50' Change

0.0 This trail starts about 100 yds. north of the Visitor Center and climbs slightly to a grove of eucalyptus. Notice the woodpecker holes drilled in dead snags for storing acorns .

0.3 Kule Loklo village. This reconstruction of a Coast Miwok village was started in 1976 and continues today. Cultural demonstrations, work parties and festivals are held here every year. Check with the Visitor Center for a schedule of events.

0.4 Restroom and junction. For a longer way back, you can bear right to pick up the Horse trail as it circles the pasture adding 0.5 miles to the hike. Otherwise, head left and retrace your steps.

0.7 Back at the trailhead north of the Visitor Center.

Morgan - Woodpecker Trails - 0.8 miles and 150' Change

0.0 Start at the main Bear Valley trailhead located at the south end of the parking lot. Take the Morgan trail east as it parallels the road up to the red buildings of the Morgan horse ranch.

0.1 Junction and museum. For an interesting side trip, you can tour the museum that explains the history and workings of the Morgan horse ranch. After that, head left and follow the Woodpecker trail as it skirts the meadow under a canopy of oaks and bays.

0.8 Bear Valley trailhead and Visitor Center.

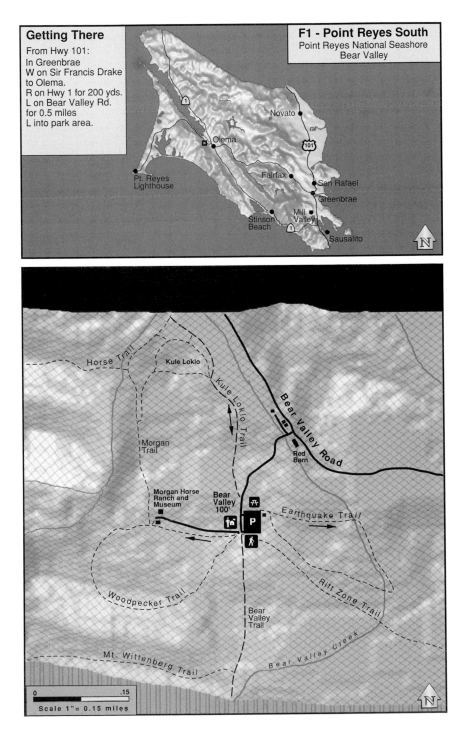

Getting There

From Hwy 101:
In Greenbrae
W on Sir Francis Drake
to Olema.
R on Hwy 1 for 200 yds.
L on Bear Valley Rd.
for 0.5 miles
L into park area.

F1 - Point Reyes South
Point Reyes National Seashore
Bear Valley

Novato

Olema

101

Pt. Reyes
Lighthouse

Fairfax

San Rafael

Greenbrae

Stinson
Beach

Mill
Valley

1

Sausalito

N

Horse Trail

Kule Loklo

Kule Loklo Trail

Bear Valley Road

Morgan
Trail

Red
Barn

Morgan Horse
Ranch and
Museum

Bear
Valley
100'

P

Earthquake Trail

Woodpecker Trail

Rift Zone Trail

Bear
Valley
Trail

Mt. Wittenberg Trail

Bear Valley Creek

0   .15

Scale 1"= 0.15 miles

N

189

F2 Bear Valley - Meadow - Horse Trails

Distance: 6.1 miles   Shaded: 70%
Elevation Change: 1300'   Can be dusty in fall.
Rating: Hiking - 9   Difficulty - 7   Steep in parts.
When to Go: Good anytime, best on clear days in spring.
This hike makes a round trip to the top of Mt. Wittenberg and back.
Great views when clear and good wildflowers in May and June.

0.0 Start at the Bear Valley trailhead south of the parking area.

0.8 Junction #1 with the Meadow trail. Cross the bridge to the right and notice the fallen bay tree straddling the creek. The bay, or California laurel, is very adaptable. It can grow in sun or shade and, when downed, often starts new shoots. Although there are occasional bay trees here, this is primarily a Douglas fir forest.

1.5 The meadow of the Meadow trail. On the right, you can see the deer-graze line about three feet up on the fir trees. At the north end of the meadow, a fir tree, loaded with cones, provides food for squirrels and seeds for new trees. Douglas fir seeds germinate and survive only when they root in mineral soil and receive direct sunlight. These conditions often occur following a fire. Deer, which are common here, munch new seedlings and help maintain the meadow.

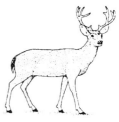

Mule Deer

The trail reenters the forest and circles a huge bowl-shaped canyon on the left. The understory is lush with huckleberry, sword fern, tanoak and elderberry.

2.3 Two junctions #2. Head right on the Mt. Wittenberg trail. At this point, the trail leaves the forest and enters an open hillside. Up ahead, the trail provides great views of Drakes Bay and the Point Reyes headlands.

2.7 Junction #3. Take the trail uphill to the top of Mt. Wittenberg for views of Olema Valley. After exploring the hilltop, return here.

3.1 Junction #3. Take the Z Ranch trail right.

3.8 Junction. Take the Horse trail right downhill.

5.6 Bridge and junction #4. Go left 100 yds., then right into Kule Loklo. Head for the large mound and the road through the eucalyptus.

6.1 Bear Valley trailhead. Water and restrooms.

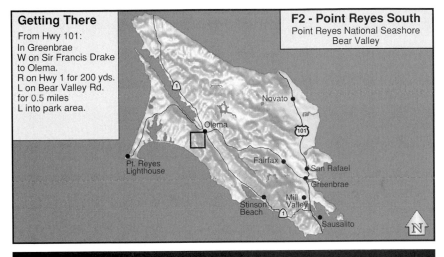

Getting There

From Hwy 101:
In Greenbrae
W on Sir Francis Drake
to Olema.
R on Hwy 1 for 200 yds.
L on Bear Valley Rd.
for 0.5 miles
L into park area.

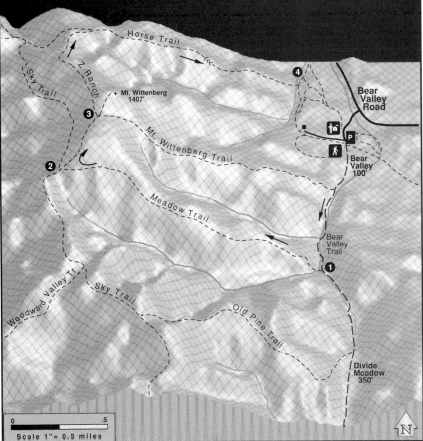

F3 Bear Valley - Old Pine - Mt. Wittenberg

Distance: 6.9 miles   Shaded: 80%
Elevation Change: 1300'
Rating: Hiking - 10   Difficulty - 7   Steep downhill.
When to Go: Excellent anytime, best from March to June.
This is the best and easiest hike to Inverness Ridge. It provides great views, forest vegetation, good berries and spring wildflowers.

0.0 Start at the Bear Valley trailhead at the south end of the parking area and head into the meadow. Most of the grasses are non-native, imported from Mediterranean countries to feed livestock.

1.0 About 300 yds. past the junction to the Meadow trail, just before starting uphill, there are two interesting plants growing along the left bank, trillium and wild ginger. Trillium has three symmetrical leaves and in late February and March, produces a beautiful flower with three white petals. Ginger has a dark-green, heart-shaped leaf, and from March to June produces deep-purple flowers that are hidden beneath the leaves.

Wild Ginger

1.6 Divide Meadow and junction #1. Take the Old Pine trail right, which provides the easiest climb to the crest of Inverness Ridge. Although called "Old Pine Trail", the trail passes through a magnificent Douglas fir forest.

2.5 Huckleberry lane. Winter rains and summer fog create a luxurious understory, dominated by tall huckleberry shrubs. The small black, edible berries are ripe for picking in August and September.

3.5 Junction #2 with the Sky trail. Head right, to the north.

3.8 Junction with the Woodward Valley trail. In spring, this verdant meadow, edged with firs offers a peaceful rest stop and picnic area.

4.5 Two junctions #3. The trail leaves the forest here; continue right on the Mt. Wittenberg trail.

4.9 Junction #4 with the Z Ranch trail. If the weather is clear, head uphill to Mt. Wittenberg for dramatic views. Good wildflowers in May.

5.1 Mt. Wittenberg, at 1407'. Often, you will see deer grazing the hillside to the south. Fifty years ago, the entire hilltop was grass. Now, Douglas fir trees are moving in.

5.3 Junction #4. Take the Mt. Wittenberg trail left downhill.

6.9 Back at the Bear Valley trailhead. Water and restrooms.

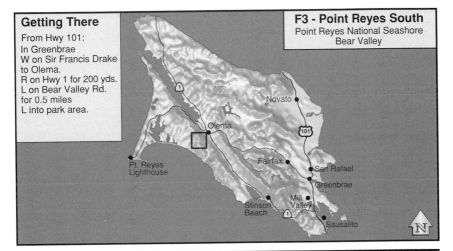

Getting There

From Hwy 101:
In Greenbrae
W on Sir Francis Drake
to Olema.
R on Hwy 1 for 200 yds.
L on Bear Valley Rd.
for 0.5 miles
L into park area.

F3 - Point Reyes South
Point Reyes National Seashore
Bear Valley

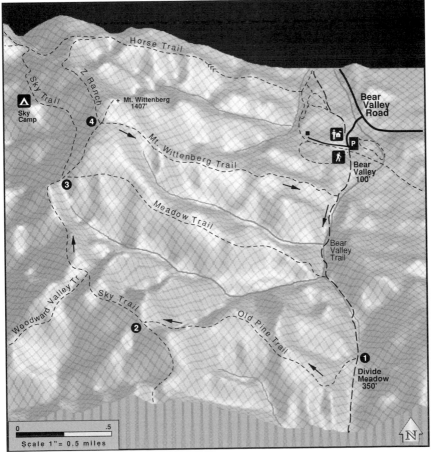

F4 Bear Valley Trail to Arch Rock

Distance: 8.2 miles   Shaded: 70%
Elevation Change: 400'   Bicycles allowed part way.
Rating: Hiking - 10   Difficulty - 3
When to Go: Excellent anytime. Best when the coast is clear. This is the most popular hike on Point Reyes. It is an out and back hike so you can turn around anytime. Great views at Arch Rock.

0.0 Start at the main trailhead south of the parking area.

1.6 Junction #1 at Divide Meadow. In the early 1890s, the Pacific Union Club of San Francisco built a sportsman's lodge here with 35 rooms, stables and kennels. The original plans included a golf course, tennis courts and swimming pool. Fortunately, the entire resort was never built. The lodge building deteriorated and was removed in 1950. You might be able to discover its location on the east side of the meadow hilltop. Look for amaryllis and other plantings nearby.

3.2 Junction #2 with the Glen and Baldy trails. Bicycles stop here. Continue towards the ocean.

Bear Valley Country Club c. 1895

4.0 Junction with the Coast trail. Head north along the Coast trail for 100 yds. and then take the trail to Arch Rock.

4.1 Arch Rock overlook with great views of the coast. To the south, you can see along Wildcat Beach to Double Point. To the north, you can see Drakes Bay and the Point Reyes headlands.

4.1 Side trip down near the beach. About 50' from the overlook, a short, well-used trail drops steeply down to Coast Creek and out to the beach and ocean. It is worth the trip down to glimpse the sea tunnel (the "arch" of Arch Rock) where the creek meets the ocean.

If conditions are right - low tide, calm ocean and low creek flow - the adventurous hiker can cross the creek and explore the small beach below Arch Rock. **Note**: Proceed with caution and at your own risk! This is not a park trail. The crossing can be slippery and dangerous. Also be aware of the tide. Do not get yourself trapped on the beach. When you are ready to return, retrace your steps.

8.2 Bear Valley trailhead and Visitor Center.

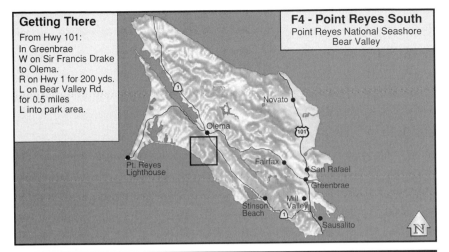

Getting There

From Hwy 101:
In Greenbrae
W on Sir Francis Drake
to Olema.
R on Hwy 1 for 200 yds.
L on Bear Valley Rd.
for 0.5 miles
L into park area.

F4 - Point Reyes South
Point Reyes National Seashore
Bear Valley

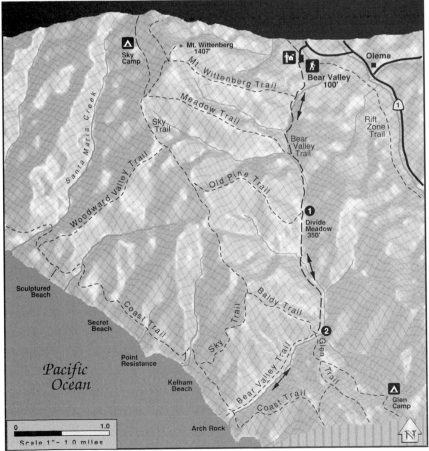

195

F5 Bear Valley - Mt. Wittenberg - Sky

Distance: 10.5 miles   Shaded: 60%
Elevation Change: 1500'   Some mud possible on the ridge.
Rating: Hiking - 9   Difficulty - 7   Steep in places.
When to Go: Excellent anytime, best in May.
This hike takes the steepest route to the Inverness Ridge and then follows the ridge to the coast. Great views and magnificent forests.

0.0 Start at the Bear Valley trailhead, south of the parking area.

0.2 Junction #1 with the Mt. Wittenberg trail, which is guarded by a large bay tree. Turn right and set a slow steady pace to climb the moderately steep trail to the ridge. Occasionally, in the open areas, stop and enjoy the views back east across Olema Valley.

1.6 Junction #2. The trail crests Inverness Ridge at 1250' offering spectacular views of Drakes Bay and the headlands with Sky Camp below in the foreground. For a side trip, you can climb to the top of Mt. Wittenberg. Otherwise, head left on the Mt. Wittenberg trail.

2.0 Two junctions. Head south on the Sky trail as it enters a dramatic Douglas fir forest kept refreshingly moist by winter rains and summer fog. The luxuriant understory is filled with ferns, elderberry, hedge nettle and huckleberry.

2.7 Junction #3 with the Woodward Valley trail. Continue south past this picturesque meadow edged with Douglas fir. Over the next half-mile, look for gooseberry, elderberry, huckleberry and thimbleberry.

Coyote Bush

4.4 Junction #4 with the Baldy trail. Continue straight. This area produces some of the densest stands of coyote bush on Point Reyes. Coyote bush, called "fuzzy wuzzy" because of the white fluff produced on the seeds of the female plant in early summer, dominates the coastal scrub community. Other plants in this "soft chaparral" community include coffeeberry, blackberry, poison oak and sword fern. This is a good place to find brush rabbits, wrentits and the white-crowned sparrow. Up ahead, the trail descends steeply towards the ocean.

5.6 Junction #5. Take the Coast trail left.

6.3 Junction #6. Head right to explore Arch Rock. (See Hike F4 for details.) The hike continues left on the Bear Valley trail.

10.5 Bear Valley trailhead with full facilities.

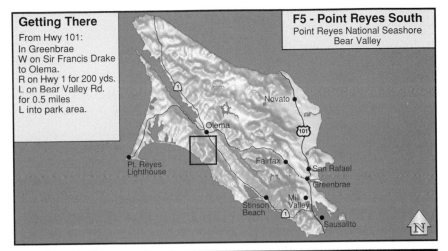

Getting There

From Hwy 101:
In Greenbrae
W on Sir Francis Drake
to Olema.
R on Hwy 1 for 200 yds.
L on Bear Valley Rd.
for 0.5 miles
L into park area.

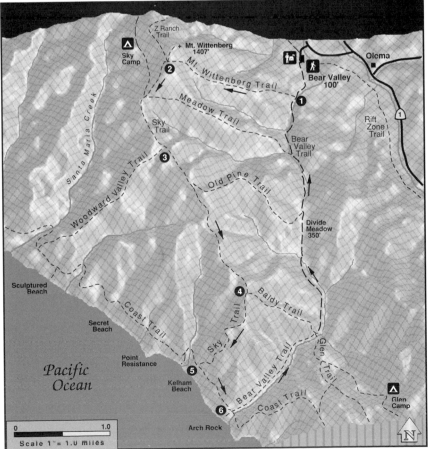

F6 Bear Valley - Glen Camp - Coast

Distance: 11.6 miles   Shaded: 70%
Elevation Change: 950'   Can be standing water when wet.
Rating: Hiking - 10   Difficulty - 6   Steep downhill.
When to Go: Excellent anytime, best when calm and clear.

This is one of the premier hikes on Point Reyes that includes a riparian corridor, lush forest, breathtaking views and spring flowers.

0.0 Start at the Bear Valley trailhead, south of the parking area.

0.5 Floods and alders. People still talk about the storm of 1982. Bear Valley was completely blocked by flood debris and over one-half of the trail was destroyed. One of the few remaining signs of the flood are groves of young red alders that seeded the following spring. In time, these alders will get much larger, once again shading the trail.

3.2 Junction #1 with Glen trail. Take the Glen trail across the creek and head uphill out of the lush riparian corridor of alder, elderberry, ferns and mosses and into firs, bays, hazelnut, and forget-me-nots.

3.7 Junction #2. Take the Glen Camp Loop trail left. **Option:** You can short-cut the hike by 0.7 miles by staying on the Glen trail.

4.6 Glen Camp with tables and water. This is the prettiest of the backpacking camps, nestled in a small meadow surrounded by oaks and firs. Look for iris under the oaks in spring. Campers will find lots of wildlife, especially at dusk. The trail continues from the west side of the meadow where it begins a moderately steep climb to the ridge.

5.3 Two junctions. Take the second right, the signed Coast/Glen spur trail west towards the ocean.

5.5 Junction #3 with Coast trail. Bear right. You may have to wade through one to two inches of water in winter time. The trail heads north across open coastal grasslands. Watch for deer.

6.0 Junction and seasonal pond. Continue left on the Coast trail.

6.3 Outcropping, wildflowers, picnic spot and viewpoint. As you look north along Drakes Bay, the largest prominence is Pt. Resistance. The trail begins a moderate descent. Down below and further west, look for a breathtaking view south towards Double Point.

7.4 Junction #4 with Arch Rock trail. Head left to explore Arch Rock.

7.5 Arch Rock. (See Hike F4 for details on getting to the beach.) To return, follow the signs back along the Bear Valley trail.

11.6 Bear Valley trailhead and Visitor Center.

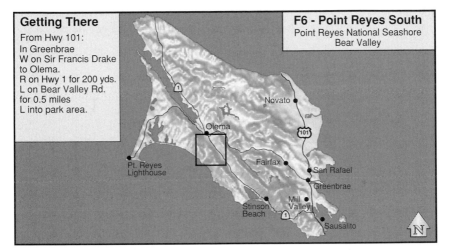

Getting There

From Hwy 101:
In Greenbrae
W on Sir Francis Drake
to Olema.
R on Hwy 1 for 200 yds.
L on Bear Valley Rd.
for 0.5 miles
L into park area.

F6 - Point Reyes South

Point Reyes National Seashore
Bear Valley

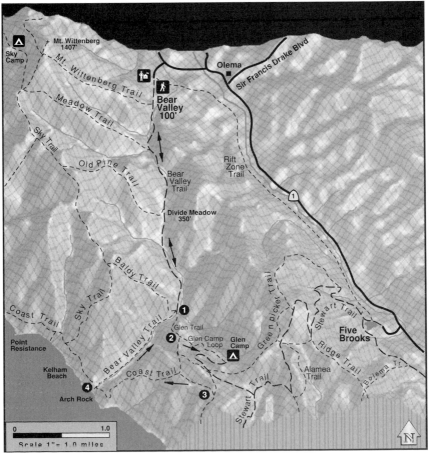

199

F7 Bear Valley - Sky - Woodward Valley

Distance: 11.6 miles   Shaded: 60%
Elevation Change: 1700'   Can be overgrown. Can be windy.
Rating: Hiking - 10   Difficulty - 7   Steep in places.
When to Go: Excellent anytime, best when clear and calm.
This hike has it all! Meadows, forests, creeks, beaches, rolling hills, wildflowers and panoramic views all await the vigorous hiker.

0.0 Start at the Bear Valley trailhead at the south end of the parking area. Look for deer in the meadow, especially in the early morning.

0.2 Junction #1 with the Mt. Wittenberg trail. Head right and start a moderately steep climb under tanoak and Douglas fir.

1.6 Junction #2. The trail crests Inverness Ridge offering dramatic views over Sky Camp to Drakes Bay and the headlands. If the weather is clear, you can take a short side trip and climb 300' to the top of Mt. Wittenberg. Otherwise, head left on the Mt. Wittenberg trail.

2.0 Two junctions. Head south on the Sky trail as it enters a dense Douglas fir forest. In the understory, lush, light-green elderberry presents a striking contrast to the tall, dark fir canopy.

2.7 Junction #3 with Woodward Valley trail. Turn right and head west to follow the trail as it rolls downhill through meadow, forest and open coastal ridges. Tall grass crowds the trail in summer.

3.7 Ocean views. The trail levels off along a rocky outcrop above the ocean. This scenic viewpoint offers a panoramic sweep from the Point Reyes headlands to Double Point.

4.5 Junction #4 with Coast trail. Bear left and head south.

6.5 Kelham Beach access trail. Continue south on the Coast trail. **Option:** In the summer and fall, at tides below plus one foot, the adventurous hiker can walk along Kelham Beach and take the sea tunnel up to Arch Rock. (See Hike F4 for more details).

7.4 Junction #5 with Arch Rock trail. Head right.

7.5 Arch Rock. (See Hike F4 for exploring Arch Rock.) To complete the hike, follow the Bear Valley trail inland as it parallels the creek.

7.7 Buckeye trees. Two large, gnarled buckeyes with twisted trunks stand guard along the right of the trail. Buckeyes produce fragrant flowers in late spring, then soon after, in early summer, begin losing their leaves. The nut is large, brown and shiny like a buck's eye.

11.6 Bear Valley trailhead. Visitor Center, water and restrooms.

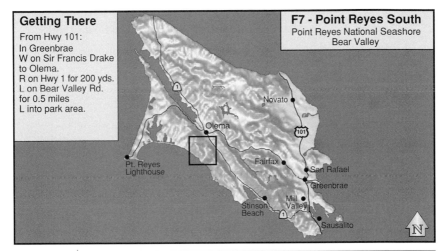

Getting There

From Hwy 101:
In Greenbrae
W on Sir Francis Drake
to Olema.
R on Hwy 1 for 200 yds.
L on Bear Valley Rd.
for 0.5 miles
L into park area.

F7 - Point Reyes South

Point Reyes National Seashore
Bear Valley

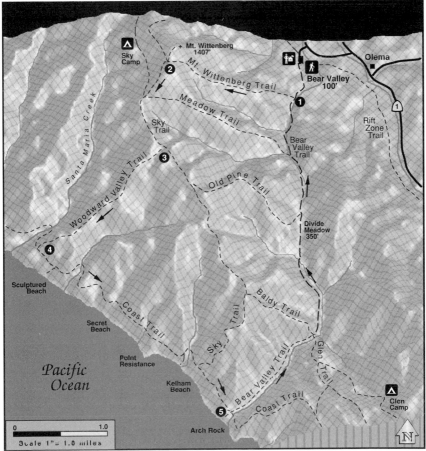

F8 Five Brooks Trailhead to Bear Valley*

Distance: 4.6 miles   Shaded: 40%
Elevation Change: 200'   Trail can be muddy or dusty.
Rating: Hiking - 8   Difficulty - 3
When to Go: Best in winter and spring, but not when real wet.
This one-way hike explores the terrain of the San Andreas rift zone. Vegetation includes forest, meadow, pasture and wildflowers.

*Shuttle Hike. Leave pickup cars at Bear Valley and shuttle all hikers to the Five Brooks parking area and trailhead.

0.0 Go through the gate and head west towards Inverness Ridge.

0.1 Junction. Continue past the Rift Zone trail.

0.2 Junction #1. Take the Stewart trail right towards the north.

0.3 Junction. Go through the metal gate and head downhill towards the Rift Zone trail. California hazelnut dominates the understory here. At the bottom of the hill continue straight through a 4-way junction to a meadow, then head left to cross the creek.

0.4 Creek. At the creek, take the signed Rift Zone trail left.

1.4 Private property. A sign indicates that the trail is now crossing land owned by the Vedanta Society, a religious retreat organization.

3.1 Junction #2. Go through the gate, head right 100' and then left across the pasture. Up ahead, look for a glimpse of the Vedanta retreat house about one-half mile on your left. This magnificent old Victorian, called "The Oaks", was solidly built out of redwood by James Shafter in 1869 and easily survived the 1906 earthquake. James Shafter, and his brother, Oscar, two lawyers from Vermont, at one time owned most of the Point Reyes peninsula.

The Oaks c. 1920s

4.0 Road. The hike passes through two gates and crosses the main road to the Vedanta house. The area before the gates can be very muddy if cows have churned up the soil. After passing through the second gate, the trail skirts a marshy area, climbs a knoll, then drops into a meadow leading to Bear Valley.

4.6 Bear Valley trailhead with full facilities.

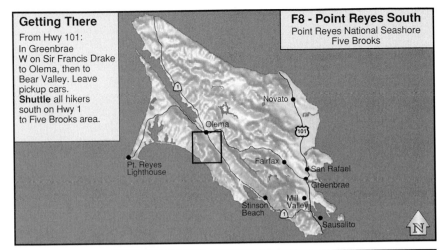

Getting There

From Hwy 101:
In Greenbrae
W on Sir Francis Drake
to Olema, then to
Bear Valley. Leave
pickup cars.
Shuttle all hikers
south on Hwy 1
to Five Brooks area.

F8 - Point Reyes South
Point Reyes National Seashore
Five Brooks

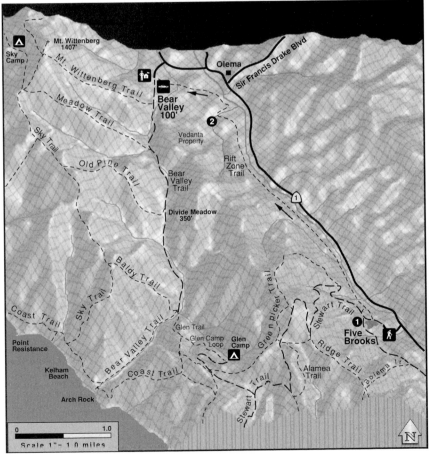

F9 Olema Valley - Bolema - Stewart

Distance: 6.2 miles   Shaded: 90%
Elevation Change: 1100'   Bicycles possible.
Rating: Hiking - 9   Difficulty - 5   Can be dusty or muddy.
When to Go: Best in spring, good anytime.

This hike makes a loop around the eastern side of Inverness Ridge through a dense Douglas fir forest.

0.0 Start at the Five Brooks trailhead and take the main trail northwest past the old logging pond towards Inverness Ridge.

0.2 Junction #1. Take the Olema Valley trail left around the pond 100 yds., then bear right at the second junction. The trail heads south through an enchanting forest of Douglas fir, bay and alder with a dense understory of ferns, hazelnut, ginger, nettles and blackberry.

Up ahead, the trail crosses a bridge, then starts a moderately steep climb in more open forest.

1.4 Junction #2. Head right on the Bolema trail and continue to climb. Farther up the trail, you'll see the first stand of Monterey pines that were seeded after logging operations in the late 1950s.

2.5 Junction #3, and the highest point of the hike at 1180'. Head right on the Ridge trail. Occasionally, you get glimpses west to the ocean.

3.1 Forest and berries. The trail enters a dark Douglas fir forest with lots of huckleberries that ripen from July through September. The forest is often damp in the summertime due to heavy fog drip.

3.2 Junction #4. The Ridge trail goes left. Continue straight here and right at the next junction 100 yds. ahead.

3.3 Junction. Take the Stewart trail downhill to the right. The old roadbed was once paved and wide enough for two lanes of traffic. Watch for an occasional large, old-growth Douglas fir on the edge of the roadbed. These trees were left by loggers to support the road and to provide seeds for future trees.

5.2 Junction #5 with the Greenpicker trail. Continue downhill. Up ahead, the trail makes a large hairpin turn in a steep canyon and creek. Look for five-finger ferns along the bank. In June, an aralia with large 12" leaves, and even larger flower stalks, blooms along the moist banks.

6.0 Junction #1 and mill pond. Head left.

6.2 Trailhead with picnic tables, water and restrooms.

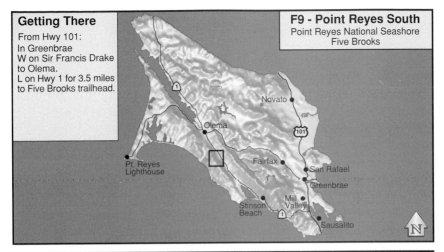

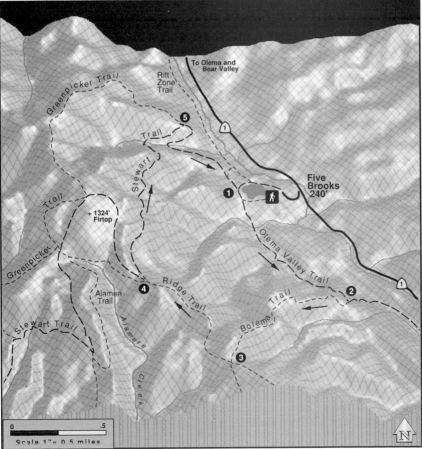

F10 Stewart - Greenpicker Trails

Distance: 6.9 miles   Shaded: 90%
Elevation Change: 1300'   Dusty when dry. Bicycles possible.
Rating: Hiking - 7   Difficulty - 7   Moderately steep in places.
When to Go: Good anytime, best in February and March.

This hike stays entirely in a scenic Douglas fir forest as it climbs the eastern slopes of Inverness Ridge.

0.0 Start at the Five Brooks parking area and head northwest through the gate. Circle the pond surrounded by willows and alders.

0.2 Junction #1 with the Olema Valley and Stewart trails. Head right and follow the signs to Firtop. The Stewart trail is really a wide road that makes a moderate climb through a Douglas fir forest with occasional bay, alder and tanoak. Ferns and elderberry dominate the understory.

0.7 Hairpin turn. Just past the turn, look for four different ferns on the steep bank - lady fern, sword fern, five-finger fern and chain fern.

Five-finger Fern

1.0 Junction with the Greenpicker trail. Continue left towards Firtop. Up ahead, you'll find stumps of Douglas fir, remnants of the logging operations that ended in the early 1960s.

2.9 Junction #2 with the Ridge trail. Continue on the Stewart trail.

3.7 Junction and Firtop at 1324'. The small meadow at Firtop is surrounded by firs, blocking what were once magnificent views. You can cut the hike short by returning on the Greenpicker trail. Otherwise, continue across the meadow and head downhill.

4.0 Two junctions #3. Go right about 100' on the Ridge trail and pick up the Greenpicker trail to head back towards Five Brooks. The trail first makes a moderate descent for 0.2 miles, then climbs steeply through a very dense forest back up to Firtop.

4.4 Junction #4 with the spur trail to Stewart trail. Continue left on the Greenpicker trail. This part of the hike borders the private property of the Vedanta Society. Up ahead, the terrain becomes more difficult and leaves the road to enter an old growth forest with lots of huckleberries and sword ferns.

5.9 Junction. Head left, downhill on the Stewart trail.

6.9 Five Brooks trailhead with water and restrooms.

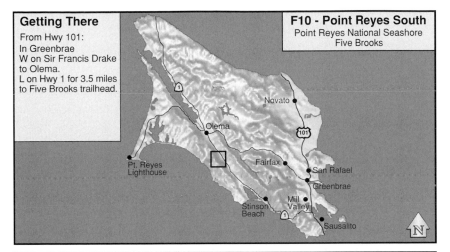

Getting There

From Hwy 101:
In Greenbrae
W on Sir Francis Drake
to Olema.
L on Hwy 1 for 3.5 miles
to Five Brooks trailhead.

F10 - Point Reyes South

Point Reyes National Seashore
Five Brooks

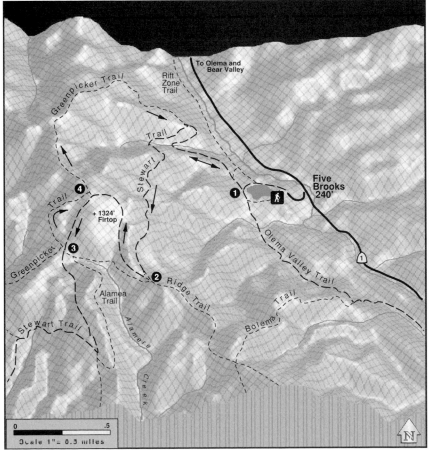

F11 Greenpicker - Coast - Stewart Trails

Distance: 10.3 miles   Shaded: 70%
Elevation Change: 1600'   Bicycles possible on Stewart trail.
Rating: Hiking - 8   Difficulty - 6   Poison oak may crowd trail.
When to Go: Good anytime, best when clear.

This is a rugged hike that makes a moderately steep climb through dense forest, then provides dramatic views along the coast.

0.0 Start at the Five Brooks parking area and circle the pond bordered by willows and alders. Look for ducks and turtles.

0.2 Junction #1. Head right on the Stewart trail.

1.0 Junction #2. Take the Greenpicker trail right as it heads uphill, then skirts the private Vedanta property. The trail climbs through rugged terrain that supports a luxuriant Douglas fir forest. The tall canopy allows light for a dense growth of ferns and huckleberry.

2.5 Junction with the Stewart trail and Firtop at 1324'. A spur trail leads left to the meadow at Firtop. Continue on the Greenpicker trail.

2.8 Junction #3 with Ridge and Stewart trails. Continue on the Greenpicker trail as it goes right downhill.

3.8 Junction #4 with Glen trail. Go left up the road.

3.9 Two junctions. Take the second right, the Coast Spur trail.

4.1 Junction with Coast trail. Head left. Watch out for poison oak.

4.4 Wildcat Camp overlook. Here is one of the premier viewing spots on Point Reyes. The wild-looking, jumbled hills from Wildcat Camp to Bass Lake are mostly the result of massive landslides. See if you can spot evidence of old scarps, large cuts and slides on the western slopes of Inverness Ridge.

5.0 Junction #5 with the Stewart trail. Bear left. **Option**: Head right for 0.7 miles for a side trip to Wildcat Camp and the beach.

5.5 Junction with Glen trail. Stay right on the Stewart trail.

5.8 Two uncommon shrubs. Just 20' past an exposed cliff, look for a white ceanothus, which flowers in May and below it, a silk tassel shrub, with hanging catkins. Both plants are seldom seen on Point Reyes. Continue on the Stewart trail.

6.7 Junction #3. Take the Ridge trail right to circle Firtop.

7.3 Junction #6. Head left 200' to pick up the Stewart trail.

10.3 Five Brooks trailhead with water and restrooms.

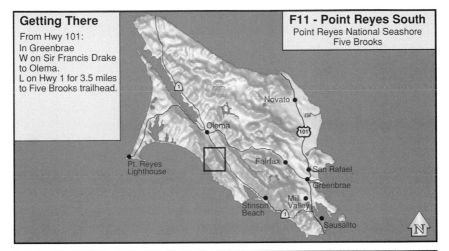

Getting There

From Hwy 101:
In Greenbrae
W on Sir Francis Drake
to Olema.
L on Hwy 1 for 3.5 miles
to Five Brooks trailhead.

F11 - Point Reyes South
Point Reyes National Seashore
Five Brooks

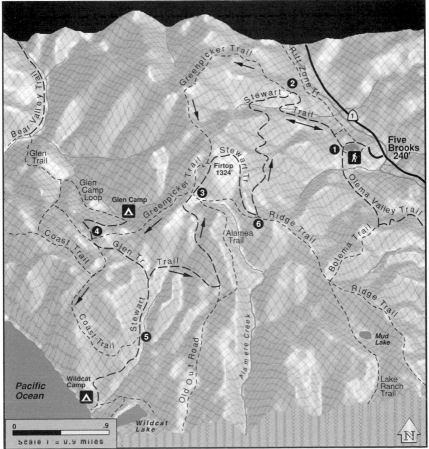

F12 Randall - Olema Valley - Bolema

Distance: 9.8 miles   Shaded: 70%
Elevation Change: 1200'   Trail may be closed. See Note.
Rating: Hiking - 7   Difficulty - 8   Steep and rutted in places.
When to Go: Best in April and May after the ground dries a bit.
This loop hike follows the earthquake terrain of Olema Valley, then climbs the heavily forested Inverness Ridge.

Note: The Teixeira trail can be steep with exposed roots and deep ruts. It has often been closed. Check with the Visitor Center before going. Also, see the note for Hike F13 about the Olema Valley trail.

0.0 Start at the Randall trailhead located near mile marker 20.53 on Highway 1. Take the Randall Spur trail west along a bank of willows heading towards Inverness Ridge. Look for warblers in the willows.

0.4 Junction #1. Head right on the Olema Valley trail and start a gentle climb through a mixture of open grassland and oak, bay, and fir trees. The trail can be muddy or dusty depending on the season.

Occasionally, look back to view the jumbled topography of the San Andreas rift zone. It is estimated that the Inverness Ridge to the west is moving 1.3" per year relative to the Bolinas Ridge to the east. This motion adds up to more than 1000' over the last 10,000 years.

1.7 Junction #2 with the Bolema trail. Head left to climb the old ranch road towards the ridge. This is mostly Douglas fir forest with ferns, hazelnut, hedge nettle and thimbleberries in the understory.

2.8 Junction #3. Take the Ridge trail left and head south on the ridge.

3.1 Tree stumps and succession. Clearcut logging along the ridge in the late 1950s opened the way for manzanita to establish itself. Now, the second generation firs have formed a dense canopy shading out the manzanita and causing dieback.

5.3 Junction #4. Take the Teixeira trail left. Watch for stinging nettles.

6.0 Junction with the Pablo Point trail. Continue downhill on the Teixeira trail. Ahead, trail conditions deteriorate as horses and water have created deep ruts with exposed roots and jagged rocks.

7.1 Junction #5. The trail crosses a bog right before the junction. (A bypass trail can be taken around the bog 0.1 mile before the junction.) Head left on the Olema Valley trail through an open meadow.

9.4 Junction. Take the Randall Spur trail east.

9.8 Back at the trailhead. If grass crowded the trail, check for ticks.

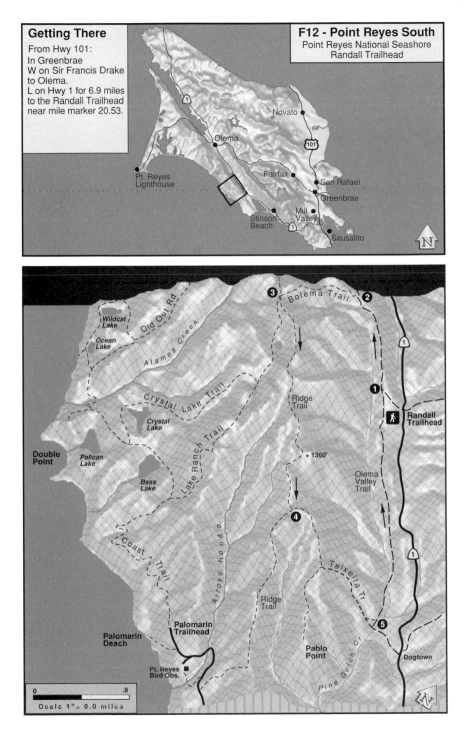

Getting There
From Hwy 101:
In Greenbrae
W on Sir Francis Drake
to Olema.
L on Hwy 1 for 6.9 miles
to the Randall Trailhead
near mile marker 20.53.

F12 - Point Reyes South
Point Reyes National Seashore
Randall Trailhead

Novato

Olema

Pt. Reyes
Lighthouse

Fairfax

San Rafael

Greenbrae

Stinson
Beach

Mill
Valley

Sausalito

Wildcat
Lake

Old Out Rd

Ocean
Lake

Alamea Creek

Bolema Trail

Crystal Lake Trail

Crystal
Lake

Ridge
Trail

Randall
Trailhead

Double
Point

Pelican
Lake

Lake Ranch Trail

+ 1360'

Olema
Valley
Trail

Bass
Lake

Coast Trail

Arroyo Hondo

Palomarin
Beach

Palomarin
Trailhead

Ridge
Trail

Teixeira Tr

Pablo
Point

Pine Gulch Cr

Dogtown

Pt. Reyes
Bird Obs.

0   .8

Scale 1" = 0.0 miles

F13 Olema Valley to Five Brooks*

Distance: 5.5 miles   Shaded: 30%
Elevation Change: 600'   Trail can be impassable. Poison oak.
Rating: Hiking - 9   Difficulty - 8   Moderately steep.
When to Go: Excellent anytime, best when the hills are green.

This one-way hike meanders, like the local creeks, through a mixture of vegetation along the San Andreas fault zone.

*Shuttle Hike. Leave pickup cars at Five Brooks and shuttle all hikers to the Olema Valley trailhead at mile marker 18.17, north of Dogtown.

Note: The trail passes through a marshy area that can have 1-3" of standing water in winter and spring. Also, there are many deep holes along the trail created by horses' hooves sinking into soft mud. Within the first mile, the trail crosses two creeks that can be 3-6" deep during wet weather (more if raining). Rocks can make the crossing easier.

0.0 The trail starts in a meadow and heads northwest with good views to Inverness Ridge to the west.

0.4 Junction #1 with the Teixeira trail. Continue north through the marsh area, past grasses and tall, deadly nightshade.

0.8 Creek crossings. The trail crosses Pine Gulch Creek which follows an old faultline on its way to Bolinas Lagoon.

1.6 Earthquake country. Rolling hills, sag ponds, small scarps (slides) and slumps provide topographic evidence of the thousands of earthquakes that have formed the Olema Valley rift zone.

This variety of terrain supports a variety of vegetation. Alders line the creeks. Douglas fir and bay trees compete for light along the moist hillsides. Meadows, dotted with coyote bush and coffeeberry, offer good views to the surrounding hills.

2.7 Junction #2 with a spur trail to the highway and the Randall trail. Continue north. If the trail is damp, look for animal tracks.

4.0 Junction #3 with the Bolema trail. This is the highest point on the hike at 700'. Bear right and start a moderately steep descent through dense cover of Douglas fir with ferns, hazelnut, vines and nettles.

4.8 Small bridge. Up ahead, the creek widens into a broad, flat streambed shaded by a thicket of alders and bays.

5.2 Junction. The trail right heads to the stables. Continue left.

5.3 Junction #4. Bear right to skirt the lake back to the trailhead.

5.5 Five Brooks trailhead. Pickup cars, tables, water and restrooms.

Getting There
From Hwy 101:
In Greenbrae
W on Sir Francis Drake
to Olema.
L on Hwy 1 for 3.5 miles
to Five Brooks.
Shuttle hikers 5.8 miles
to the Olema Valley
trailhead near
mile marker 18.17.

F13 - Point Reyes South
Point Reyes National Seashore
Olema Valley Trailhead

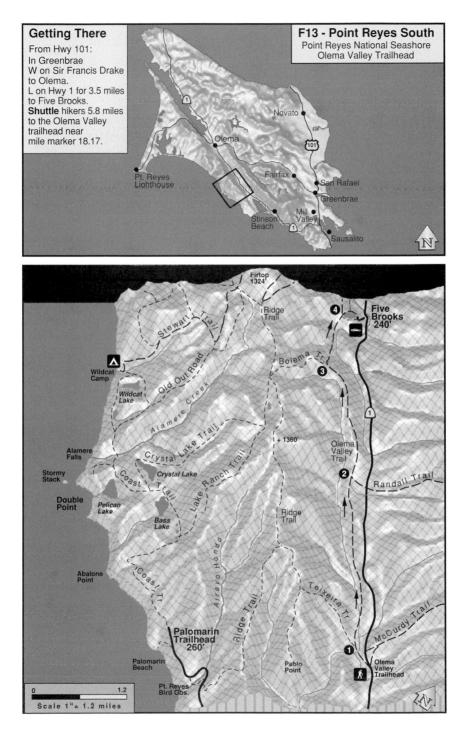

213

F14 PRBO and Palomarin Beach Trails

Distance: 0.5 and 0.8 miles   Shaded: 60% and 10%
Elevation Change: 250' for the Palomarin Beach trail.
Rating: Hiking - 10   Difficulty - 5   Both moderately steep.
When to Go: Excellent anytime, beach trail best at low tide.

The Point Reyes Bird Observatory Nature trail explores a magnificent small canyon with dense growth. The beach trail leads to tidepools.

Point Reyes Bird Observatory Nature Trail - 0.5 miles and 50'

Note: A pamphlet is available at the PRBO Visitor Center.

0.0 Start at the PRBO parking lot and take the nature trail south past coyote bush and wind-pruned fir trees. At 100 yds., notice the tough, scrub oak trees growing close to the ground.

Up ahead, the trail heads steeply down into Fern Canyon guarded by twisted buckeye trees covered with old man's beard, a grey-green lichen hanging in the branches. This little canyon provides a rain forest habitat of robust flora and noisy birds. Look for several kinds of ferns and berries - sword fern, five-finger fern, chain fern, blackberries and thimbleberries - under a canopy of buckeye trees.

0.1 The trail crosses the creek and climbs out the other side. A multi-trunked buckeye stands over patches of Solomon's seal.

Continue across the bluff to a 4-way junction marked by three posts on your left. If the trail is not overgrown with blackberries and thimbleberries, head left through the posts to the road. Otherwise retrace your steps.

0.2 Road. Go left past the exposed shale cliffs.

0.5 Entrance to PRBO.

Palomarin Beach Trail - 0.8 miles and 250' Change

0.0 Start at the trailhead 0.3 miles north of the Point Reyes Bird Observatory. Follow the trail as it heads down past eucalyptus, sage and coastal scrub towards the beach. Look for wildflowers in spring. Up ahead, a sign cautions visitors to watch for slippery rocks and large waves. This spot also offers great views south down the coast and northwest across Drakes Bay to the Point Reyes headlands.

0.3 Hollow. The trail skirts the edge of a wet hollow, then drops down to the beach.

0.4 Beach. You can explore in both directions from here.

0.8 Parking area.

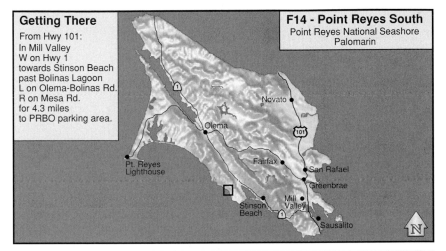

Getting There

From Hwy 101:
In Mill Valley
W on Hwy 1
towards Stinson Beach
past Bolinas Lagoon
L on Olema-Bolinas Rd.
R on Mesa Rd.
for 4.3 miles
to PRBO parking area.

F14 - Point Reyes South
Point Reyes National Seashore
Palomarin

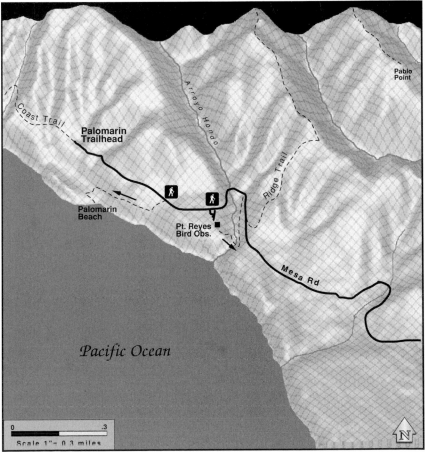

F15 Coast Trail to Double Point

Distance: 8.0 miles   Shaded: 20%
Elevation Change: 1000'   Poison oak crowds trail in places.
Rating: Hiking - 9   Difficulty - 6   Trail rutted. Steep cliffs.
When to Go: Excellent anytime, best from December to July.

Double Point provides one of the best view spots on the west coast. In season, look for whales, seals and wildflowers. Can be windy.

0.0 Start at 260' at the Palomarin parking area. Take the dirt road up towards the eucalyptus grove. In spring, look for lupine, cow parsnip, Indian paintbrush, iris, wild cucumber and poppies.

2.0 Small pass. After heading inland into a large ravine, the trail makes a long climb up through a narrow rocky pass at 580'. These outcroppings of chert, shale and sandstone are marine deposits, part of a sedimentary layer that covers most of the southern seashore.

2.2 Junction #1 with the Lake Ranch Trail. Continue left.

2.7 Bass Lake. The first glimpse through the willows and coyote bush provides an enticing view of this lovely lake.

2.8 Unmarked junction. A spur trail left explores the lake shoreline. On warm days, you'll often find picnickers and swimmers here. The hike continues uphill into a small fir forest where ferns, ceanothus and coffeeberry offer a nice change of pace from the open hillsides.

3.3 Pelican Lake. Across the lake, a small notch between Double Point allows overflow in wet years. Pelican Lake and the lakes in this area were formed by landslides that blocked normal drainage.

3.6 Two junctions #2 (see map - inset). At the first junction at the north end of the lake, take the spur trail left. **Note:** At the second junction 150' beyond, another spur trail goes left 0.5 miles to the top of Alamere Falls. This trail is unmaintained and may be overgrown with poison oak.

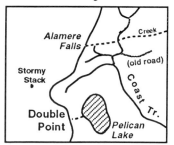

4.0 Double Point at 490'. This spot provides commanding views of the coastline and hills inland. (Stay well back from the cliffs edge!) In winter and spring, look for whales in the ocean. Also check the beaches below for harbor seals that breed here from May to July. When done, retrace your steps.

8.0 Palomarin trailhead. Restrooms, but no water.

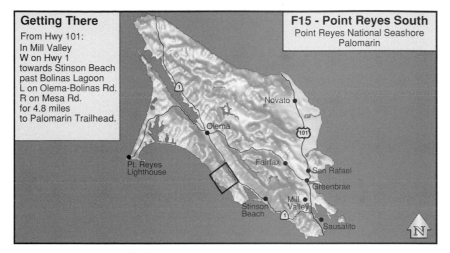

Getting There

From Hwy 101:
In Mill Valley
W on Hwy 1
towards Stinson Beach
past Bolinas Lagoon
L on Olema-Bolinas Rd.
R on Mesa Rd.
for 4.8 miles
to Palomarin Trailhead.

F15 - Point Reyes South
Point Reyes National Seashore
Palomarin

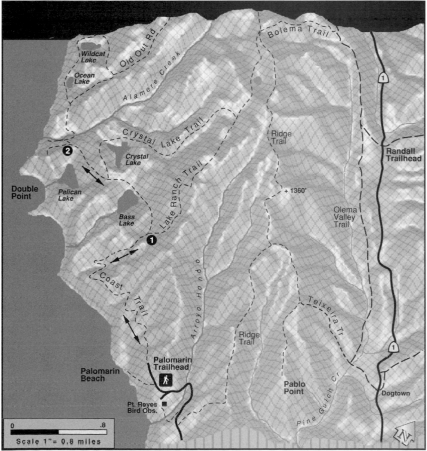

F16 Ridge - Lake Ranch - Coast Trails

Distance: 11.2 miles   Shaded: 70%
Elevation Change: 1300'   Some poison oak.
Rating: Hiking - 9   Difficulty - 6   Can be muddy.
When to Go: Excellent anytime, best in spring when clear.

This hike climbs the southern end of Inverness Ridge into a magnificent fir forest, then drops through a massive landslide area.

0.0 Park in the Point Reyes Bird Observatory parking lot. Take the signed Nature trail down into a small canyon featuring luxuriant growth and striking buckeye trees. Cross the creek and immediately head up the other side. Follow the trail across the plateau to a four-way junction marked by three short poles on your left. Head left past the poles and through dense blackberry vines towards the road.

0.2 Junction with Mesa Rd. Head right down the dirt road.

0.4 Junction #1 with the Ridge trail. Turn left and start a moderately steep climb through coastal scrub dotted with wind-pruned Douglas fir. The trail may be overgrown in places. Watch out for poison oak.

1.6 Views. Good views east to Pablo Point and beyond to Bolinas Ridge and south to Bolinas Lagoon.

Up ahead, the trail enters a dense conifer forest that covers the Inverness Ridge from here to Point Reyes Hill ten miles north.

2.7 Junction #2 with the Teixeira trail. Continue north on the ridge.

3.6 Mountain top at 1360'. A large moss-covered Douglas fir stands at the highest point on the southern ridge. This area was heavily logged in the late '50s which allowed manzanita to spread. Now the manzanita is dying out under the shade of the second growth of fir.

5.2 Junction #3. Take the Lake Ranch trail to the left. Up ahead, Mud Lake provides a home to red-winged blackbirds.

6.0 Junction with Crystal Lake trail. Continue on the Lake Ranch trail.

7.1 Views and landslides. The trail heads south into open grassland providing great views of the coast below and of the headlands north. On your left, look for evidence of the massive slides that reshaped the landscape and created a series of ponds and lakes below. For the next mile, try to imagine how these slides took place.

8.3 Junction #4. Head left on the Coast trail.

10.5 Palomarin trailhead #5. Continue on the road south.

11.2 PRBO parking area. No facilities.

Getting There

From Hwy 101:
In Mill Valley
W on Hwy 1
towards Stinson Beach
past Bolinas Lagoon
L on Olema-Bolinas Rd.
R on Mesa Rd.
for 4.3 miles
to PRBO parking area.

F16 - Point Reyes South

Point Reyes National Seashore
Palomarin

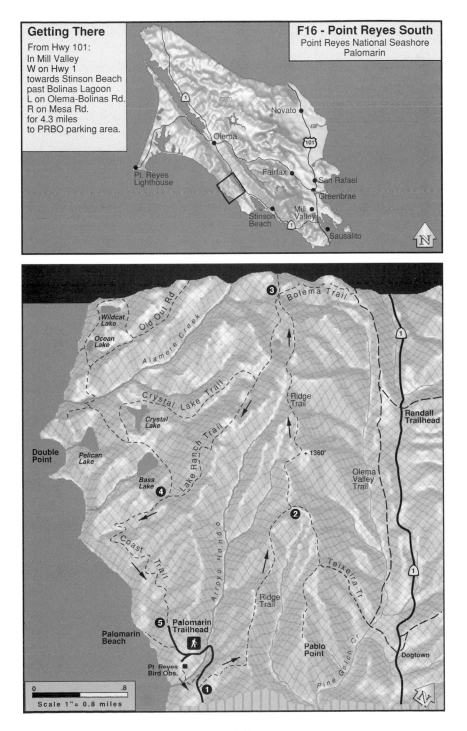

219

F17 Coast Trail to Wildcat Camp

Distance: 11.6 miles   Shaded: 20%
Elevation Change: 1200'   Trail lies along steep cliffs.
Rating: Hiking - 9   Difficulty - 6   Poison oak possible.
When to Go: Good anytime, best in April and May.

This hike follows the Coast trail past ponds and lakes to Wildcat Camp where you can make a side trip to Alamere Falls. Good views.

0.0 Start at 260' at the Palomarin parking area. Take the dirt road up towards the eucalyptus grove. A National Park interpretive sign is located at the entrance to the grove.

0.6 Coastal views. The trail skirts the cliff offering dramatic views both north and south. In spring, the green hills are dotted with blue lupine, white cow parsnip and the red or yellow Indian paintbrush. Other spring wildflowers include iris, wild cucumber and poppy.

2.2 Junction #1 with Lake Ranch trail. Continue left. Up ahead, the trail passes several small ponds formed by slumping soil. All of the ponds and lakes in this area were formed thousands of years ago by massive landslides that blocked normal creek drainage.

2.7 Bass Lake. Coastal scrub edges the southern shore of Point Reyes' most picturesque lake while Douglas fir frames the north side.

2.8 Unmarked junction. A spur trail left explores Bass Lake.

3.3 Views of Pelican Lake.

3.6 Three junctions. (See map inset Hike F15.) Continue on Coast trail.

4.2 Junction #2 with Ocean Lake Loop. Head left. Good views ahead.

Bass Lake

5.4 Junction #3 with the Coast trail. Head left.

6.1 Wildcat Camp. Water and restrooms available. Be sure to go down the ravine to the beach for a view south to Alamere Falls.

Option: If the tide is out, walk south along the beach 1.1 miles to the 40' Alamere Falls. Alamere Creek flows all year, but is most spectacular in the spring and after heavy rains.

For the return trip, take the Coast trail south towards Palomarin.

11.6 Palomarin trailhead. Restrooms, but no water.

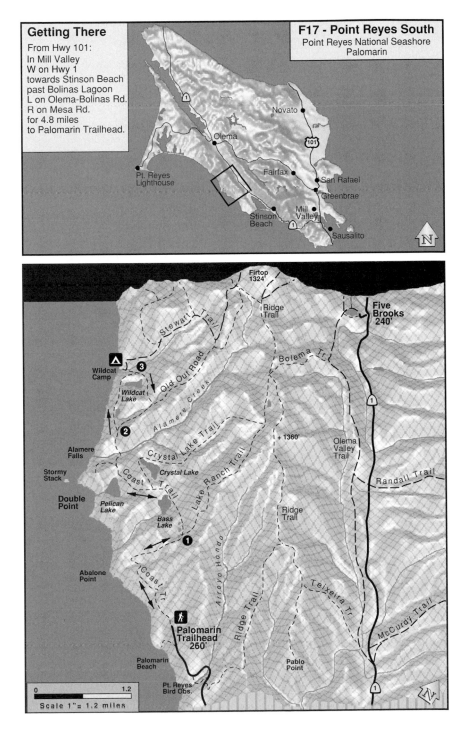

Getting There

From Hwy 101:
In Mill Valley
W on Hwy 1
towards Stinson Beach
past Bolinas Lagoon
L on Olema-Bolinas Rd.
R on Mesa Rd.
for 4.8 miles
to Palomarin Trailhead.

F17 - Point Reyes South
Point Reyes National Seashore
Palomarin

Novato

Olema

101

Pt. Reyes
Lighthouse

Fairfax

San Rafael

Greenbrae

Stinson
Beach

Mill
Valley

Sausalito

N

Firtop
1324'

Ridge
Trail

Five
Brooks
240'

Stewart Trail

Bolema Trl

Wildcat
Camp

3

Old Out Road

1

Wildcat
Lake

Alamere Creek

2

Crystal Lake Trail

+ 1360'

Olema
Valley
Trail

Alamere
Falls

Crystal Lake Trail

Stormy
Stack

Coast Trail

Crystal Lake

Lake Ranch Trail

Randall Trail

Double
Point

Pelican
Lake

Bass
Lake

Ridge
Trail

1

Abalone
Point

Coast Tr.

Arroro Hondo

Teixeira Tr

McCurdy Trail

Palomarin
Trailhead
260'

Ridge Trail

Palomarin
Beach

Pablo
Point

Pt. Reyes
Bird Obs.

0   1.2

Scale 1"= 1.2 miles

N

221

F18 Griffin Loop - Bird Overlook Trails

Distance: 2.9 miles   Shaded: 70%
Elevation Change: 700'   Call 415-868-9244 for information.
Rating: Hiking - 9   Difficulty - 4   Moderately steep.
When to Go: Open mid-March to mid-July, weekends 10-4.

This hike leads to an overlook that offers a rare and unforgettable view of great blue herons and egrets in their tree-top colonies.

0.0 Park at the Audubon Canyon Ranch parking area. Before beginning, register at the welcoming table and pick up brochures that describe the preserve. The hike starts by taking the Griffin Loop trail. 0.1 Junction, bench and Clem Miller Overlook. Good view to Bolinas Lagoon. Continue towards the Overlook.

0.3 Junction. A connecting trail heads left. Continue right.

0.5 Junction #1. Take the trail right to the overlook.

0.5 Henderson Overlook, benches and spotting scopes. Audubon volunteers with telescopes show visitors the herons and egrets in their nesting sites in the tops of redwood trees. Both herons and egrets display elaborate courtship rituals at the beginning of nesting season. Both species lay two to five eggs that take about four weeks to hatch. Young egret chicks start flying at about seven weeks of age, the young heron chicks at nine weeks. Typically, there are about 60-100 egret nests and 7-15 heron nests. One year, raccoons and an eagle raided the nests, significantly reducing the population.

Around the turn of the century, great egrets were nearly hunted to extinction for their courting plumes or feathers. The Audubon Society in the United States was first formed to stop their decimation.

0.6 Junction #1. The hike continues by heading up the ridge on the Griffin Loop trail. (Some signs may call it the Canyon trail).

1.3 Junction #2. Take the Griffin Loop trail right, which circles above Audubon Canyon in a redwood forest. **Option**: The North Loop trail heads left. It offers a more riparian, more diverse hike and is best in March and April. Both routes present great views.

2.9 Back at the Ranch with water, restrooms and a very agreeable picnic area. Be sure to visit the bookstore and exhibit hall. Also, a bird hide located next to the picnic area lets you watch birds feeding.

Option: If you would like more hiking. Take the Harwell Nature trail which makes a pleasant 0.8 mile loop into Garden Club Canyon. In early June, look for sweet-smelling buckeye trees and tiger lilies.

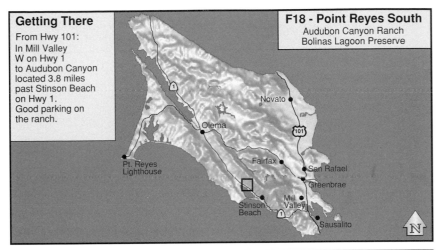

Getting There

From Hwy 101:
In Mill Valley
W on Hwy 1
to Audubon Canyon
located 3.8 miles
past Stinson Beach
on Hwy 1.
Good parking on
the ranch.

F18 - Point Reyes South
Audubon Canyon Ranch
Bolinas Lagoon Preserve

Novato

Olema

101

Pt. Reyes
Lighthouse

Fairfax

San Rafael

Greenbrae

Stinson
Beach

Mill
Valley

Sausalito

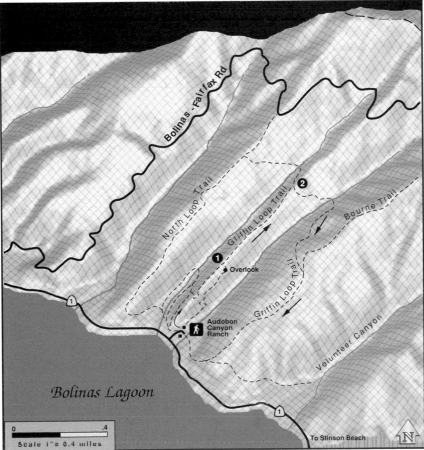

Bolinas - Fairfax Rd

North Loop Trail

Griffin Loop Trail

❷

Bourne Trail

❶
Overlook

Griffin Loop Trail

Audubon
Canyon
Ranch

Volunteer Canyon

Bolinas Lagoon

0   .4

Scale 1" = 0.4 miles

To Stinson Beach

223

G - Point Reyes North - 19 Hikes

Starting from Sky Trailhead at 680'
G1..... Sky - Horse - Z Ranch Trails 4.5
G2..... Sky - Fire Lane - Laguna Trails 6.2
G3..... Sky Trailhead to Bear Valley 7.1*
G4..... Sky - Woodward Valley - Coast - Fire Lane Trails 9.4

Starting from Bayview Trailhead at 720'
G5..... Bayview - Muddy Hollow - Laguna Trails 5.3
G6..... Inverness Ridge - Bucklin - Bayview Trials 7.9

Starting from Muddy Hollow at 160'
G7..... Coast - Beach - Muddy Hollow Trails 4.8
G8..... Muddy Hollow - Estero Trails 6.4

Starting from Limantour Beach at 40'
G9..... Limantour Spit - Beach Trails 2.0
G10... Beach Trail to Sculptured Beach at Low Tide 5.4

Starting from along Sir Francis Drake Hwy
G11... Estero - Drakes Head Trails 8.8
G12... Drakes Beach Trail 2.5
G13... PR Lighthouse and Chimney Rock Trails 1.2 and 1.6

Starting from Tomales State Park
G14... Johnstone - Jepson Trails 4.5
G15... Pierce Point Road to Shell Beach 5.6*

Starting from along Pierce Point Road
G16... Beach and Lagoon Trails 2.4, 4.0, 1.2 and 1.2
G17... Kehoe Beach Trailhead to Abbotts Lagoon 5.1*
G18... Tomales Point Trail 9.4

Starting from Tomales State Park along Hwy 1
G19... Tomales Bay Trail and Millerton Point Loop 2.2 and 1.2

* Shuttle Hike

Pets are not allowed on any hikes.

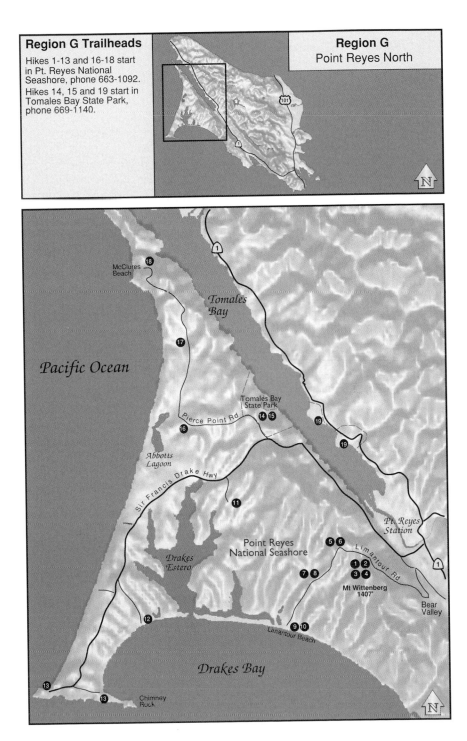

Region G Trailheads

Hikes 1-13 and 16-18 start in Pt. Reyes National Seashore, phone 663-1092.

Hikes 14, 15 and 19 start in Tomales Bay State Park, phone 669-1140.

Region G
Point Reyes North

McClures Beach

18

Tomales Bay

17

Pacific Ocean

Tomales Bay State Park

Pierce Point Rd

16

14 15

19

19

Abbotts Lagoon

Sir Francis Drake Hwy

11

Drakes Estero

Point Reyes National Seashore

5 6

Limantour Rd

1 2
3 4

7 8

Pt. Reyes Station

1

Mt Wittenberg 1407'

Bear Valley

12

9 10

Limantour Beach

Drakes Bay

13

13

Chimney Rock

225

G1 Sky - Horse - Z Ranch Trails

Distance: 4.5 miles   Shaded: 50%
Elevation Change: 750'   Can be muddy.
Rating: Hiking - 10   Difficulty - 7   Steep up Mt. Wittenberg.
When to Go: Excellent anytime, best in late spring.
This is the easiest hike to the top of Mt. Wittenberg. When clear, the hike provides great views in all directions. Good wildflowers in May.

0.0 Start at the Sky trailhead about 3.5 miles out the Limantour Road. The trail is an old ranch road that climbs south through a mostly Douglas fir forest lush with berries, nettles and ferns.

0.7 Junction #1. Take the Horse trail left. At the start of the trail, notice the large patch of salal with bright green, shiny leaves . Up ahead, the trail circles a steep canyon bare of conifers. The canyon's bowl shape suggests that a large slide occurred. In winter, water from a spring seeps out of the hillside, and may cause further soil erosion.

1.1 Junction #2. The vegetation opens up to provide good views north. The large flat mountain due north is Point Reyes Hill at 1336'. Turn right and head uphill on the Z Ranch trail.

1.2 More evidence of slides. The trail doubles back above the large canyon. Here is where the slide must have started. Notice the large firs above the trail. Also, notice there is much less seepage. Up ahead, the view north gets better. You can just get a glimpse of Mt. Saint Helena 40 miles northeast in Sonoma County.

1.8 Junction #3 and more views. Drakes Bay and the Point Reyes headlands provide a nice background to the grassy slopes of Mt. Wittenberg and Sky Camp below. Take the spur trail up to the top of Mt. Wittenberg. Look for tidy tips and lupine in May and June.

2.0 Mt. Wittenberg at 1407'. This is the highest point on Point Reyes. Circle the broad mountain top and enjoy the views before heading back down. Look for deer along the southern hilltops.

2.2 Junction #3. Take the Mt. Wittenberg trail south along the ridge.

2.8 Two junctions #4. Take the Sky trail right towards Sky Camp.

3.3 Sky Camp and spring. To explore the spring take the short spur trail to the left. When done, continue down the road past the restroom.

3.8 Junction #1 and rock exposure. Just before the junction, slabs of sedimentary rock, called Monterey shale, lie exposed along the trail.

4.5 Back at the trailhead. No facilities.

Getting There

From Hwy 101:
In Greenbrae
W on Sir Francis Drake
to Olema.
R on Hwy 1 for 200 yds.
L on Bear Valley Rd.
for 1.9 miles,
L on Limantour Rd.
for 3.5 miles
to the Sky trailhead.

G1 - Point Reyes South

Point Reyes National Seashore
Sky Trailhead

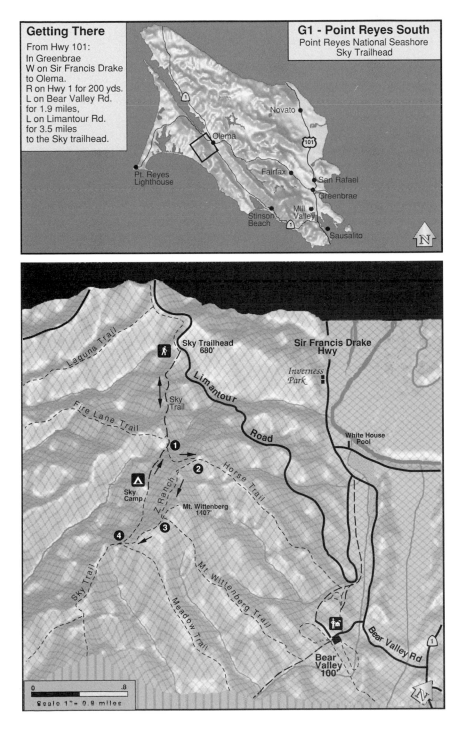

227

G2 Sky - Fire Lane - Laguna Trails

Distance: 6.2 miles   Shaded: 60%
Elevation Change: 850'   Can be wet.
Rating: Hiking - 9   Difficulty - 6   Moderately steep in places.
When to Go: Good anytime. Try early morning in winter for views.

This trail provides interesting terrain as it rolls down a ridgeline from Mt. Wittenberg. Early morning sunshine makes the headlands glow.

0.0   Start at the Sky trailhead about 3.5 miles along the Limantour Road. About 200 yds. up the trail, where it breaks into the open, look for Bishop pine to the right of the trail. This is a good hike for comparing Douglas fir and Bishop pine. Douglas fir have small, one-inch needles sprayed around a stem. Bishop Pine have two needles per bunch, each three inches long. The cones of the Bishop pine are bigger, harder and heavier.

Most of this hike takes place in a transition zone between Douglas fir and Bishop pine communities.

Bishop Pine   Douglas Fir

0.7   Junction #1 with Fire Lane trail. Take a right and follow the trail as it skirts the hilltop. The trail climbs slightly to 1090' then starts a moderate descent towards the ocean.

1.0   Great views. The trail descends through a mixture of forest and coastal scrub opening up great views of the rolling hills, Drakes Bay and the Farallon Islands.

2.0   The trail is deceptive. You expect it to be all downhill, but it climbs several knolls, each one bringing different views.

2.9   Junction #2. Often, you can hear frogs from a marsh 300 yds. to the south. The Laguna trail heads north here. After heavy rains, there may be standing water up ahead. In some places, the trail consists of fine, sandy soil. When wet, look for animal tracks.

3.7   Junction #3 with the road and the ranger residence at 140'. Stay on the Laguna trail as it heads uphill to the right. Notice the large, old buckeye trees with their multiple trunks covered with moss and lichen. Up ahead, look for trillium and Solomon's seal in early spring.

4.0   Junction with the Hidden Valley trail. Continue straight. At the end of the grassy meadow, the trail starts a moderate climb northeast.

5.5   Junction #4 with the Bayview trail. Turn right and head southeast.

6.2   Sky trailhead. No facilities.

Getting There

From Hwy 101:
In Greenbrae
W on Sir Francis Drake
to Olema
R on Hwy 1 for 200 yds.
L on Bear Valley Rd.
L on Limantour Rd.
for 3.5 miles
to the Sky trailhead.

G2 - Point Reyes South
Point Reyes National Seashore
Sky Trailhead

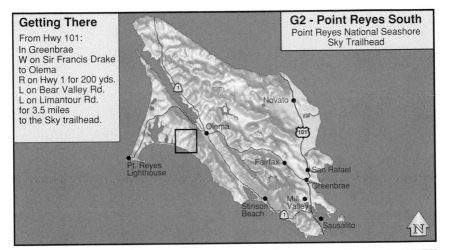

229

G3 Sky Trailhead to Bear Valley*

Distance: 7.1 miles   Shaded: 80%
Elevation Change: 750' up and 1300' down
Rating: Hiking - 10   Difficulty - 7   Steep up Mt. Wittenberg.
When to Go: Excellent anytime, best when clear.

This is the easiest and best all-around hike for exploring the forested Inverness Ridge and Bear Valley. Good views too.

*Shuttle Hike. Leave pickup cars at Bear Valley and shuttle all hikers to the Sky trailhead about 3.5 miles along the Limantour Road.

0.0 The Sky trail starts by heading south up an old ranch road.

0.7 Junction #1. Take the Horse trail left through dense vegetation along the moist, north-facing slope of Mt. Wittenberg. Up ahead, the trail circles a landslide that occurred in 1982.

1.1 Junction. Turn right and head uphill on the Z Ranch trail.

1.8 Junction #2 and more views. The grassy slopes of Mt. Wittenberg and Sky Camp below provide a picturesque foreground to Drakes Bay and the Point Reyes headlands. Take the spur trail left up to the top. Look for tidy tips and lupine in May and June.

2.0 Mt. Wittenberg at 1407' is the highest spot on Point Reyes. Retrace your steps down the mountain when ready to continue.

2.2 Junction. Take the Mt. Wittenberg trail south along the ridge line.

2.6 Two junctions. Continue south on the Sky trail, which now enters a magnificent forest of Douglas fir towering over a smaller forest of elderberry. In early spring, the light-green leaves of the elderberry provide a striking contrast to the darker colors of the fir. Later in spring, cream-colored blossoms and inedible red berries create changing patterns in this woodsy setting.

Red Elderberry

3.3 Junction #3 and meadow. The Woodward Valley trail heads right through a beautiful meadow, ideal for picnics. Continue straight along the ridgetop.

3.6 Junction #4. Take the Old Pine trail left as it leaves the Inverness Ridge and makes a long, gradual descent down to Bear Valley.

5.5 Junction #5 and Divide Meadow. Head downhill to the left.

7.1 Bear Valley trailhead with water, restrooms and pickup cars.

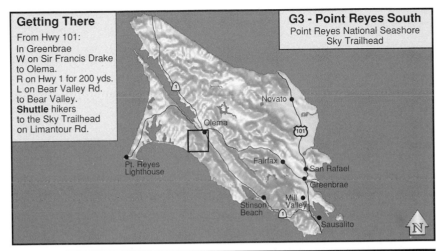

Getting There

From Hwy 101:
In Greenbrae
W on Sir Francis Drake
to Olema.
R on Hwy 1 for 200 yds.
L on Bear Valley Rd.
to Bear Valley.
Shuttle hikers
to the Sky Trailhead
on Limantour Rd.

G3 - Point Reyes South
Point Reyes National Seashore
Sky Trailhead

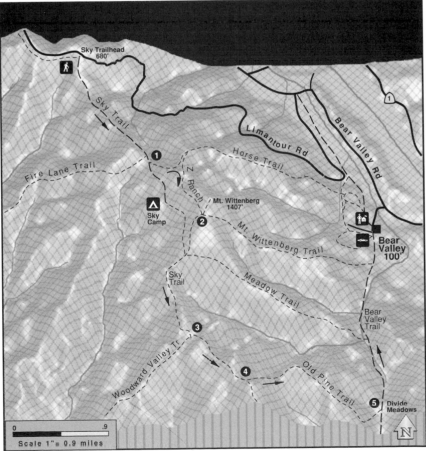

G4 Sky-Woodward Valley-Coast Trails

Distance: 9.4 miles   Shaded: 50%
Elevation Change: 1300'   Wet in winter, overgrown in summer.
Rating: Hiking - 9   Difficulty - 8   Steep downhill.
When to Go: Excellent anytime, best when clear and calm.
This hike explores the western slopes of Mt. Wittenberg down to the ocean. It offers a variety of terrain and views, and beach access.

0.0 Start at the Sky trailhead located 3.5 miles out the Limantour Road and take the trail south as it climbs towards Sky Camp.

0.7 Two junctions #1. Continue uphill past both the Fire Lane trail and the Horse trail, which is located 100 yds. farther up the road.

1.2 Sky Camp. Near the restroom, you can climb a small knoll to the right to get good views of Drakes Bay. The trail continues south.

1.7 Two junctions #2. Bear right and head south past the Meadow trail. The Sky trail rolls downhill along the Inverness Ridge and enters a magnificent Douglas fir forest. Huckleberry, elderberry, ferns and nettles make up the lush understory.

2.4 Junction #3 and meadow. Take the Woodward Valley trail as it heads down through the oval-shaped meadow.

3.9 View point. The trail levels off along a rocky outcrop offering commanding views of the coastline. To the south, you can see all the way to Double Point and just below it, Alamere Falls. To the north, you see the sweeping arc of Drakes Bay culminating in the Point Reyes headlands and Chimney Rock.

4.2 Junction. Take the Coast trail north. Up ahead, the trail turns inland to cross Santa Maria Creek, then returns to the coast. Look for a large, granite outcropping high above the trail.

5.4 Coast Camp. Water, restrooms and beach access. **Option:** Take the trail west along the creek to explore the beach.

5.5 Junction #4. Take the Fire Lane trail to the right and start a moderate climb through open grassland. Up ahead, the trail passes a marshy area where you may hear frogs croaking.

6.5 Junction #5 with the Laguna trail. Continue right on the Fire Lane trail which climbs more steeply. Watch for two kinds of conifers, the short-needle Douglas fir and the longer-needle Bishop Pine.

8.7 Junction #1. Head left on the Sky trail.

9.4 Back at the Sky trailhead. No facilities.

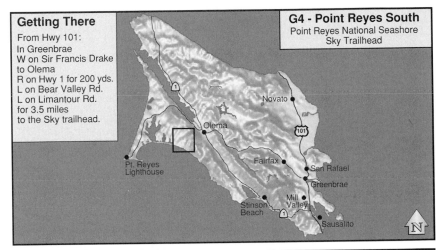

Getting There

From Hwy 101:
In Greenbrae
W on Sir Francis Drake
to Olema
R on Hwy 1 for 200 yds.
L on Bear Valley Rd.
L on Limantour Rd.
for 3.5 miles
to the Sky trailhead.

G4 - Point Reyes South
Point Reyes National Seashore
Sky Trailhead

233

G5 Bayview - Muddy Hollow - Laguna

Distance: 5.3 miles   Shaded: 50%
Elevation Change: 600'   Some poison oak possible.
Rating: Hiking - 9   Difficulty - 5   Trail can be wet in winter.
When to Go: Excellent anytime, best in April and May.

This hike descends the slope of Inverness Ridge offering great views to the west, then enters a lush riparian corridor.

0.0   Start at the Bayview trailhead about 4.7 miles along the Limantour Road. There is parking here for about a dozen cars in an open area adjacent to an old rock quarry. Take Bayview trail west.

The hike starts in a mixture of Bishop pine forest and coastal scrub. The latter includes huckleberry, coffeeberry, coyote bush, ferns, monkeyflower, salal and blackberry. Good views to the ocean.

1.5   The trail drops down into a scenic canyon and riparian corridor dominated by red alder. Nettles, miner's lettuce, sedges and cow parsnip provide a lush, green understory.

The succulent leaves and stems of miner's lettuce, also known as Indian lettuce, provided a nourishing treat for earlier inhabitants.

1.9   Junction with Drakes View trail. Continue left. Up ahead, the trail crosses a wooden bridge, then passes through a small marshy area. Farther ahead, majestic old buckeyes, their

Miner's Lettuce

contorted branches covered with lichen, overhang the trail.

2.3   Junction #1 with the Muddy Hollow road. Head left and watch for birds along the creek and in the marsh.

2.6   Junction with the Limantour Road. Cross the road and continue along the pavement past the hostel. Follow the signs to the Laguna trailhead.

3.0   Junction #2 with the Laguna trail. Just past the residence, take the Laguna trail left. Up ahead, the trail enters an open, grassy meadow. The Clem Miller Environmental Center can be seen on the left. A short loop trail up Hidden Valley takes off on the right.

At the end of the meadow, the trail starts a moderately steep climb up the slopes of Inverness Ridge.

4.8   Junction #3 with the Bayview trail. Head left.

5.3   Bayview trailhead. No facilities.

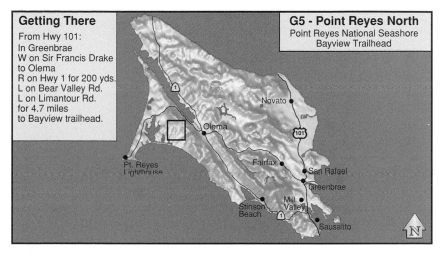

Getting There

From Hwy 101:
In Greenbrae
W on Sir Francis Drake
to Olema
R on Hwy 1 for 200 yds.
L on Bear Valley Rd.
L on Limantour Rd.
for 4.7 miles
to Bayview trailhead.

G5 - Point Reyes North
Point Reyes National Seashore
Bayview Trailhead

Novato

Olema

Fairfax

101

San Rafael

Greenbrae

Pt. Reyes
Lighthouse

Stinson
Beach

Mill
Valley

1

Sausalito

N

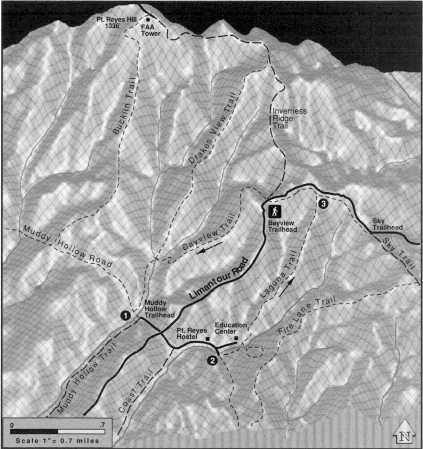

Pt. Reyes Hill
1336'

FAA
Tower

Bucklin Trail

Drakes View Trail

Inverness
Ridge
Trail

Muddy Hollow Road

Bayview Trail

Bayview
Trailhead

3

Sky
Trailhead

Sky Trail

Limantour Road

Laguna Trail

1

Muddy
Hollow
Trailhead

Pt. Reyes
Hostel

Education
Center

Fire Lane Trail

2

Muddy Hollow Trail

Coast Trail

0 .7

Scale 1" = 0.7 miles

N

235

G6 Inverness Ridge - Bucklin - Bayview

Distance: 7.9 miles   Shaded: 40%
Elevation Change: 1400'   Rocky, crowded with grasses.
Rating: Hiking - 8   Difficulty - 7   Moderately steep.
When to Go: Good when clear, best in spring.
This is the best hike for exploring the Bishop pine forests along Inverness Ridge. It also offers great views, both east and west.

0.0 Start at the Bayview trailhead located 4.7 miles along the Limantour Road. Take the signed Inverness Ridge trail north through the gate and head downhill through coastal scrub and Bishop pine.

Up ahead, the trail levels out on an open ridgetop covered with dense coastal scrub, an ideal home for brush rabbits.

0.7 Gate. Go 100 yds. past the gate and up the paved road to pick up the trail to the left, which now climbs steeply through a Bishop pine forest.

Brush Rabbit

1.3 Junction #1. Continue straight to pass through a luxuriant mix of forest and coastal scrub that includes ceanothus, coyote bush, manzanita, oak, madrone, blackberry, coffeeberry, bracken fern, salal, monkeyflower and Bishop pine.

Up ahead, the trail enters a dense stand of tall Bishop pine with long slender trunks and few side branches. This forest is similar to the Douglas fir forests further south. Both have lots of huckleberries in the understory and both are supported by heavy, summer fog drip.

2.1 Good views. After crossing an open saddle, the trail heads steeply uphill through coastal scrub and grasses that occasionally crowd the narrow rutted path. Great views to Tomales Bay.

2.6 FAA Station and junction #2 on Point Reyes Hill at elevation 1336'. Continue along the paved road about 50 yds. to pick up the Bucklin trail which follows the green fence west, then heads downhill. The hike now rolls down a mostly open ridgeline offering great views of Drakes Bay and the headlands. In the spring, look for the white, hairy star tulip.

5.0 Junction #3 with the Muddy Hollow Road. Head left.

5.6 Junction #4 with the Bayview trail. Head left and start the long easy climb towards Inverness Ridge.

7.9 Back at the trailhead. No facilities.

Getting There

From Hwy 101:
In Greenbrae
W on Sir Francis Drake
to Olema
R on Hwy 1 for 200 yds.
L on Bear Valley Rd.
L on Limantour Rd.
for 4.7 miles
to Bayview trailhead.

G6 - Point Reyes North
Point Reyes National Seashore
Bayview Trailhead

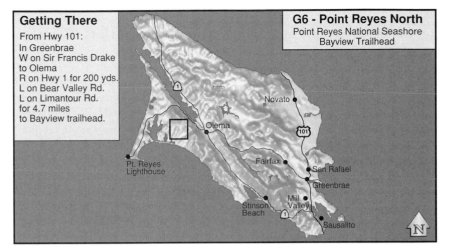

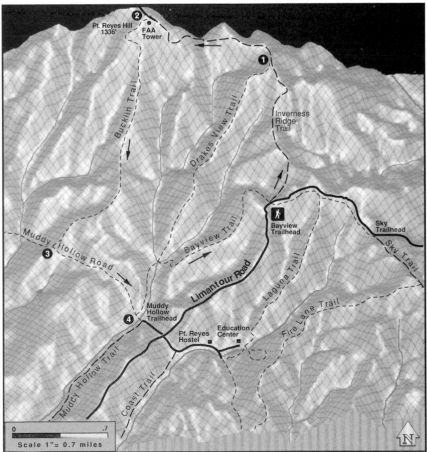

237

G7 Coast - Beach - Muddy Hollow Trails

Distance: 4.8 miles   Shaded: 30%
Elevation Change: 200'
Rating: Hiking - 9   Difficulty - 2   Trail may be muddy.
When to Go: Best in fall and winter for birds.

This hike travels along creeks, fresh and saltwater marshes and the ocean to offer a variety of habitats and good birding locations.

0.0 Park at the Muddy Hollow parking area 0.2 mile north of the Limantour Road. The hike starts by heading back up toward the road.

0.2 Limantour Road. Continue across the road towards the hostel.

0.4 Junction #1. Before reaching the hostel, take the Coast trail south towards Drakes Bay. The Coast trail parallels a riparian corridor following a small creek into Limantour Marsh. In the early morning, the chatter of birds fills the air. Look for Indian paintbrush, Douglas iris and buttercups in spring.

1.3 Creek crossing and alders. Up ahead, the trail skirts the marsh, then doglegs to the right towards the ocean.

2.1 Junction #2 with the beach. Take the signed trail 30' through the dunes and head right along the beach. If it's not too windy, this can be an exhilarating walk with views of Drakes Bay, refreshing ocean breakers and much beach activity. Watch for pelicans, willets and plovers. Keep an eye out for sand crabs and rock louse. On occasion, sea lions will follow your progress along the beach.

Brown Pelican

2.9 Trail inland #3. Look for the greatest concentration of people or a break in the dunes and head inland towards the Limantour parking area. This beach is popular for sunning and wading.

Willet

3.0 Junction, water and restroom. At the restroom, head left to pick up the Muddy Hollow trail. Look for sandpipers, willets, egrets and herons in Limantour Estero to the west.

3.4 Junction #4 with the Estero trail. Continue heading inland. The Muddy Hollow trail passes in and out of a riparian community with creeks and marshes lined with red alders.

4.8 Back at the Muddy Hollow parking area. No facilities.

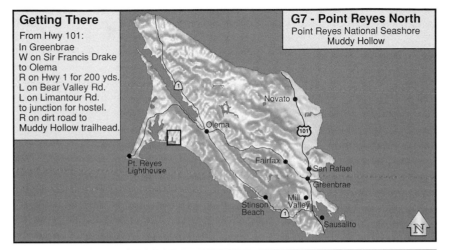

Getting There

From Hwy 101:
In Greenbrae
W on Sir Francis Drake
to Olema
R on Hwy 1 for 200 yds.
L on Bear Valley Rd.
L on Limantour Rd.
to junction for hostel.
R on dirt road to
Muddy Hollow trailhead.

G7 - Point Reyes North
Point Reyes National Seashore
Muddy Hollow

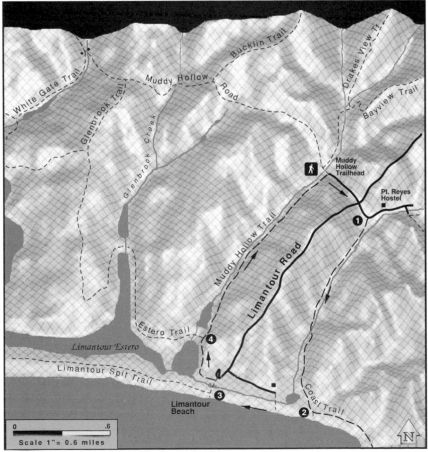

Scale 1"= 0.6 miles

G8 Muddy Hollow - Estero Trails

Distance: 6.2 miles   Shaded: 20%
Elevation Change: 450'   Some poison oak and nettles.
Rating: Hiking - 7   Difficulty - 4   Ruts and mud possible.
When to Go: Good when clear skies, best in spring, but not too wet.

This hike traverses open coastal hills offering excellent views of Drakes Bay and Limantour Estero, then returns via Muddy Hollow.

0.0 Start at the Muddy Hollow trailhead located 0.2 mile north of Limantour Road. Take the dirt road northeast through the gate.

0.1 Junction. Continue past the Bayview trail and the site of the old Muddy Hollow ranch, which was located near the cypress trees. If the road is wet, look for deer tracks in the wet sandy soil.

0.7 Junction #1 with the Bucklin trail. Continue straight and follow the road as it heads down into the Glenbrook Creek drainage basin. After crossing the creek and starting to climb, look south to see if you can spot the broken dam where the creek enters Limantour Estero.

1.3 Junction #2. Take the Glenbrook trail left and make a short climb to a rise offering great views of the coast. As you start down a long run towards the ocean, the view of Drakes Bay keeps getting better.

2.0 Junction #3 with the Estero trail. Continue towards the ocean.

2.7 Turning point. The trail now reverses direction to head back inland. **Option:** For a side trip, take the unmarked trail 0.1 to 0.4 miles to various views overlooking the estero and Limantour Beach.

3.5 Bridge. As you head inland, the trail drops down past eucalyptus trees. The first dairy on Point Reyes was established here in 1857 by the Steele brothers. Up ahead, the trail crosses a bridge on Glenbrook Creek. This section of trail can be muddy and overgrown with stinging nettles. After crossing the bridge, the trail makes a short climb over a ridge and drops down into Muddy Hollow. The last section of trail that crosses another bridge and dam can also be overgrown. Watch out for poison oak in this last section.

4.8 Junction #4 and side trip. Take the Muddy Hollow trail to the left. **Option:** For a side trip, go right 0.4 miles to Limantour Beach.

The Muddy Hollow trail skirts a pond and then a creek that provide riparian habitat, good for birding. The trail can be muddy when wet. However, it has been greatly improved since the time it was named.

6.2 Back at the Muddy Hollow trailhead. No facilities.

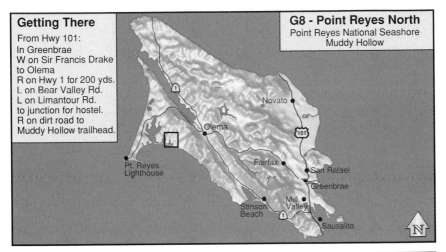

Getting There

From Hwy 101:
In Greenbrae
W on Sir Francis Drake
to Olema
R on Hwy 1 for 200 yds.
L on Bear Valley Rd.
L on Limantour Rd.
to junction for hostel.
R on dirt road to
Muddy Hollow trailhead.

G8 - Point Reyes North
Point Reyes National Seashore
Muddy Hollow

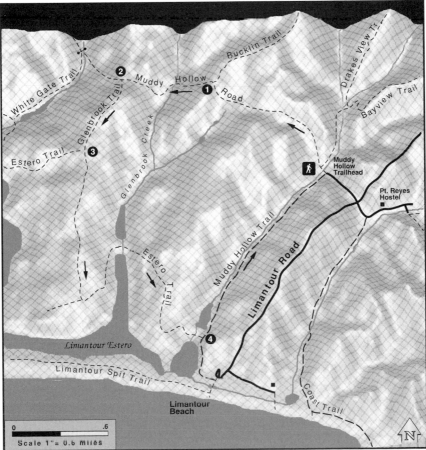

241

G9 Limantour Spit - Beach Trails

Distance: 2.0 miles   Shaded: 0%
Elevation Change: less than 100'
Rating: Hiking - 8   Difficulty - 2   Can be windy.
When to Go: Anytime, best when calm and clear.
This refreshing hike along the dunes and beach provides good views, lots of birds and a reminder of the historic struggle to create a park.

0.0 Start at the Limantour parking area and head down past the restroom towards the ocean. Just after passing the marsh area, turn right and head north along the trail in the dunes.

This trail was once called Limantour Drive, which led into a subdivision called Drakes Bay Estates.This area of the development had been divided into over one hundred lots. When the National Seashore formed in 1962, six of the lots already had homes built. As you walk along, you'll see an occasional pipe or concrete pad, reminders of the heroic efforts of the early conservationists.

Modern landowners were not the first to use this spit. Before the developers moved in, archeologists had uncovered three middens or shell mounds that were garbage dumps of the Coastal Miwoks. Not only did the middens contain shells, but archeologists also found dozens of pieces of Chinese Ming porcelain and other artifacts that indicate that Cermeno may have camped on the spit after the shipwreck of the San Agustin in 1595.

0.5 Birds of the estero. Look for egrets, herons, willets, and plovers especially in winter.

1.0 End of the road. Head out across the dunes to the beach, then go left again. **Option**: To add to the hike, continue northwest 1.8 miles to the end of the spit. (You might see an old shipwreck about 1.5 miles out.)

Harbor Seal

1.5 Harbor seal or sea lion? The two most common marine mammals at Point Reyes are harbor seals and sea lions. Harbor seals are smaller and have a mottled coat. They have large eyes and no ears. When they go under, they often sink straight down, while sea lions tend to dive forward.

Sea Lion

2.0 Limantour parking area, restrooms and water.

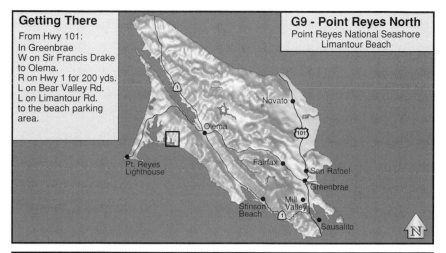

Getting There

From Hwy 101:
In Greenbrae
W on Sir Francis Drake
to Olema.
R on Hwy 1 for 200 yds.
L on Bear Valley Rd.
L on Limantour Rd.
to the beach parking
area.

G9 - Point Reyes North

Point Reyes National Seashore
Limantour Beach

Novato

1

Olema

Pt. Reyes
Lighthouse

Fairfax

San Rafael

101

Greenbrae

Mill
Valley

Stinson
Beach

1

Sausalito

N

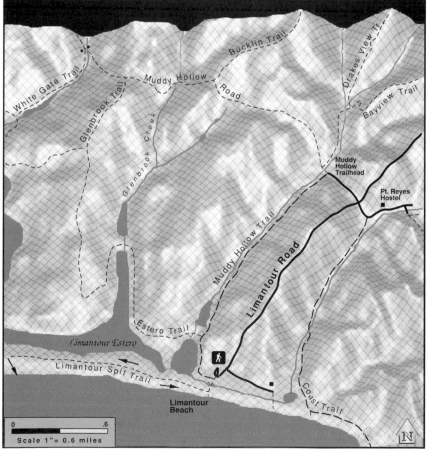

White Gate Trail

Bucklin Trail

Muddy Hollow

Road

Drakes View Tr.

Bayview Trail

Glenbrook Trail

Glenbrook Creek

Muddy
Hollow
Trailhead

Pt. Reyes
Hostel

Muddy Hollow Trail

Limantour Road

Estero Trail

Limantour Estero

Limantour Spit Trail

Coast Trail

Limantour
Beach

0   .6

Scale 1"= 0.6 miles

N

243

G10 Beach Trail to Sculptured Beach

Distance: 5.4 miles   Shaded: 0%
Elevation Change: 50'   Check tide tables before taking this hike.
Rating: Hiking - 7   Difficulty - 2 to 5 (See text below.)
When to Go: Best at low tide in the summer and fall.
This hike explores the interesting rock formations and tidepools on the beaches south of Limantour. Conditions vary with beach level.

0.0 Park in the auxiliary parking area south of the main parking lot at Limantour Beach. Take the trail across the dunes to the beach and head south. Before leaving the dunes, look back and note the trees and ranger residence, which provide a landmark for returning.

1.4 Creek, Coast Camp and junction #1. Continue along the beach.

1.8 Santa Maria Creek and Sculptured Beach. The sandy beach here changes with the seasons. In winter, large wave action moves sand offshore lowering the level of the beach and making travel over the rocky terraces difficult. In the summer and fall, smaller wave action brings the sand back ashore and it is easier to walk along here and explore the rocks and tidepools.

2.5 Junction #2. You can climb up to a small rocky terrace and scan the beach south to Pt. Resistance. Usually, this is as far as you can go. When done exploring, retrace your steps.

Option: If the beach sand level is high enough and there is a minus tide, you may be able to explore the beach south. You will probably have to climb down off the terrace 4-6 feet to reach the beach. If you can safely do this, there are interesting caves and tunnels ahead. (This is not an approved park trail. Hike at your own risk and be sure to watch the tide!)

Low Tide
Low tide at Point Reyes occurs 35-40 minutes earlier than Golden Gate low tide, which is usually given in the tide tables.
Also, the tide comes in slowly at first, then rises more quickly about two hours after the minimum. You should plan to have a clear, safe route off any beach by this time.

3.6 Junction #1 and Coast Camp. Head inland, veer left and follow the Coast trail towards Limantour Beach.

4.8 Junction #3. Leave the Coast trail and take the beach north.

5.3 Junction. Look for the trees and residence and head inland again.

5.4 Parking area. Restrooms and water at the main parking area.

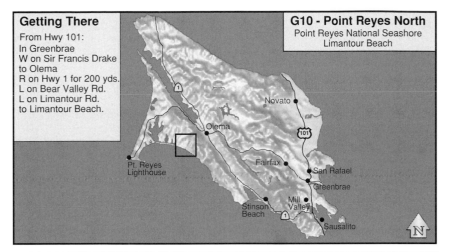

Getting There

From Hwy 101:
In Greenbrae
W on Sir Francis Drake
to Olema
R on Hwy 1 for 200 yds.
L on Bear Valley Rd.
L on Limantour Rd.
to Limantour Beach.

G10 - Point Reyes North
Point Reyes National Seashore
Limantour Beach

Novato

Olema

Pt. Reyes
Lighthouse

Fairfax

San Rafael

Greenbrae

Stinson
Beach

Mill
Valley

Sausalito

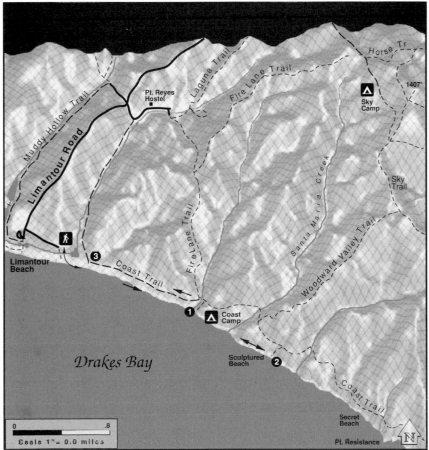

Muddy Hollow Trail

Laguna Trail

Fire Lane Trail

Horse Tr

Pt. Reyes
Hostel

Limantour Road

1407'

Sky
Camp

Santa Maria Creek

Sky
Trail

Fire Lane Trail

Woodward Valley Trail

Limantour
Beach

Coast Trail

3

1

Coast
Camp

Drakes Bay

Sculptured
Beach

2

Coast Trail

Secret
Beach

0   .8

Scale 1" = 0.0 miles

Pt. Resistance

G11   Estero - Drakes Head Trails

Distance: 8.8 miles   Shaded: 0%
Elevation Change: 750'
Rating: Hiking - 8   Difficulty - 4   Trail can be muddy in parts.
When to Go: Best in late fall and winter when calm and clear.

This is an out and back hike through rolling pastureland to the best viewpoint on Point Reyes. A good hike to see birds and mammals.

0.0 Start at the parking area off the paved road. Go through the fence and follow the Estero trail south towards the pine forest. This rangeland is part of Home Ranch which has been grazed since the 1850s. In spring, patches of deep-blue iris dot the hillsides.

1.0 Dam and bridge at point #1. Crossing the bridge of Home Bay, notice the Home Ranch farm buildings to the east. James Shafter's ranch, started in 1857, is the oldest surviving ranch on Point Reyes.

The trail now heads uphill past lupine and coyote bush. Watch for wildlife along the way - deer, rabbits, osprey, ducks and egrets.

1.5 Plateau and view of Drakes Estero. The point across the water was one of two Schooner Landing sites. The estero and bay were deeper in earlier days allowing small schooners, like the *Point Reyes*, to deliver highly-prized butter to San Francisco.

Schooner Point Reyes

Johnson's Oyster Farm now uses the shallower estero waters.

2.4 Junction #2 with the Sunset Beach trail. Bear left, head uphill.

3.0 Junction #3 and corral. Turn right and follow the signed Drakes Head trail towards the ocean.

4.0 Water tank and trees. This is the site of the Drakes Head Ranch, which operated from the 1850s to 1960. Keep to the right.

4.4 Drakes Head. On a clear day this is the best view spot on all of Point Reyes! (Caution: The cliff edge may be unstable.) It offers a panoramic sweep of Drakes Bay from the headlands to Double Point. Look for harbor seals sunning at the end of the spit. When you are ready to return, retrace your steps.

8.8 Back at the parking lot. Restrooms available.

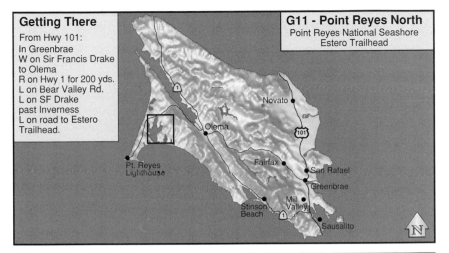

Getting There

From Hwy 101:
In Greenbrae
W on Sir Francis Drake
to Olema
R on Hwy 1 for 200 yds.
L on Bear Valley Rd.
L on SF Drake
past Inverness
L on road to Estero
Trailhead.

G11 - Point Reyes North
Point Reyes National Seashore
Estero Trailhead

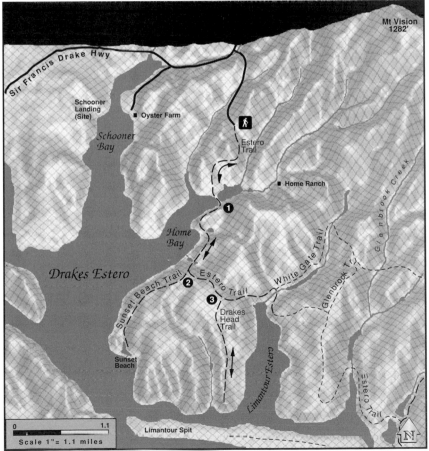

247

G12 Drakes Beach Trail

Distance: 2.5 miles   Shaded: 0%
Elevation Change: 300'   Some parts may not be passable.
Rating: Hiking - 9   Difficulty - 7   Rutted hillside. Creek crossing.
When to Go: Best at low tide, good wildflowers in April and May.

This hike makes a figure-eight traveling on the beach and coastal bluffs to visit the historic marker commemorating Drake's landing.

0.0 Start at the Ken Patrick Visitor Center picnic area and take the trail left up the cliff to the bluffs above. At the top of the cliff, you have two choices. You can either follow the cliff, staying well back from the edge, or head inland to pick up a grass-covered road heading east.

0.3 Crest. The trail reaches a high point overlooking Horseshoe Pond. Follow the road down towards the pond.

0.5 Dam and beach. **Note:** As you cross the dam towards the beach, look carefully at the road coming down the hill slightly to your left. This is your return route. Check the creek level connecting the road to the beach. If this looks too difficult, you should return via the beach. Also, check the hillside for cows or bulls. See note below.

0.6 Beach. If the tide is not too high, continue down the beach past the cliffs and dunes to the estero.

1.1 Drakes Estero. If possible, circle the dunes and head towards the cliff and trees.

1.3 Drake's Memorial. Look for the pole and monument about 50' inland. Most experts believe that this is the spot where Drake careened the Golden Hinde for repairs in 1579. **Note:** The hike continues through the gate and up the road into pastureland. If you are concerned about cows or bulls, then return via the beach. However, the pasture has great wildflowers in spring.

One of two monuments to Drake. This one is located next to the parking lot.

1.8 Horseshoe Pond. Look for a creek crossing. Do not go up on the bluff for a crossing. It is unsafe. As you walk along the beach and terraces, see if you can spot fault lines in the cliff above. These show up as shifts in the horizontal lines.

2.5 Back at the Visitor Center with restrooms and snack bar.

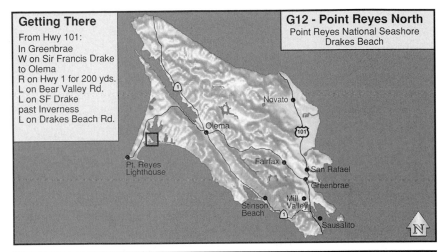

Getting There

From Hwy 101:
In Greenbrae
W on Sir Francis Drake
to Olema
R on Hwy 1 for 200 yds.
L on Bear Valley Rd.
L on SF Drake
past Inverness
L on Drakes Beach Rd.

G12 - Point Reyes North
Point Reyes National Seashore
Drakes Beach

Novato

Olema

101

Fairfax

Pt. Reyes
Lighthouse

San Rafael

Greenbrae

Stinson
Beach

Mill
Valley

1

Sausalito

N

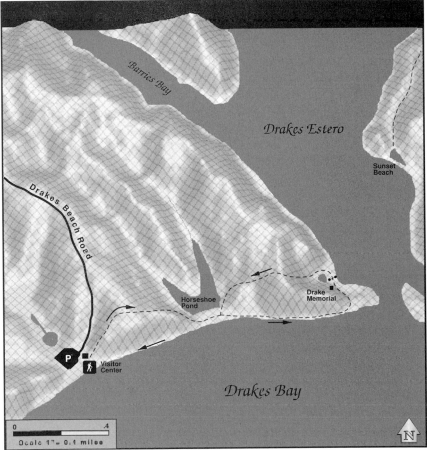

Barries Bay

Drakes Estero

Sunset
Beach

Drakes Beach Road

Horseshoe
Pond

Drake
Memorial

P

Visitor
Center

Drakes Bay

0   .4

Scale 1" = 0.1 miles

N

G13 PR Lighthouse and Chimney Rock

Distance: 1.2 and 1.6 miles   Shaded: 0%
Elevation Change: 400' and 100'   Check weather at 663-9029.
Rating: Hiking - 10   Difficulty - 3   Wind and fog likely.
When to Go: Best in early January and again in March-April.

These are exhilarating hikes. The lighthouse offers whale watching. Chimney Rock has the best wildflowers on the coast. Great views.

Note: During peak whale watching and wildflower times, usually January to April, the park service restricts traffic to the lighthouse and Chimney Rock, and runs a bus shuttle from the South Beach parking lot during the hours 10 am to 2 pm. Call the above number for info.

To the PR Lighthouse and Back - 1.2 miles and 400' Change.

0.0 Start at the lighthouse parking lot and head uphill past the gate.

The view north along Point Reyes Beach, which runs 11 miles, offers a classic picture-taking spot.

0.5 Visitor Center. The center is open Thursday to Monday, 10 am to 5 pm. The lighthouse stairs, all 308 of them, are open from 10 am to 4:30 pm Th-M, weather permitting. Check the Visitor Center for tours of the lighthouse itself. The lighthouse platform is the best place in Marin to watch grey whales migrating from Alaska to Baja California.

To Chimney Rock and Back - 1.6 miles and 100' Change

0.0 From the Chimney Rock trailhead, follow the trail as it skirts the hillside above the cypress trees and ranger residence.

0.3 Junction with Underhill road. Continue straight. The US Coast Guard Lifeboat Station, below, operated between 1927 and 1968. Dozens of people were saved after shipwrecks near here.

0.4 Junction #1. Take the Overlook trail to the right.

0.5 Overlook and views. Towering 500' cliffs provide spectacular coastline scenery. Head back, then right towards Chimney Rock.

0.9 Chimney Rock and wildflowers. Expert observers have counted over 60 species of flowers along the trail including hairy cat's-ears, Johnny-tuck, paintbrush, lupine, iris and checkerbloom.

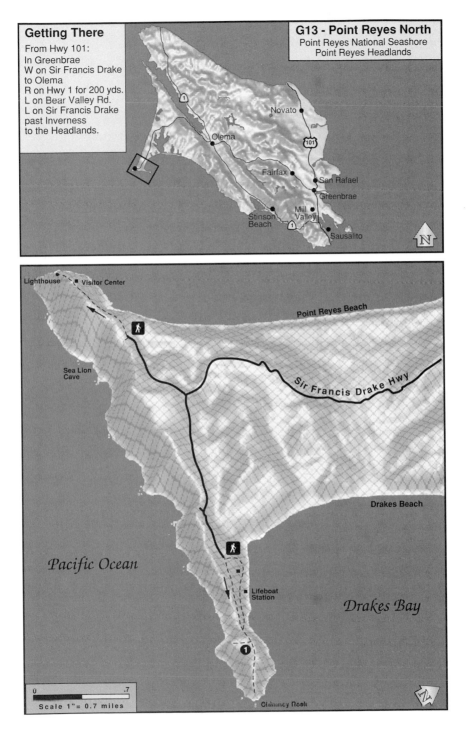

Getting There

From Hwy 101:
In Greenbrae
W on Sir Francis Drake
to Olema
R on Hwy 1 for 200 yds.
L on Bear Valley Rd.
L on Sir Francis Drake
past Inverness
to the Headlands.

G13 - Point Reyes North
Point Reyes National Seashore
Point Reyes Headlands

Novato

Olema

Fairfax

San Rafael

Greenbrae

Stinson
Beach

Mill
Valley

Sausalito

Lighthouse

Visitor Center

Point Reyes Beach

Sea Lion
Cave

Sir Francis Drake Hwy

Drakes Beach

Pacific Ocean

Lifeboat
Station

Drakes Bay

0   .7
Scale 1" = 0.7 miles

Chimney Rock

G14 Johnstone - Jepson Trails

Distance: 4.5 miles   Shaded: 80%
Elevation Change: 500'
Rating: Hiking - 10   Difficulty - 4   Can be muddy in winter.
When to Go: Great anytime. Birds in winter, wading in summer.

This is a magnificent hike through Tomales Bay State Park. It features a luxuriant Bishop pine forest, Indian Nature trail and three beaches.

Option: If you want to picnic or wade in the bay after the hike, you might drive into the park (pay fee) and start the hike at mile 2.1 below.

0.0 Start at the small parking area located one mile out Pierce Point Rd. and two-tenths of a mile before the entrance to Tomales Bay State Park. Take the signed Jepson trail uphill into Bishop pine forest.

0.1 Junction. Head right towards signed Shell Beach.

0.3 Junction #1. Take the Johnstone trail left towards Pebble Beach. Up ahead, after crossing the road again, the trail enters a luxuriant forest produced by winter rain and summer fog drip.

1.6 Junction #2. Continue right past the restroom to delightful Pebble Beach. When ready to continue, return to junction #2 and take the trail towards Heart's Desire Beach. Up ahead, toyon and huckleberry shrubs are almost twice their normal size in this lush rainforest.

2.0 Junction. A trail leads left to the parking circle. Continue straight towards Heart's Desire. Great views of the bay.

2.1 Heart's Desire Beach. Continue across the beach, past the restroom and take the signed Indian Nature trail to Indian Beach.

2.3 Junction #3 with the Loop trail. Keep to the right.

2.6 Bridge and Indian Beach. Head down the beach towards the Indian kotchas. The hike continues on the road that circles the marsh.

3.2 Junction. Leave the road and take the loop trail left.

3.3 Junction #3 again. Head right.

3.5 Heart's Desire Beach. Cross the beach and take the Johnstone trail along the shoreline.

3.6 Junction. Head right up to the parking lot, then circle around counterclockwise on the paved street.

3.7 Junction. Take the signed Jepson trail uphill.

4.4 Junction with the trail to Shell Beach. Stay right.

4.5 Back at the parking area. No facilities.

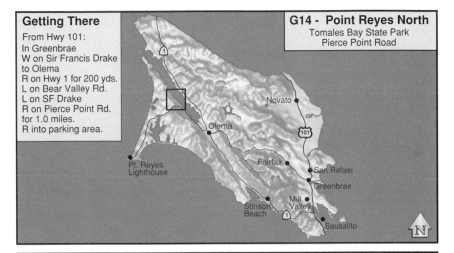

Getting There

From Hwy 101:
In Greenbrae
W on Sir Francis Drake
to Olema
R on Hwy 1 for 200 yds.
L on Bear Valley Rd.
L on SF Drake
R on Pierce Point Rd.
for 1.0 miles.
R into parking area.

G14 - Point Reyes North
Tomales Bay State Park
Pierce Point Road

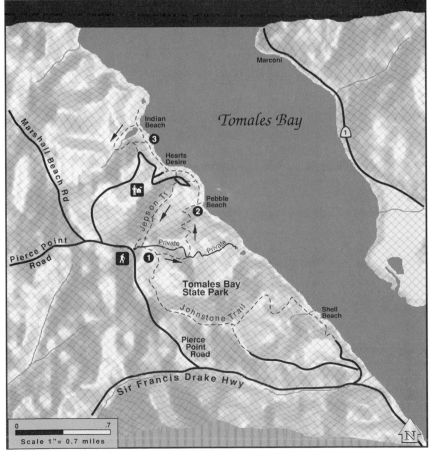

253

G15 Pierce Point Road to Shell Beach*

Distance: 5.6 miles   Shaded: 90%
Elevation Change: 1100' down, 600' up.   Poison oak possible.
Rating: Hiking - 9   Difficulty - 5   Beaches crowded in summer.
When to Go: Great anytime. Best early fall for swimming and berries.

This one-way hike in Tomales Bay State Park makes a loop down to Heart's Desire Beach, then heads towards Shell Beach.

*Shuttle Hike. Leave pickup cars in the parking area in Tomales Bay State Park at the end of Camino Del Mar. Shuttle all hikers to the small parking area located one mile out Pierce Point Rd.

0.0 Take the signed Jepson trail uphill into Bishop pine forest.

0.1 Junction. Head left towards signed Heart's Desire Beach. Ahead, the trail enters the Jepson Memorial Grove, one of the finest groves of Bishop pine in California. Bishop pine are smaller than most pines. They have two needles per bunch, each about 3" long. Cones are tightly bound to branches.

Bishop Pine

Option: You can cut the hike short by 2.5 miles and save 500' of climbing by heading right towards Shell Beach (switch to jct #3 below).

0.8 Parking lot. Head left around the parking circle to find the trail.

0.9 Junction #1 with the Johnstone trail. Head left.

1.0 Heart's Desire Beach. Return to junction #1.

1.1 Continue on the signed Johnstone trail towards Pebble Beach.

1.5 Junction #2. Head left past the restroom to Pebble Beach. Return here to continue the hike towards Shell Beach.

2.8 Junction #3. Head left on the Johnstone trail to Shell Beach. Down below, the trail crosses the upper end of a lush ravine.

Huckleberry

3.3 Bench and viewpoint. Good views east to Tomales Bay. Caution: Poison oak crowds the trail, but is sometimes difficult to spot. Up ahead, good huckleberries in the fall.

4.0 Junction #4. Continue left to start a long gradual descent.

5.3 Shell Beach and restroom. This small sandy beach offers good picnicking and swimming. Continue the hike across the beach.

5.6 Beach. Continue across the beach to the parking area and cars.

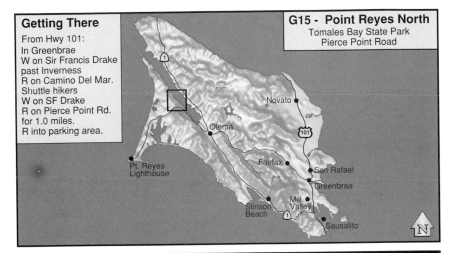

Getting There

From Hwy 101:
In Greenbrae
W on Sir Francis Drake
past Inverness
R on Camino Del Mar.
Shuttle hikers
W on SF Drake
R on Pierce Point Rd.
for 1.0 miles.
R into parking area.

G15 - Point Reyes North
Tomales Bay State Park
Pierce Point Road

Novato

Olema

Pt. Reyes
Lighthouse

Fairfax

San Rafael

Greenbrae

Stinson
Beach

Mill
Valley

Sausalito

N

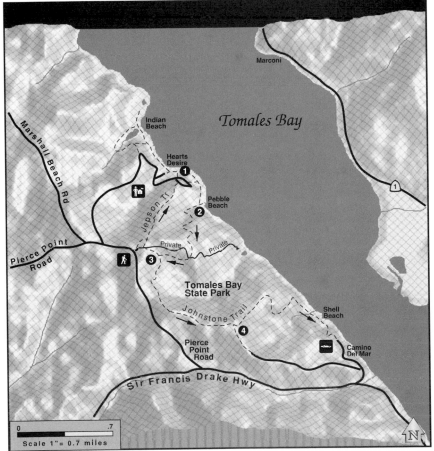

Marconi

Tomales Bay

Marshall Beach Rd

Indian
Beach

Hearts
Desire

1

Pebble
Beach

2

Jepson Tr

Private

Private

Pierce Point
Road

3

Tomales Bay
State Park

Johnstone Trail

Shell
Beach

4

Pierce
Point
Road

Camino
Del Mar

Sir Francis Drake Hwy

1

0   .7

Scale 1"= 0.7 miles

N

G16 Beach and Lagoon Trails

Distance: 1.2 to 4.0 miles   Shaded: 0%
Elevation Change: 100' to 350'
Rating: Hiking - 8   Difficulty - 3   Kehoe trail can be wet.
When to Go: Best weather in fall and winter, best flowers in spring.

All four of these trails provide access to great beaches on the northern end of Point Reyes. Good birding at Abbotts Lagoon.

Note: Dangerous Surf! Do not swim or wade on ocean beaches.

Marshall Beach Trail - 2.4 miles and 350' Change

0.0 The trailhead is located 2.5 miles down the Marshall Beach Road just after the turnoff to Tomales State Park. Head north and take the trail through pastureland, then down towards a cypress grove.

1.2 Cove and beach. This picturesque beach offers sunbathing, picnicking, wading and views across Tomales Bay. If you head north along the beach, you might spot traces of a Miwok shell mound.

Abbotts Lagoon Trail - 4.0 miles and 100' Change

0.0 Start at the trailhead located 3.4 miles along the Pierce Point Road and head west across the open pastureland. In wet years, these fields are aglow with yellow poppies and fiddleneck.

1.5 Bridge, lagoon, wildflowers and birds. Yellow gold fields cover the hill on the left, while the bridge offers a good view spot for shore birds. Cross the bridge and follow the edge of the lagoon to the ocean.

2.0 Point Reyes Beach is also called Ten-mile Beach and Great Beach.

Kehoe Beach Trail - 1.2 miles and 100' Change

0.0 Start at the trailhead 5.5 miles along the Pierce Point Road. This is a level trail that parallels Kehoe Marsh out to the beach. Good birding in the winter and abundant wildflowers in the spring.

0.6 Beach and wildflowers. The cliffs on the right are often covered in gold fields, poppies, lupine and baby blue eyes in April and May.

McClures Beach Trail - 1.2 miles and 300' Change (See map G18)

0.0 The trailhead is located at the end of the Pierce Point Road, 9.5 miles from the Sir Francis Drake Hwy. junction. The trail follows a ravine as it descends 300' to the ocean.

0.6 Beach. During super-low tides, there are great tidepools at the south end of the beach. Be sure to check the tide tables and plan your return while the tide is still low.

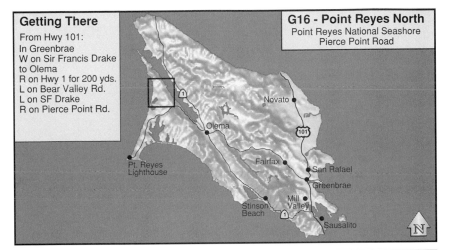

Getting There

From Hwy 101:
In Greenbrae
W on Sir Francis Drake
to Olema
R on Hwy 1 for 200 yds.
L on Bear Valley Rd.
L on SF Drake
R on Pierce Point Rd.

G16 - Point Reyes North
Point Reyes National Seashore
Pierce Point Road

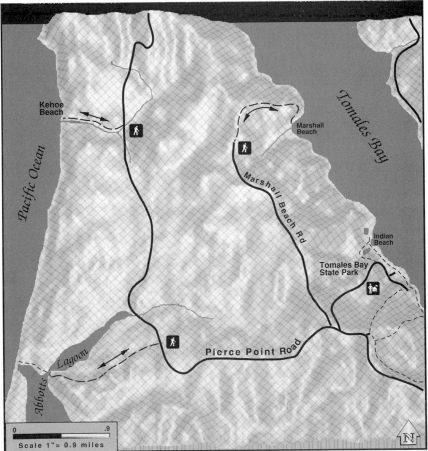

Kehoe
Beach

Pacific Ocean

Marshall
Beach

Tomales Bay

Marshall Beach Rd

Indian
Beach

Tomales Bay
State Park

Pierce Point Road

Lagoon

Abbotts

0   .9
Scale 1" = 0.9 miles

N

G17 Kehoe Beach to Abbotts Lagoon*

Distance: 5.1 miles   Shaded: 0%
Elevation Change: 100'   Trail can be wet near the marsh.
Rating: Hiking - 7   Difficulty - 3   Includes 2 miles on beach.
When to Go: Best in April and May when not too windy.

This one-way trail and beach hike is one of the three best wildflower hikes on Point Reyes. Go in the morning before winds get too strong.

*Shuttle Hike. Leave pickup cars at Abbotts Lagoon trailhead, 3.4 miles along the Pierce Point Road and shuttle hikers another 2.1 miles to the Kehoe Beach trailhead.

0.0 The trail starts next to an exposed slab of Monterey shale on the northern hillside and follows a mostly level path through sandy soil to the beach. On the left, Kehoe Marsh provides freshwater habitat for sedges, reeds and birds. In spring, the grassy hills on the right are dotted with fragrant bush lupine and occasional patches of iris.

0.5 Dunes, cliffs and wildflowers. Take the narrow path towards the right along the exposed cliff to view gold fields, poppies, tidy tips, baby blue eyes and blue lupine.

At the beach, head down by the water and hike along the wet sand south towards Abbotts Lagoon.

3.1 Abbotts Lagoon. You should be able to spot the lagoon from the beach by looking for a low-lying opening in the dunes. The lagoon is close to the ocean

Gold Fields

and low enough in elevation that heavy breakers enter it at high tide to create brackish water. Follow the northern edge of the lagoon inland. Look for the yellow flowers of lizard tail along the way.

3.6 Bridge and wildflowers. Cross the bridge and enjoy another hillside covered in gold. Just like Chimney Rock and Kehoe Beach, the best wildflower displays often appear in the most hostile environments. Up ahead, notice the wind-pruned coastal scrub on the hillside opposite the lagoon. Also, keep an eye out for birds.

Continue following the trail as it heads inland to the east. After crossing a small swale, the trail passes through fields of poppies, lupine, mustard and orange fiddleneck.

5.1 Abbotts Lagoon trailhead with pickup cars and restrooms.

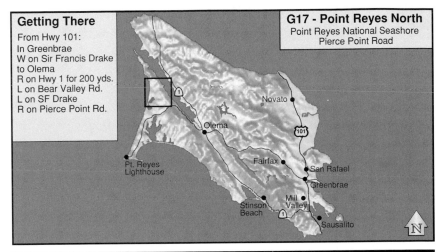

Getting There

From Hwy 101:
In Greenbrae
W on Sir Francis Drake
to Olema
R on Hwy 1 for 200 yds.
L on Bear Valley Rd.
L on SF Drake
R on Pierce Point Rd.

G17 - Point Reyes North
Point Reyes National Seashore
Pierce Point Road

Novato

101

Olema

Pt. Reyes
Lighthouse

Fairfax

San Rafael

Greenbrae

Mill
Valley

Stinson
Beach

Sausalito

N

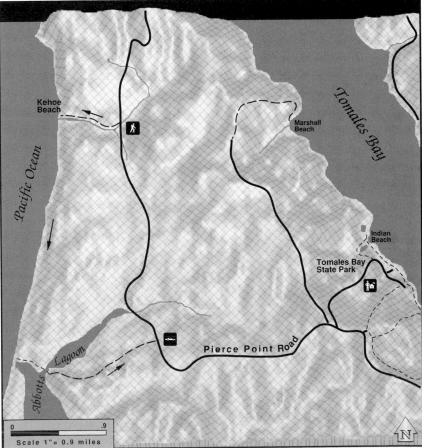

Kehoe
Beach

Marshall
Beach

Tomales Bay

Pacific Ocean

Indian
Beach

Tomales Bay
State Park

Pierce Point Road

Abbotts

Lagoon

0   .9

Scale 1" = 0.9 miles

N

259

G18 Tomales Point Trail

Distance: 9.4 miles   Shaded: 0%
Elevation Change: 1000'   Can be very windy.
Rating: Hiking - 9   Difficulty - 4
When to Go: Winter is good; best flowers in April and May.
This hike along an open, exposed ridge can be spectacular or miserable depending on the weather. Carry ponchos in case of fog.

0.0 Start at the parking lot at the end of Pierce Point Road. Follow the signs around the old dairy ranch. If fog cuts your hike short, you can tour the ranch when you get back.

0.8 Point #1 with spectacular coastal views. Just before the trail turns inland, you can see the dramatic coastal cliffs to the north rising over 400' above the ocean. In spring, this spot also provides a great wildflower display with yellow gold fields, tidy tips, buttercups, sun cups, poppies, lupine and wild strawberries.

1.0 The trail heads inland offering a view east down White Gulch to Hog Island in Tomales Bay.

Watch for Tule elk and for their large V-shaped tracks on the trail.

2.5 Highest point at 471'. As you climb to the highest spot on Pierce Point, you can see across Bodega Bay to the Bodega headlands and the Sonoma coast. On clear days, look for the jutting profile of Mt. Saint Helena 30 miles northeast.

Tule Elk

3.3 Lower Pierce Ranch site and unmarked junction #2. At the ravine, near the cypress trees, a small trail heads right down the right side of the ravine to a beach on Tomales Bay. Continue on the main trail.

4.0 Bird Rock viewpoint. If the tide is right, you can see a blowhole on the left side of the rock. From here, the trail climbs through a sandy area and dunes.

4.7 Tomales Point. In 1852, the English merchant ship, *Oxford*, mistaking Tomales Bay for San Francisco Bay, came full sail into the bay until she ran permanently aground just before Hog Island. After enjoying the view, retrace your steps back south.

9.4 Back at Pierce Point trailhead. Restrooms available.

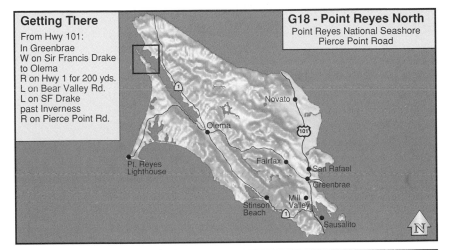

Getting There

From Hwy 101:
In Greenbrae
W on Sir Francis Drake
to Olema
R on Hwy 1 for 200 yds.
L on Bear Valley Rd.
L on SF Drake
past Inverness
R on Pierce Point Rd.

G18 - Point Reyes North

Point Reyes National Seashore
Pierce Point Road

Novato

101

Olema

Fairfax

San Rafael

Pt. Reyes
Lighthouse

Greenbrae

Mill
Valley

Stinson
Beach

1

Sausalito

N

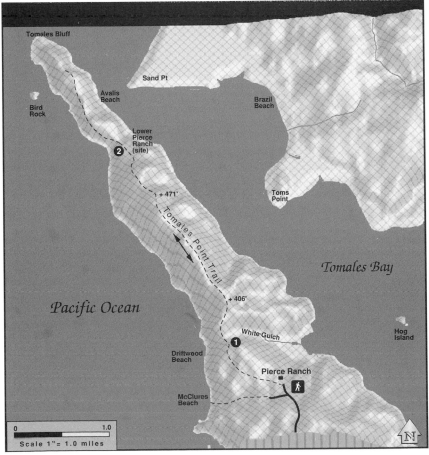

Tomales Bluff

Sand Pt

Avalis
Beach

Brazil
Beach

Bird
Rock

Lower
Pierce
Ranch
(site)

2

+ 471'

Toms
Point

Tomales Bay

Pacific Ocean

+ 406'

Hog
Island

White Gulch

1

Driftwood
Beach

Pierce Ranch

McClures
Beach

0   1.0

Scale 1"= 1.0 miles

N

G19 Tomales Bay and Millerton Point

Distance: 2.2 and 1.2 miles   Shaded: 0%
Elevation Change: 100' and 50'   Strong winds possible.
Rating: Hiking - 6   Difficulty - 3   Can be muddy.
When to Go: Best in winter for birds and spring for green hills.

These are fairly level hikes through pastureland out to bluffs overlooking Tomales Bay. Osprey nest at Millerton Point.

Tomales Bay Trail - 2.2 miles and 100' Change

0.0 Park at the signed Tomales Bay Trailhead 1.5 miles north of Point Reyes Station on Hwy 1. The hike starts by passing through a gate into pasture that may have cows grazing in it.

0.4 Overlook. The cliff edge provides a good view of the mudflats of Tomales Bay and shore birds. The levee running north was the bed of the North Pacific Coast Railroad that was originally built to haul lumber from the Russian River and west Marin to San Francisco.

To continue the hike, backtrack 100' and head right down past the fence and across the dam to the next knoll.

0.9 Junction #1. At a Y, bear right up to the knoll, then head north as far as you can go. **Option**: At the north end of the knoll, it may be possible to follow a cowtrail down a short steep section through brush to the levee. If not, head back. The downhill section can be muddy.

Millerton Point Loop - 1.2 miles and 50' Change

0.0 Park at the signed Millerton Point area located about 5 miles north of Point Reyes Station. The picnic area is on the left. The hike starts by heading uphill along the fence towards the knoll.

A sign at the trailhead describes an osprey nest that was relocated from a PG&E utility pole to a new non-electrical pole. This nest is one of 18 nests on Tomales Bay. Another 20 or so nests are located along Kent Lake making this area one of the most important osprey nesting regions on the west coast.

0.1 Junction #1. At the top of the knoll, head right to parallel the highway north. This knoll offers good views across the bay to the Inverness Yacht Club and to the heavily forested Inverness Ridge.

0.4 Clifftop #2. The edge of the cliff provides a nice view north up Tomales Bay. The white stakes mark the position of oyster beds.

0.7 Junction #3. Head back. **Option:** At low tide, it is possible to walk down to the beach, then north towards the oyster beds.

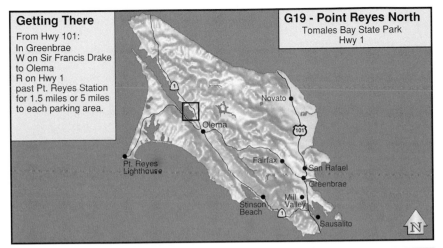

Getting There

From Hwy 101:
In Greenbrae
W on Sir Francis Drake
to Olema
R on Hwy 1
past Pt. Reyes Station
for 1.5 miles or 5 miles
to each parking area.

G19 - Point Reyes North
Tomales Bay State Park
Hwy 1

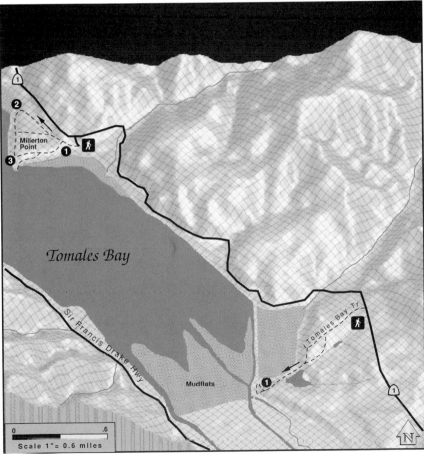

263

H1 A Trail For All Seasons

December - January
The sun is at its lowest angle of the year and it's often cold and wet or foggy. This is the rainiest period in Marin County with rainfall averaging 20 inches on the wettest areas of Mt. Tamalpais. But you can beat the indoor blues by getting out and looking for views, coastal hills and beaches, creeks, waterfalls, mosses and lichens, whales, wintering birds and southern exposures. Here are a few suggestions:

Southern Marin - Hikes A2, A4, A7, A10, A15
Mt. Tamalpais South - Hikes B1, B4, B8, B10, B14, B20
Mt. Tamalpais North - Hikes C3, C4, C8, C10, C11, C12, C16
Central Marin - Hikes D2, D3, D5, D9, D12
North Marin - Hikes E1, E2, E4, E5, E8, E11, E13
Point Reyes South - Hikes F7, F14, F15,
Point Reyes North - Hikes G6, G10, G11, G12, G13

February - March
This is the premier hiking time of the year. Even though rainfall averages 16 inches in the wettest areas, the weather is getting better, and water runoff is high. Trillium, milkmaids and hound's tongue start the wildflower parade. All the hikes are at their best.

Southern Marin - Hikes A3, A5, A11, A12, A14, A15
Mt. Tamalpais South - Hikes B2, B4, B9, B12, B14, B15, B16, B18
Mt. Tamalpais North - Hikes C2, C8, C9, C11, C17
Central Marin - Hikes D2, D4, D10, D11, D13
North Marin - Hikes E3, E6, E8, E10, E11, E14
Point Reyes South - Hikes F3, F6, F7, F14, F17
Point Reyes North - Hikes G1, G2, G11, G12, G13, G17, G18

April - May
More great hiking time. The weather is at its best, the hills are green and the late wildflowers reach their peak. Be sure to visit the rolling hills around Pt. Reyes, Mt. Burdell and the MMWD lakes area. Look for iris peaking in April. All the hikes are great.

Southern Marin - Hikes A3, A5, A6, A11, A12
Mt. Tamalpais South - Hikes B14, B15, B16, B17, B19, B21
Mt. Tamalpais North - Hikes C1, C3, C4, C5, C7, C10, C12, C17
Central Marin - Hikes D3, D5, D11, D12, D14
North Marin - Hikes E1, E6, E7, E9, E10, E11, E12, E13
Point Reyes South - Hikes F4, F6, F8, F13, F16, F18
Point Reyes North - Hikes G2, G4, G5, G6, G8, G11, G12, G13, G17

June - July
While much of Marin is hot and dry, Marin Headlands, Muir Woods, Steep Ravine and the Pt. Reyes coast are often cool and foggy as the bay area air-conditioning system runs full blast. Some summer wildflowers, yellow mariposa lily, monkeyflower, poppy, yarrow and clarkia hang on while the hills turn brown.

Southern Marin - Hikes A4, A5, A6, A7, A8, A10, A11, A12
Mt. Tamalpais South - Hikes B4, B16
Mt. Tamalpais North - Hikes C2, C14
Central Marin - Hikes D7, D15
North Marin - Hikes E6
Point Reyes South - Hikes F4, F14, F15, F16, F17, F18
Point Reyes North - Hikes G5, G6, G7, G8, G9, G10

August - September
Now is the time to avoid the dry, dusty roads. Head for the coast and beaches, north-facing trails, creeks, conifer forests and ripe huckleberries. Try an early morning hike. Caution: During hot, dry and windy days, fire danger is high. Avoid Mt. Tamalpais and the ridges of central and north Marin.

Southern Marin - Hikes A2, A4, A5, A10, A13
Mt. Tamalpais South - Hikes B4, B14
Mt. Tamalpais North - Hikes C17
Central Marin - Hikes D11, D13, D14, D15
North Marin - Hike E2
Point Reyes South - Hikes F5, F7, F10, F15
Point Reyes North - Hikes G4, G6, G10, G14, G15

October - November
Look for fall red color from poison oak, and yellow and brown colors from big-leaf maple and deciduous oaks. First winter storms arrive. Rainfall, averaging 8 inches around Mt. Tamalpais, settles the dust and brings out mushrooms. This is great weather time with gusty winds, clear days and marvelous views. It's a good time to head for the coast, south-facing trails and the oak-bay woodlands in central Marin and around the lakes.

Southern Marin - Hikes A2, A4, A5, A9, A10, A12
Mt. Tamalpais South - Hikes B1, B2, B8, B10, B12, B14, B16
Mt. Tamalpais North - Hikes C3, C4, C13, C16, C18
Central Marin - Hikes D5, D11, D12, D13
North Marin - Hikes E1, E4, E5, E8, E9, E12, E13
Point Reyes South - Hikes F2, F4, F6, F11, F16, F17
Point Reyes North - Hikes G1, G4, G5, G6, G9, G10, G14

H2 A Selection Of Best Trails

Not sure where to go? Here is our selection of best trails. Remember that the season and weather influence trail conditions.

Where to See Waterfalls

Marin County is blessed with an amazing number of waterfalls. The best time to visit these falls is in winter and early spring. Here's a list with our favorites near the top.

1. Cataract Creek - Scenery from Hawaii - Hike C11
2. Steep Ravine - Falls under the redwoods - Hikes B14 and B16
3. Cascade Falls - An easy hike, but difficult parking - Hikes D2 and D3
4. Little Carson Falls - Over 100' total drop - Hikes C8 and C9
5. Alamere Falls - Can only be seen from the beach - Hike F17

Cascade Falls

6. Dawn Falls - Easy hike to Baltimore Canyon - Hike A15
7. Redwood Creek - Start in Muir Woods and climb- Hike B6
8. Tucker Trail - Several small cascades - Hike C5
9. Loma Alta Falls - You'd never expect falls like this here - Hike D5
10. Stairstep Falls - Samuel P. Taylor Park - Hike D10
11. Troop 80 Trail - South side of Mt. Tamalpais - Hike B9
12. Indian Valley Falls - Only after rains - Hike E6
13. Warner Canyon Falls - Small, but nice - Hike A14

Great Views from High Up

Every once in a while, maybe two or three times a year, the air gets crystal clear with visibilities over 50 miles. When that happens, drop everything and head for the peaks.

1. East Peak - On top of the mountain - Hikes B8, B20 and C19
2. Mt. Livermore on Angel Island - Best bay area location - Hike A12
3. Big Rock Ridge - Marin's 2nd tallest peak - Hike E4
4. Old Mine Trail - More Tamalpais Views - Hikes B13 or B15
5. Coastal Trail - Marin Headlands - Hike A3
6. China Camp Nike Missile Site - Hike D12
7. Ring Mountain - Tiburon Peninsula - Hike A11
8. Hawk Hill - Marin Headlands - Hike A2
9. Mt. Barnabe - Samuel P. Taylor Park - Hikes D9 and D11
10. Blithedale Ridge - Mill Valley - Hike B1

11. Mt. Burdell - Verdant rolling hills - Hike E13 and E14
12. Bald Hill - Outside San Anselmo - Hike C3

Looking for Local Views

Not all views require hiking to the top of a mountain. Marin offers lots of great views of hills, valleys and spectacular coastline. In fact, there are too many to list them all. Here are some of the best.

1. Estero Trail - Tremendous view of coast and beaches - Hike G11
2. Northside trails - Views north from Mt. Tamalpais - Hikes B21 and C18
3. Matt Davis Trail - Above Stinson Beach - Hike B16
4. Tomales Point Trail - Coastline, hills and elk - Hike G18
5. Coast Trail - Marin Headlands - Hikes A5 and A10
6. Drakes Bay - White cliffs of Marin - Hike G12

Drakes Bay

7. Double Point - Spectacular views at Pt. Reyes - Hike F15
8. Coastal Trail - More coastal views on Pt. Reyes - Hike F6
9. Kent Trail - Views of Alpine Lake - Hike C14
10. Chimney Rock, Pt. Reyes Lighthouse - Glorious - Hike G13
11. Loma Alta - Views of Ross Valley - Hike D5
12. Mt. Wittenberg - Views of Pt. Reyes - Hike F2, F3 and G1

The Best Wildflower Trails

There are many kinds of wildflower hikes. Some hikes, like Chimney Rock, provide a splendid variety of flowers. Other hikes visit areas with great abundance or carpets of wildflowers. Many hikes lead to old-time favorites like trillium or iris. And a few hikes offer the discovery of rare jewels like the lovely calypso orchid or the Tiburon *Calochortus*.

1. Chimney Rock - One of the best wildflower hikes on the west coast - Hike G13
2. Ring Mountain - Variety, abundance and the rare Tiburon *Calochortus* - Hike A11
3. Coastal Trail - Marin Headlands in March for variety - Hike A3
4. Benstein Trail - Mar-Apr for rare calypso orchid - Hike B18
5. Baltimore Canyon - March for trillium - Hike A15
6. Olompali - March for early spring flowers - Hike E14
7. Tomales Pt. - Mar-Apr for possible carpets - Hike G18
8. Cascade Canyon - March for great spring flowers - Hike D2

Best Wildflower Trails (continued)

9. Yolanda Trail, both north and south - Hikes C4 and C6
10. Pumpkin Ridge Trail - April for iris - Hike C17
11. Sun Trail - Late Feb-Mar for early flowers - Hike B5
12. Kehoe Beach and Abbotts Lagoon - Can be carpets - Hike G17
13. Wolf Ridge - Marin Headlands Mar-May for variety - Hike A5
14. Concrete Pipe Rd. - Lakes area in Apr-May for variety - Hike C12
15. Coastal Trail - Mt. Tamalpais in April for variety - Hike B15

Best Birding Trails

Marin County is one of the premier birding areas on the West Coast. Of the almost 1000 species of birds in the United States, more than 180 have been spotted at Las Gallinas, more than 300 on Mt. Tamalpais and over 450 species have been counted on Pt. Reyes. However, birds are not as easy to find as flowers and waterfalls. Birding locations that are good for experienced birders are not always best for beginners. Here's where we suggest beginners go. Winter is usually the best time unless otherwise indicated. Be sure to bring binoculars.

1. Hawk Hill - Sept-Oct migration reaches 2000 per day - Hike A2
2. Las Gallinas Wild Life Ponds - Can always find birds - Hike E2
3. Pt. Reyes Bird Observatory - May see banding - Hike F14
4. Audubon Canyon Ranch - Open March-July weekends - Hike F18
5. Muddy Hollow - Pt. Reyes - Hikes G5 and G7
6. Limantour Spit - Pt. Reyes - Hike G9
7. Rodeo Lagoon - Marin Headlands - Hike A4
8. Lake Lagunitas - Hike C15
9. Simmons Trail - Mt. Tamalpais - Hike B17
10. Bon Tempe Lake Trail - Hike C13

Great Blue Heron

Hiking on the Beach

Like to walk on the beach? All of these hikes start on or lead to a sandy beach. All are great year-round, except when too foggy or windy. Bring a picnic in the fall when weather is often best. Listings are by area rather than ranking.

1. Kirby Cove - Good views to San Francisco - Hike A2
2. Rodeo Beach - Look for semi-precious stones - Hike A3
3. Tennessee Cove - Easy hike, but dangerous surf - Hike A7
4. Muir Beach - Start at the beach - Hike A10
5. Stinson Beach - Strenuous seven mile hike - Hike B16

6. China Camp Village - Swimming and picnicking - Hike D13
7. Palomarin Beach - South Pt. Reyes - F14
8. Wildcat Beach and Alamere Falls- Twelve mile hike - Hike F17
9. Limantour Beach - Wading possible - Hike G9
10. Sculptured Beach - Long beach hike. Best at low tide - Hike G10
11. Drakes Beach - Best beach on Pt. Reyes. Wading - Hike G12
12. Kehoe and McClures Beach - Dangerous surf - Hike G16
13. Kehoe Beach to Abbotts Lagoon - Long beach hike - Hike G17
14. Tomales Bay beaches - Good swimming - Hikes G14 and G15

Historical Hikes

Marin County has a rich human history that began with Native Americans over 7000 years ago. And long before the pilgrims landed at Plymouth Rock, Drake and Cermano both beached at Drakes Bay. Some hikes, especially those that include a Visitor Center, provide a glimpse of that history.

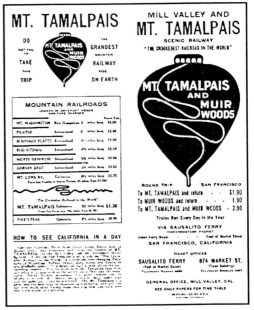

Old Railroad Ad

1. Miwok Village - Kule Loklo Trail at Pt. Reyes - Hike F1
2. Francis Drake - Pt. Reyes Visitor Center and Hikes G12 and G13
3. Olompali - Miwoks and early Marinites - Hike E14
4. China Camp Village - Old buildings and Museum - Hike D13
5. Military fortifications - Headlands Visitor Center and Hike A4
6. Shipwrecks on the coast - Tennessee Valley - Hike A7
7. Crookedest Railroad in the World - Mt. Tam - Hikes B2 and B10
8. Mountain Theater - Outdoor amphitheater - Hikes B12 and B13
9. Pioneer cabin - Phoenix Lake - Hike C1
10. The First Paper Mill - SP Taylor State Park - Hike D7
11. Historical Dairy Ranch - Tomales Point - Museum and Hike G18
12. Earthquake Evidence - Pt. Reyes - Visitor Center and Hike F1
13. East Peak Museum - Weekends on Mt. Tam - Hikes B20 and B21
14. Angel Island - Military History - Museum and Hike A12
15. Pt. Reyes Lighthouse - Museum and Hike G13

H3 Plant Communities

Marin County offers a magnificent diversity of plant life that can be described by several plant communities.

Redwood Forest

The mature redwood forest is one of nature's masterpieces as a visit to Muir Woods will attest. Branches of redwoods form flat sprays with dark, shiny green, one inch pointed needles. The cones are small, from 1-2 inches long. Redwoods have a shallow root system spreading out from the base and in severe winters, a few trees will topple.

Redwoods form a dense canopy that shades and restricts growth on the forest floor. Decomposition of its needles produces a rich humus that favors acid-loving plants like redwood sorrel, trillium, clintonia and several species of ferns. Other plants in the understory include hazelnut, huckleberry, tanoak and occasionally bay trees.

Redwood

Redwoods need winter rain and summer moisture (fog), conditions that are found in Muir Woods, Samuel P. Taylor State Park, Baltimore Canyon and many of the smaller canyons on Mt. Tamalpais.

Douglas Fir Forest

The Douglas fir is a majestic tree that can reach heights of 200' with a pyramid shaped crown. The one inch needles are sprayed out at various angles and the 2-3 inch cones have bracts that resemble mouse tails. These characteristics clearly distinguish Douglas fir trees from other conifers.

Elderberry, huckleberry and ferns comprise most of the understory in the Douglas fir forest. The Douglas fir forest dominates the more moist ridges, canyons and valleys of the southern half of the Point Reyes peninsula. You can get a good feel for the forest by hiking any of the trails out of Bear Valley and Five Brooks. Smaller stands of Douglas fir can be found on the north slopes of Mt. Tam.

Douglas Fir

Bishop Pine Forest

North of the Douglas fir forest on Point Reyes, on slightly drier slopes, the Bishop pine forest grows on the exposed granite of Inverness

270

Ridge. Bishop pine grow to about 70' in height and are similar in shape to Monterey pines. The needles of the Bishop pine are 2-4 inches long and come two to a bunch. (Monterey pines have slightly longer needles, three to a bunch.) The asymmetrical cones are tight swirls 3-5 inches in size that open to release seeds in hot weather or after fires.

Bishop Pine

Other plants found in the Bishop pine understory include coffeeberry, huckleberry, salal and in drier areas, manzanita and ceanothus.

A good place to see Bishop pine is in Tomales Bay State Park.

The Oak - Bay Hardwood Forest

The oak-bay hardwood community, composed primarily of oaks and bay, with some madrone and tanoak, is also referred to as the broadleaf evergreen community.

Several oaks grow in this community with the coast live oak, the most common. It is a large 30-75 foot tree with a broad round crown and 1-2 inch oval, cup-shaped leaves. The acorns are slender and pointed, and mature in one season.

Coast Live Oak

Other oaks include the evergreen canyon live oak (or goldcup oak), chaparral oak and the deciduous California black oak.

California bay or laurel, has a dark green, lance shaped leaf with a distinctive odor when crushed. The tree is adaptable to most light conditions and appears to be increasing in Marin.

Two common, evergreen members of this community are the madrone, with its distinctive smooth red bark and shiny leaves, and the tanoak, which ranges in size from a small 3' shrub to a tall 100' tree.

California Bay

Many shrubs, herbs and grasses are found in the understory of the hardwood forest, including coffeeberry, California hazel, ocean spray, poison oak, bracken fern and wood rose.

The oak-bay hardwood forest can best be seen around the lakes in the Marin Municipal Water District.

The Mixed Forest Communities

Most of the communities listed above are small and often intermixed.

Thus, you may find Douglas fir in an oak-bay community or conversely, oaks and bay mixed into a Douglas fir forest. Likewise, it is common to find redwoods and Douglas fir mixed together around Mt. Tamalpais (not Point Reyes - redwoods do not appear to grow on the Point Reyes peninsula because of soil conditions.)

The Oak Woodland and Oak Savannah Communities

Mt. Burdell, in northern Marin provides a striking example of the oak woodland community that features majestic oaks standing in a sea of grasses. Five of the nine species of oaks in California are found at Mt. Burdell with valley oak being the most common. Oak woodland has a tree cover of more than 30%, while the oak savannah consists of more widely spaced trees and a tree cover of less than 30%. Northern Marin offers fine examples of each community.

Chaparral Community

The chaparral community, comprised mostly of chamise, manzanita, ceanothus and oaks are dense, drought resistant shrubs. Most of them have small, evergreen leaves with a waxy, shiny or hairy covering to prevent water loss and long roots to tap moisture from surrounding soil.

Chamise is the most common shrub of the chaparral community. It is a member of the rose

Chamise

family and ranges in height from 3-10 feet with tiny, needle-like leaves and small white flowers that start blooming in May. In the fall, the flowers dry to a reddish-brown color and give Mt. Tamalpais its characteristic autumn hue.

There are several species of manzanita found in Marin. They range from 3-10 feet tall with simple, oval-shaped leaves and small, urn-shaped, waxy flowers that start blooming in December. The trunks of manzanita shrubs are very distinctive with a smooth, deep reddish-brown bark that resembles the madrone tree.

Manzanita

Several species of *Ceanothus*, or California lilac, are found in Marin and these shrubs range in size from 1-15 feet. They have shiny leaves, often with 3 veins diverging from the base. The fragrant flower clusters vary from white to blue to purple and blooming begins in February.

Four species of oaks are found in the chaparral community in Marin. These include the leather oak, chaparral oak, canyon live oak and

272

scrub oak. The leather oak, *Quercus durata*, is restricted to serpentine soil. Surprisingly, the canyon live oak is the same species that becomes a majestic 50 foot hilltop oak under better conditions.

Other common chaparral plants include toyon, bush monkeyflower, yerba santa, chaparral pea, huckleberry, tree poppy, poison oak, pitcher sage and Indian paintbrush.

Ceanothus

The largest chaparral stands in Marin County are located high on the south-facing slopes of Mt. Tamalpais. Although the chaparral communities of Mt. Tamalpais are healthy, they are decreasing in area, especially at lower elevations. Because there has not been a large fire on the mountain in a long time, oak-bay hardwoods and Douglas fir trees have invaded many chaparral areas where soil and moisture conditions are adequate.

Coastal Scrub

Coyote bush is the dominant shrub in the coastal scrub community. It consists primarily of 4-6' shrubs that range from impenetrable thickets to isolated shrubs dotting grassy hillsides. Coyote bush, also called "fuzzy wuzzy" is a nondescript shrub that forms white flowers in summer.

Coyote Bush

Joining the coyote bush in this community are sword fern, bracken fern, coffeeberry, bush lupine, monkeyflower and poison oak. California sagebrush with grey-green needle-like leaves can also be found on drier slopes.

The best place to see this community is on the the Sky trail on Inverness Ridge at Point Reyes.

Grass, Prairie and Pastureland

The largest area of Marin, including about 50% of Point Reyes, is covered with grasses. Historically, much of this land has been used for dairy and cattle grazing and many of the native, perennial bunch grasses have been replaced with non-native, annual grasses like wild oats.

Other Communities

Other plant communities in Marin include the salt marsh, sand dune, riparian and freshwater marsh. Each has its own environmental conditions and distinctive plants.

Oakland Star Tulip 3-10"
Calochortus umbellatus
March-May

Milkmaids 12-16"
Cardamine californica
January-March

Modesty 6-12"
Whipplea modesta
March-May

Popcorn Flower 8-12"
Plagiobothrys nothofolvus
April-May

False Solomon's Seal 12-24"
Smilacina stellata
February-April

Other common white - cream wildflowers are
Fairy Bells ..... Feb-Jul, 2 feet, white, bell-shaped flowers
Alum-root ..... May-Jul, 2 feet, small white flowers
Yarrow ..... Apr-Sep, 18 inches, fern-like leaves, white flower cluster

Morning glory 4-8'
Convolvulus occidentalis
April-August

Wallflower 8-12"
Erysimum concinnum
February-July

Cow Parsnip 3-8'
Heracleum lanatum
March-May

Wild Cucumber 5-20'
Marah fabaceous
April-July

Zigadene 12-18"
Zigadenus fremontii
February-April

Woodland Star 8-16"
Lithophragma affine
March-May

275

H5 Yellow - Orange Wildflowers

Buttercup 8-16"
Ranunculus californicus
February-May

California Poppy 8-16"
Eschscholzia californica
March-October

Cream Cups 4-12"
Platystemon californicus
March-May

Gold Fields 6-10"
Lasthenia californica
March-June

Bush Monkeyflower 24-60"
Mimulus aurantiacus
March-August

Other common yellow - orange wildflowers are
Brass Buttons ..... Mar-Dec, 10 inches, yellow button-like flowers
Footsteps of Spring ..... Jan-May, 14 inches, early flower
False Lupine ..... Mar-May, 2 feet, yellow pea flower, 3 leaflets

Mules Ears 12-18"
Wyethia glabra
March-June

Sun Cup 3-7"
Camissonia ovata
February-May

Lizard Tail 12-48"
Eriophyllum staechadifolium
February-July

Hairy Cat's Ear 3-16"
Hypochoeris radicata
April-December

Yellow Mariposa 8-12"
Calochortus luteus
May-July

Fiddleneck 8-24"
Amsinckia intermedia
March-June

H6 Pink - Red Wildflowers

Chinese Houses 8-12"
Collinsia heterophylla
April-May

Checkerbloom 12-18"
Sidalcea malvaeflora
March-May

Farewell to Spring 8-16"
Clarkia purpurea ssp. *quadrivulnera*
May-August

Columbine 12-24"
Aquilegia formosa
April-June

Indian Paintbrush 8-16"
Castilleja subinclusa ssp. *franciscana*
March-June

Other common pink-red wildflowers are:
Clintonia ..... Apr-June, 18 inches, shiny leaves, pink flower clusters
Red Larkspur .....Mar-June, 18 inches, red 1-inch flower with spur
Wood Rose ..... May-July, 30 inches, shrub with prickles on branches

Shooting Star 8-14"
Dodecatheon hendersonii
February-April

Buckwheat 12-18"
Eriogonum latifolium ssp. *nudum*
June-November

Sea Pink 12-24"
Armeria maritima var. *californica*
April-August

Trillium 6-12"
Trillium chloropetalum
February -March

Owls Clover 3-6"
Castilleja densiflora
March-May

Indian Warrior 8-12"
Pedicularis densiflora
January-March

279

H7 Blue - Purple Wildflowers

Blue Dicks 12-24"
Dichelostemma capitatum
March-June

Blue-eyed Grass 6-12"
Sisyrinchium bellum
March-May

Douglas Iris 6-18"
Iris douglasiana
March-May

Hound's Tongue 24-36"
Cynoglossum grande
February-April

Larkspur 12-18"
Delphinium hesperium
April-May

Other common blue-purple wildflowers are:
Forget-me-not ..... Feb-June, 12 inches, clusters of small flowers
Slink Pod .....Jan-Feb, 4 inches, broad spotted leaves, purple flower
California Phacelia ..... Apr-Jul, 1 foot, coil of lavender flowers

Lupine 4-20"
Lupinus nanus
March-May

Mission Bells 12-18"
Fritillaria affinis
January-March

Hedge Nettle 12-24"
Stachys rigida var. *quercetorum*
May-August

Ithuriels Spear 12-18"
Brodiaea laxa
April-June

Seaside Daisy 4-12"
Erigeron glaucus
May-August

Baby Blue Eyes 6-8"
Nemophila menziesii
February-June

H8 Berries and Ferns

Two favorite groups of plants found in Marin County are berries and ferns. Ferns are treasured for their symmetry and delicate shape. Berries provide showy flowers and colorful fruit. All of the species shown below, except the blackberry, thrive in the shady canyons and ridges of the conifer forest or along shady wet banks and creeks where they are kept moist.

Berries

Berries grow on trees, shrubs, vines and ground covers and come in a variety of flavors. Some are edible, some slightly toxic and some downright poisonous. An important Berry Rule is,

"Never taste a berry unless you know what it is."

Here are five of the most common berries found in Marin County and their suitability for eating.

*Red elderberry, to 15'
White flowers - spring
Red berries may be
toxic.*

*Huckleberry, to 10'
White flowers - spring
Blue-black berries in
fall are edible.*

*Thimbleberry, to 8'
White flowers - spring
Red berries in
summer are edible
when soft.*

*Red-flowering currant,
to 10' Red flowers -
early spring. Purple
berries are barely
edible.*

*Blackberry, vine to 5'
White flowers - spring
Blackberries range
from tart to sweet.*

Ferns

Ferns are unusual in that the main part of the fern is a leaf, called a frond. More complex ferns, like the bracken fern, are a classic example of a fractal shape in nature. Fractals maintain similarity as you zoom in on them. Look closely at a bracken fern. The side leaflets are shaped just like the whole leaf. Likewise, the shape is repeated in the subleaflets.

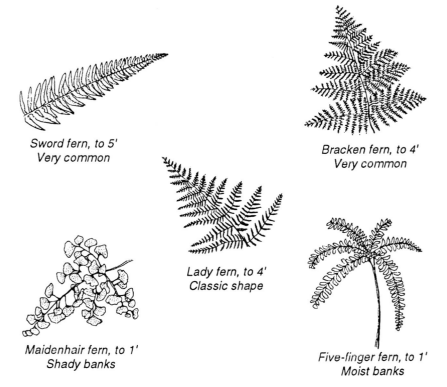

Sword fern, to 5'
Very common

Bracken fern, to 4'
Very common

Lady fern, to 4'
Classic shape

Maidenhair fern, to 1'
Shady banks

Five-finger fern, to 1'
Moist banks

Ferns are different from most plants in that they reproduce by spores rather than flowers and seeds. The life cycle of a fern includes two separate plants: a small, rarely-seen plant called a gametophyte and the sporophyte which we call a fern.

An individual fern can produce hundreds of thousands of spores in small capsules on the underside of each leaflet. After the capsule springs open, the spores are released and, if conditions are right, grow into a gametophyte about 1/4" in size with male and female parts. If fertilization occurs, the fertilized egg develops into a new fern.

H9 Animals and Animal Tracks

In the days before the Europeans came, the San Francisco bay area and Marin County were rich in wild life. Among the large animals, there were grizzly and black bear, mountain lions, coyotes, tule elk and deer. Today, the bear are gone. The coyotes and mountain lion may be returning. A tule elk herd has been reintroduced to Point Reyes.

The only large mammal to continuously inhabit the land is the mule deer.

Mule Deer

The black-tailed or mule deer are abundant in Marin. They are most noticeable on the hills throughout Marin and on the coast. Males begin rutting in fall and should be considered dangerous. Antlers are shed in

Mule Deer

the winter. Females usually give birth to two fawns in the spring.

Smaller Animals

There are dozens of smaller animals living in Marin. These include squirrels, chipmunks, possums, shrews, weasels, moles, skunks, jack rabbits, raccoons, rats, feral pigs, bats, foxes and bobcats.

The pigs are non-native, introduced elsewhere for hunting. In the 1980s, there were as many as 200 wild pigs on Mt. Tamalpais causing considerable damage digging roots and bulbs. By the 1990s, their numbers have been reduced significantly by traps and hunters.

Grey Fox

The grey fox can sometimes be seen in oak-bay woodland hills and in the coastal grasslands. They often have a reddish hue on the front flanks and can be identified by their black-tipped tail.

Bobcats are common in Marin, but probably seen less often than foxes. They can be found in coastal canyons, oak-woodland hills and along the edges of meadows. They are slightly larger than a domestic cat and are identified by their short ears and stubby tail.

Bobcat

Animal Tracks

Most animals are not easily seen. They are wary of open areas and many only appear at dusk or at night. Their footprints are the primary evidence we see during the daytime.

The first thing to check when looking at animal tracks is the number of toes. Deer have two toes. Dogs, foxes, cats, mountain lions,bobcats and rabbits have four toes. Raccoons, weasels and skunks have five toes.

Track size depends on several factors, the size and age of the animal, whether it's the front or hind foot, condition of the ground and whether the animal is walking or running. The tracks shown here are about 3/4 actual size for an adult animal.

Raccoon 2-3"

Bobcat 1.5-2"

Skunk 1-1.5"

Grey Fox 1.5-2"

Walking Deer 2-3"

Mountain Lion 3-4"

Running Deer 2-3"

285

H10 Sea and Shore Birds

Common Goldeneye 18"
Bucephala clangula

Killdeer 10"
Charadrius vociferus

Willet 15"
*Catoptrophorus
semipalmatus*

Bufflehead 14"
Bucephala albeola

Western Sandpiper 7"
Calidris mauri

**American
Oystercatcher 16"**
Haematopus palliatus

Ruddy Duck 15"
Oxyura jamaicensis

Common Murre 16"
Uria aalge

Species	Spr	Sum	Fall	Wint	General Habitat
Common Goldeneye	2	5	2	2	Lagoons
Bufflehead	2	5	2	1	Lagoons - Ponds
Ruddy Duck	2	5	2	1	Lagoons
Killdeer	2	2	2	2	Grasslands - Ponds - Coastal
Amer. Oystercatcher	4	3	4	4	Coastal
Willet	2	5	1	1	Lagoons - Coastal
Western Sandpiper	1	5	1	1	Lagoons - Ponds
Common Murre	1	1	2	2	Coastal - Ocean

1 = Abundant, 2 = Common, 3 = Fairly Common, 4 = Uncommon, 5 = Rare

Common Loon 32"
Gavia immer

Great Egret 39"
Casmerodius albus

Brandt's Cormorant 34"
Phalaccrocorax penicillatus

Western Grebe 25"
Aechmophorus occidentalis

Northern Pintail 27"
Anas acuta

Great Blue Heron 47"
Ardea herodias

Surf Scoter 19"
Melanitta perspicillata

Brown Pelican 50"
Pelecanus occidentalis

Species	Spr	Sum	Fall	Wint	General Habitat
Common Loon	3	5	3	1	Lagoons - Coastal
Western Grebe	3	5	3	2	Coastal - Lagoons
Brown Pelican	5	4	2	4	Lagoons - Coastal
Brandt's Cormorant	2	2	2	1	Coastal
Great Blue Heron	3	3	3	3	Lagoons
Great Egret	3	3	3	3	Lagoons
Northern Pintail	3	5	2	1	Lagoons - Ponds
Surf Scoter	2	4	3	1	Ocean - Lagoons - Coastal
1 = Abundant, 2 = Common, 3 = Fairly Common, 4 = Uncommon, 5 = Rare					

H11 Land Birds

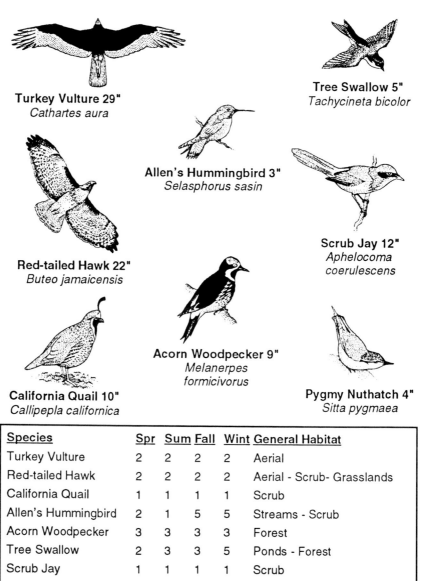

Turkey Vulture 29"
Cathartes aura

Tree Swallow 5"
Tachycineta bicolor

Allen's Hummingbird 3"
Selasphorus sasin

Red-tailed Hawk 22"
Buteo jamaicensis

Scrub Jay 12"
Aphelocoma coerulescens

Acorn Woodpecker 9"
Melanerpes formicivorus

California Quail 10"
Callipepla californica

Pygmy Nuthatch 4"
Sitta pygmaea

Species	Spr	Sum	Fall	Wint	General Habitat
Turkey Vulture	2	2	2	2	Aerial
Red-tailed Hawk	2	2	2	2	Aerial - Scrub- Grasslands
California Quail	1	1	1	1	Scrub
Allen's Hummingbird	2	1	5	5	Streams - Scrub
Acorn Woodpecker	3	3	3	3	Forest
Tree Swallow	2	3	3	5	Ponds - Forest
Scrub Jay	1	1	1	1	Scrub
Pygmy Nuthatch	3	3	3	3	Forest
1 = Abundant, 2 = Common, 3 = Fairly Common, 4 = Uncommon, 5 = Rare					

Wrentit 6"
Chamaea fasciata

Golden-crowned Sparrow 6"
Zonotrichia atricapilla

Rufous-sided Towhee 8"
Pipilo erythrophthalmus

Hutton's Vireo 4"
Vireo huttoni

Tricolored Blackbird 8"
Agelaius tricolor

White-crowned Sparrow 6"
Zonotrichia leucophrys

American Goldfinch 5"
Carduelis tristis

Wilson's Warbler 4"
Wilsonia pusilla

Species	Spr	Sum	Fall	Wint	General Habitat
Wrentit	2	2	2	2	Scrub
Hutton's Vireo	3	3	3	3	Forest - Streams
Wilson's Warbler	2	1	2	5	Streams - Forest
Rufous-sided Towhee	2	1	2	2	Scrub
White-crown Sparrow	2	2	1	1	Scrub
Golden-crown Sparrow	3	5	2	2	Scrub - Grasslands
Tricolored Blackbird	5	5	3	3	Pastures - Ponds
American Goldfinch	2	2	2	5	Grasslands - Scrub

1 = Abundant, 2 = Common, 3 – Fairly Common, 4 – Uncommon, 5 = Rare

H12 Natives Versus Non-Natives

There have been hundreds of non-native species introduced into the San Francisco bay area since the time of the Spanish missionaries. These range from roses to tomatoes, from German shepherds to parakeets. Usually, non-native introductions, called escaped exotics or aliens, are not a problem.

Occasionally, non-native introductions do create problems. The non-native may thrive, reproduce and outcompete native populations. Or, the non-native may bring new diseases or parasites that severely affect local species or damage the habitat. Or, the non-native can cause a population explosion of a native species by reducing or removing a predator.

Examples of Non-Native Invasions

One of the most famous and costliest introductions of a non-native species occurred in Australia in 1859, when a farmer imported a dozen pair of wild rabbits for hunting. Within six years, the population reached 20 million and by the 1930s, the population was estimated at 750 million rabbits. These rabbits devoured crops, fouled water holes and caused soil erosion, consequently reducing the local sheep population by over 50%. It was not until the 1950s that the rabbit population was brought partially under control through the introduction of a viral disease.

There are many, many more examples of destructive alien invasions: Starlings, intentionally brought to the United States from Europe in 1890, thrived and replaced several native songbirds. Water hyacinth, intentionally brought in from Central America in 1884, clogged inland waterways and replaced native aquatic vegetation. Mongooses, brought into Hawaii in 1883 to control the rodent population, instead killed the rats natural predators.

The Japanese beetle was accidentally imported into the United States in 1911 and now defoliates more than 250 species of trees and shrubs. Dutch elm disease was accidentally imported on timber from Europe in the 1930s and will eventually destroy millions of elm trees.

One of the quickest, most costliest invasions in history took place in the late 1980s in the Great Lakes. The zebra mussel, which hitched a ride on a ship from Europe, exploded in numbers, reaching concentrations as high as 700,000 per square meter. These little mussels clogged ten-foot-diameter intake pipes, sunk boats and buoys with their weight and smothered countless numbers of native mussels. Their economic costs may reach as high as two billion dollars annually. Their ecological costs are difficult to measure.

Non-Natives in Marin

The biggest non-native problem in Marin is French broom. It is a member of the legume family that has yellow pea-shaped flowers and bean-like pods. French broom is a drought resistant, evergreen shrub that was introduced for landscaping over 100 years ago. The shrub forms impenetrable thickets that range in height from 6-12'. It reproduces vigorously. In the fall, individual seed pods explode, ejecting up to 300 long-lived seeds in a wide circle.

French broom spreads aggressively and and can replace many native grasses and shrubs. Its thick cover can shade out and prevent tree seedlings from getting started.

French broom has no local predators or diseases to keep it in check. The only known controls are to pull it, cut it or set fire to it.

Another fast-growing problem in Marin is yellow star thistle. It is a low growing plant 12-18" tall with bright yellow flowers that bloom from April to June. It has sharp thistles and spreads very rapidly. Many parks are using controlled burns to try and control it.

Other non-native plants that thrive in Marin County include Coulter pine, eucalyptus, Monterey pine, acacia, Scotch broom, pampas grass, thistles (purple, Russian, bull), fennel, poison hemlock, cotoneaster, gorse, forget-me-nots, oats, Harding grass, Himalaya berry, capeweed, field mustard, wild radish, German ivy, fireweed and vetch. There are other escaped exotics in Marin, but this is the main list.

What You Can Do

If you're concerned about non-native plant invasions and are interested in doing something about it, here are a few suggestions:

Join the Habitat Restoration teams sponsored by the National Park Service, GGNRA, Pt. Reyes and the Marin County Open Space District. Call the Park Volunteer Hotline 415-556-3535 or the Open Space number 415-499-3778 for more information.

Join the California Native Plant Society. Team up with local neighbors and clubs for non-native control parties, like broom pulls. Replace non-native plants with native plants in home gardens.

Support public agencies in Marin that are considering ordinances discouraging or prohibiting the sale of the most aggressive non-native plants.

291

H13 Jurisdictions and Resources

Angel Island State Park

Facilities include Visitor Center, Museum, snack bar, picnic areas and camping. Fee for ferry.

Angel Island Park Headquarters 415-435-1915
Angel Island Volunteer Association 415-435-1915
Tiburon Ferry Information 415-435-2131

China Camp State Park

Facilities include Ranger Station, Museum, snack bar, picnic areas and camping. Parking fee for most areas.

China Camp Park Headquarters 415-456-0766

Golden Gate National Recreation Area (GGNRA)

Facilities include Visitor Center, historical forts, Marine Mammal Center, picnic areas and camping.

Marin Headlands Visitor Center 415-331-1540
Hostel information 415-331-2777
Stinson Beach Information 415-868-0942
Golden Gate National Park Association 415-766-0693

Marin County Open Space District (MCOSD)

No facilities. Hiking, biking and picnicking only.
Marin County Open Space District Office 415-499-6387
Volunteer Program 415-499-3778

Marin Municipal Water District (MMWD)

No facilities. Hiking, biking, fishing and picnicking only. No swimming in the lakes. Entrance fee for main lakes area.

Sky Oaks Ranger Station 415-459-5267

Mt. Tamalpais State Park

Facilities include Ranger Station, Museum, outdoor theater, snack bar, picnic areas and camping. Parking fee for some areas.

Pantoll Ranger Station and Campground 415-388-2070
East Peak Visitor Center - Hours 10-4 on weekends
East Peak Snack Bar - Hours 10-4 summer and winter weekends
Steep Ravine Cabins and Campground - Mistix 1-800-444-7275
Mt. Tamalpais Interpretive Association - Weekly hikes 415-388-2070

Mountain Play Association - Plays in May and June, 415-383-0155
Tamalpais Conservation Club - 870 Market St, Room 562, SF 94102
Mt. Tamalpais History Project - c/o Mill Valley Public Library

Muir Woods National Monument

Facilities include Visitor Center, gift shop and snack bar. No biking or picnicking allowed.

Muir Woods Park Headquarters 415-388-2595

Olompali State Historic Park

Facilities include a historical display area and picnicking. Parking fee.

Olompali Park Headquarters 415-892-3383
The Olompali People - Volunteer group 415-892-3383

Point Reyes National Seashore (PRNS)

Facilities include three Visitor Centers, gift shop and snack bar.

Bear Valley Visitor Center 415-663-1092. Main Visitor Center.
Lighthouse Visitor Center 415-669-1534. Check hours.
Drakes Beach Visitor Center 415-669-1250. A cafe is located here.
Hostel information 663-8811 early morning and evenings only.
Backpacking Reservations - call the Bear Valley Visitor Center.
Recorded Weather and Whale Information 415-663-9029
Point Reyes Field Seminars 415-663-1200

Samuel P. Taylor State Park

Facilities include Ranger Station, historical display area, picnic areas and camping. Entrance fee to main area.

Samuel P. Taylor Park Headquarters 415-488-9897

Tomales Bay State Park

Facilities include Ranger Station, swimming area and picnic areas. Entrance fee to main area.

Tomales Bay Park Headquarters 415-669-1140.

Related organizations include:

Sierra Club - Weekly hikes, 6014 College, Oakland 94618
Tamalpa Runners - PO Box 701, Corte Madera 94925
Olema Ranch Campground 1-800-655-2267
Bike Trails Council of Marin - PO Box 494, Fairfax 94978
California Native Plant Society - 1 Harrison Ave, Sausalito 94965

Camping in most areas is limited. Call before planning a trip.

H14 Bibliography

Aker, R. *Sir Francis Drake at Drakes Bay*. Drakes Navigator Guild, 1978.

Arnot, Phil. *Point Reyes: Secret Places and Magic Moments*. Wide World Publishing, 1987.

Arrigoni, Patricia. *Making the Most of Marin*. Travel Publishers International, 1990.

Bakker, E.S. *An Island Called California*. University of California Press, 1971.

Bowen, O.E., Jr. *Rocks and Minerals of the San Francisco Bay Region*. University of California Press, 1966.

Brockman, C. F. *Trees of North America*. Golden Press, 1968.

Burt, William and Grossenheider, Richard. *Mammals*. Peterson Field Guides, 1980.

Cobb, Boughton. *Ferns*. Peterson Field Guides, 1956.

Conradson, Diane R. *Exploring Our Baylands*. Coastal Parks Association, 1982.

DeCoster, M. et al. *Headlands*. University of New Mexico Press, 1989.

Delgado, James P. and Haller, Stephen A. *Submerged Cultural Resources Assessment*. (for GGNRA to Point Reyes) Southwest Cultural Resources Center Professional Papers Number 18, 1989.

Dunham, Tacy. *Wandering Marin Trails*. Tacy Dunham, 1986.

Erickson's *Mount Tamalpais Trail Map*. Eureka Cartography, 1991.

Evens, Jules G. *The Natural History of the Point Reyes Peninsula*. Point Reyes National Seashore Association, 1988.

Fairley, Lincoln. *Mount Tamalpais: A History*. Scottwall Associates, 1987

Gilliam, Harold. *Island in Time*. Sierra Club, 1962.

Gilliam, H. *Weather of the San Francisco Bay Region*. University of California Press, 1962.

Gudde, E.G. *California Place Names*. University of California Press, 1969.

Hart, John. *Wilderness Next Door*. Presidio Press, 1979.

Hickman, J.C., ed. *The Jepson Manual*. University of California Press, 1993 .

Howell, J.T. *Marin Flora*. University of California Press, 1970.

Jenkins, Olaf P., ed., *Geologic Guidebook of the San Francisco Bay Counties*. Department of Natural Resources, California, 1951.

Keator, Glenn and Heady, Ruth. *Pacific Coast Fern Finder*. Nature Study Guide, 1981.

Kruckeberg, A.R. *California Serpentines.* University of California Press, 1984.

Marshall, Don B. *California Shipwrecks.* Superior Publishing Company, 1978.

Mason, Jack. *Point Reyes: The Solemn Land.* North Shore Books, 1970.

Mason, J. *The Making of Marin.* North Shore Books, 1975.

Mason, J. *Early Marin,* 1971.

McHoul, L. *Wildflowers Of Marin.* The Tamal Land Press, 1979.

Miller, G. Tyler. *Living in the Environment.* Fifth ed., Wadsworth Publishing Co., 1988.

Molenaar, Dee. *Point Reyes National Seashore: Pictorial Landform Map.* Wilderness Press, 1988.

Morrato, M.J. *California Archaeology.* Academic Press, 1984.

Munz, P.A. *A California Flora.* University of California Press, 1959.

Murie, Olaus. *A Field Guide to Animal Tracks.* Houghton Mifflin Company, 1954.

Niehaus, T.F. and Ripper, C.L. *A Field Guide to Pacific Wildflowers.* Houghton Mifflin, 1976.

Olmsted & Bros Map Co. *Trails of Mt. Tamalpais and the Marin Headlands.* 5th edition.

Olson, R. *The History of Mount Tamalpais.* A thesis presented to the faculty of the Consortium of the California State University, 1985.

Parsons, Mary Elizabeth. *The Wild Flowers of California.* California Academy of Sciences, 1960.

Pavlik, Bruce, et al. *Oaks of California.* Cachuma Press, 1991.

Peterson, Roger Tory. *A Field Guide to Western Birds.* Houghton Mifflin Company, 1961.

Rubissow, Ariel. *Park Guide.* Golden Gate National Park Association, 1990.

Shuford, W.D. and Timossi, I. C. *Plant Communities of Marin County.* California Native Plant Society, 1989.

Spitz, Barry. *Tamalpais Trails.* Potrero Meadow Publishing Co, 1995.

Teather, L. *Place Names of Marin.* Scottwall Associates, 1986.

Whitnah, D.L. *An Outdoor Guide to the San Francisco Bay Area.* Wilderness Press, 1976.

Wurm, Theodore G. and Graves, Alvin C. *The Crookedest Railroad In The World.* 2nd edition. Howell-North Books, 1960.

Handbook of North American Indians. Vol. 8, Smithsonian Institute, 1978.

Environmental Planning Study. Marin Muncipal Water District, 1976.

About the authors

Kay Martin is the managing editor for scientific publications at the California Academy of Sciences. She also works as a volunteer docent for Bay Shore Studies and is active with the California Native Plant Society. In training for five marathons, she has logged several thousand miles running the trails of Marin County.

Don Martin teaches physics and computer science at the College of Marin. He has co-authored four computer books, published by Howard Sams, and has written and published a study guide, *How to be a Successful Student*. While Kay runs, Don jogs and occasionally rides his mountain bike.

The Martins have also written and published the books, *Mt Tam* and *Point Reyes National Seashore*.

The Martins have lived in San Anselmo since 1965. They are members of the Sierra Club, Tamalpa Runners, Audubon Society and St. Anselms Church. They have four grown children.

Bob Johnson is a well-known Sonoma and Marin County illustrator. He has illustrated and designed dozens of books. In recent years, he has become very active in the wine industry, designing labels and packaging for many Sonoma and Napa wineries.

Book Ordering Information

Books available from Martin Press:

Hiking Marin
121 Great Hikes in Marin County
Don and Kay Martin
© 1995
304 Pages, $18.95

MT TAM
A Hiking, Running and Nature Guide
Don and Kay Martin
2nd edition, © 1994
128 Pages, $9.95

Point Reyes National Seashore
A Hiking and Nature Guide
Don and Kay Martin
© 1992
128 Pages, $9.95

Many of the hikes in our first two books, *Point Reyes National Seashore* and *MT TAM* also appear in the book, *Hiking Marin*. However, *Point Reyes National Seashore* and *MT TAM* include more detailed information about their respective areas.

All three books may be ordered from your local bookstore or directly from the publisher at the address below.

Please include $3.00 per book to cover shipping and tax.

Martin Press
P.O. Box 2109
San Anselmo, CA 94979